Close to the Bone

Also by Laurie Stone

Starting with Serge
Laughing in the Dark: A Decade of Subversive Comedy

Close to the Bone

Memoirs of Hurt, Rage, and Desire

EDITED BY LAURIE STONE

Grove Press
New York

810.9
Clo

Published simultaneously in Canada
Printed in the United States of America

Permissions for Close to the Bone

"Brother" by Jane Creighton previously appeared in Ploughshares, Fall 1994, Volume 20.

"I Kiss Her Goodbye" previously appeared in Seven Tattoos: A Memoir in the Flesh by Peter Trachtenberg, Crown, 1997.

"The Story of My Father" previously appeared in Portrait of My Body: Personal Essays by Phillip Lopate, Doubleday/Anchor, 1996.

FIRST EDITION

Library of Congress Cataloging-in-Publication Data

Close to the bone : memoirs of hurt, rage, and desire / edited by
   Laurie Stone.
        p.   cm.
     ISBN 0-8021-1618-3
       1. Authors, American—20th century—Biography.
   2. Autobiographies—United States.   3. United States—Biography.
   I. Stone, Laurie.
   PS135.C58   1997
   810.9—dc21
   [B]   97-17481

Design by Laura Hammond Hough

Grove Press
841 Broadway
New York, NY 10003

10 9 8 7 6 5 4 3 2 1

for Gardner and Janet

Acknowledgments

My gratitude is large to friends who believed in this project and cheered it at every stage: Bruce Benderson, Esther Hyneman, Adrian Danzig, Trudy Solin, Janet Fisher, John Leonard, Wendy Sibbison, Elizabeth Schambelan, and Ira Silverberg, without whom the book would not exist.

Contents

Introduction

RECALLED TO LIFE

by Laurie Stone

WE COULD ALL GO ON *OPRAH* FOR SOME DAMN REASON OR OTHER, and we would all know how to do the show: Start with a shocking teaser and then look pained, as if the narrative were being yanked out of us for our own, primal good. At this point, we could all write a tell-all about our tabloid childhoods and contrive an autobiographical performance about the pleasures of humiliation. Bobbing in the culture of confession, therapy, and victimization, we're assured there are no more closets, promised that drainage is revelation. But most disclosures splashing from talk shows—as well as from performance art and personal writing about addiction and abuse—don't reveal anything more than anguish. They are howls, acts of flashing, purges. The culture of recovery trades on the wishful idea that exposing shameful feelings will dissolve them. No need to weigh will, desire, and responsibility in the making of the damaged, stymied self.

The upside of the big spill is that public life has grown more candid. We no longer require that writers mask their stories as fiction in order to tell them. We're invited to indulge our curiosity about how other people really live—to stretch our knowledge, juice our senses, be happy voyeurs. In response has come a flood of personal writing, including autobiographies, letters, diaries, and memoirs. As well as anxiety about truth-telling and questions about the veracity of accounts.

This isn't new. Mary McCarthy famously accused Lillian Hellman of lying in her memoirs about her activism against Joe McCarthy. Others have cast doubts on Hellman's portrayal of herself in "Julia," as a courier for Nazi fighters. These are factual matters—she did these things or she didn't—but Hellman's emotional honesty has also been challenged, the way she romanticized her relationship with Dashiel Hammett, editing out his abusiveness and other unappetizing aspects of their relationship. Was she intentionally falsifying? Blind? Is she being judged by standards of candor that weren't hers?

Nervously tweaking the blurry border dividing fiction and memoir, a number of writers have recently published novels in the form of faux memoirs. Philip Roth's *The Counterlife* enabled the author to publicize his infidelities to his wife Claire Bloom, while puffing out the claim "Honey, it's only a novel." Paul Theroux describes *My Other Life*, in which he chronicles a fictional character called Paul Theroux, as a "true-life novel," and he comes off coy—as if we need to be instructed that memoirs aren't purely factual and novels not solid inventions.

David Leavitt enraged Stephen Spender, from whose 1951 memoir, *World within World*, he drew inspiration and facts—without permission or attribution—for his 1993 novel, *While England Sleeps*. Leavitt fictionalized Spender's account in, among other ways, writing sexually explicit scenes to dramatize a homosexual love affair. Spender protested what he called the misappropriation of his words and life, sued for plagiarism, and pressured Leavitt's British publisher into withdrawing the book. Leavitt's novella, "The Term Paper," portrays the painful episode and the writer's block that followed and inadvertently triggered another scandal when *Esquire* editor Edward Kosner at the last minute yanked it from the April '97 issue, calling his decision "a taste question." Resigning in protest, fiction editor Will Blythe said *Esquire* feared objections to the gay sex from advertisers.

"The Term Paper" portrays the Spender crisis as it happened but veers from fact to fiction when the character David Leavitt rediscovers the joy of writing by composing term papers for undergraduates in exchange for sex. In a *New York Times* interview, Leavitt explained his strategy: "I initially intended it as a comic story, and I tried to write it with an imaginary character. But it just seemed to fit in some intuitive way with my experience, the idea that a character named David Leavitt who at the end of a grueling lawsuit should find himself in this situation seemed the natural way to tell the story. It is so common to write autobiographical fiction in which your own experience is thinly disguised. I thought it would be very interesting to do the opposite with a story where even a tiny amount of research into my life would prove it did not happen and thereby turn the conventions inside out."

A writer's got to do what a writer's got to do, but does the gambit need pumping as a convention-buster? What convention on our pomo landscape hasn't already been wrestled to the mat? How about a moratorium on gamesmanship and thinking in italics. *Okay?* Just as contemporary consciousness admits our multi-gendered natures, so it accepts our multi-genred literature. The boundaries have always been tough to protect, starting with Defoe, who in *Robinson Crusoe* invented the English novel in the form of a faux true-life chronicle.

The collages of memoir and fiction that slide down easiest make no philosophical claims. In the middle of his novel *The Law of Enclosures,* Dale Peck plunks down a section of unmasked autobiography, where the author evokes his newborn self—"the harsh red and brown wrinkled skin wrapped around me like soiled butcher paper." We see his mother, who died when he was three, a woman imagined under his father's bucking thrusts, her skin white except for marks left, her body hippy and round, until the embolism that would kill her first appears as a bruise. In Peck's peculiar gamble of a novel, the drive of narrative—more than the need to distinguish reporting from fantasy—rules.

Similarly, without fanfare, Gordon Lish blends genres in his novel *Epigraph.* His wife, that is the wife of Gordon Lish, the character, has died after a long illness, and he cannot stop remembering, recording, confessing, messing her memory to retrieve her, defile her, restore her, so he obsesses about a plate, a dish, a porcelain something that she was "in the habit of demanding her morphine suppositories be brought to her on." The book is funny, lunatic, flagrant, a bundle of hot read letters from sleepless nights. We're left to assume that the novel frees this writer to be irreverent about loss, a freedom the memoir might have inhibited, demanding, as it does, emotional reliability.

Genre-blended books, presented as such—including the sports *Ragtime* and *The Seven Percent Solution*, which place historical figures on imagined landscapes—are fictions. They aren't the place to look for lies, though lying and other ethical matters are concerns in biography, autobiography, journalism, and nonfiction. Oliver Stone's movie *JFK* presented as an interpretation of history—a kind of fiction—frees him, in my opinion, from the standards of journalism. But we want to believe the accuracy of a reporter, not to discover that the subject of a profile, described as an actual person, is invented or a composite. We want to believe that quotations were uttered by the people to whom they are attributed.

Spender's complaint about Leavitt's novel was backed by plagiarism law, but in the memoir, what are the limitations on portraying other people who are part of your life? Your nearest and dearest are pretty much your prey and often become your ex-nearest and dearest after they see what you have written. Even if you were kind and fair, no matter. They didn't have a say.

Before the New York opening of *It's a Slippery Slope*, autobiographical author/performer Spalding Gray worried aloud over lunch about the ethics of profiting from the pain of his ex-wife, Renée. Unlike the "impingencies" of his earlier works *Monster in a Box*, about a man who can't write a novel, and *Gray's Anatomy*, about a man who may be going blind—both struggles with the self—the *crise* at the core of *Slippery Slope* is Gray's affair with a woman who bears him a son and the subsequent dashing of his bond with Renée.

Gray's squirminess was understandable, but the story was his life, he reasoned, and his life is his work. So the question became: Could the piece incorporate and make use of the distaste it would generate with regard to this conflict? When I saw the monologue, I thought it hilarious in many parts but that Gray didn't succeed in grappling with his moral dilemma. Spilling the beans doesn't turn him honest. Renée's suffering was mentioned but not taken in by the narrator or presented to the audience.

The memoir form raises other ethical concerns relating to what people confess, the tone of their admissions, and the question of whether they are still engaged in the reported acts. Sexual infidelity inflicts pain, but it isn't criminal, and no one in a relationship is all sinner or all doormat. But what do we think about memoirs depicting morally loathsome activities, let's say a book by a drug dealer who knows the dope pedaled will result in deaths and who in fact does sell drugs that kill people? Supposing the narrator is still dealing? We want to know about life's seamy and ambivalent aspects, but what is being served more in such a document: our knowledge or the writer's self-promotion?

Supposing a memoirist lies about the gravity of his or her acts, presenting the self as, for example, a sexual predator but omitting rape from the litany of aggressions reported and failing to disclose that the behavior purported to be under control in reality continues? It's a case-by-case call, but I would say that a memoirist who doesn't own responsibility for antisocial acts is emotionally unreliable and that a narrator who fails to report all the salient facts of the case being explored is factually unreliable. What's produced in these books isn't fiction disguised as fact but dishonest writing.

What do we mean by honesty in the memoir, when memory continually revises the past? Even memories salvaged whole are selected and edited from a jumble of contiguous events. Sometimes memories are complete fabrications, as with false recovered memories induced in patients by their therapists—a capsizing of psychoanalysis, whose quixotic quest is to winnow out fantasy from what is actually going on.

The memoirists I find inspiring have mined self-knowledge and come clean with the goods. They may change names to protect the privacy of their subjects; certainly they edit events, often fracturing chronology, the way memory does. But these writers pledge allegiance to the world, not the tribe. They aren't playing games with illusion and reality, aren't seeking to uplift or sermonize. They are working a literary genre I call the post-therapeutic memoir. Included in the array are *This Boy's Life* by Tobias Wolff, *Maus* by Art Spiegelman, *Fierce Attachments* by Vivian Gornick, *Autobiography of a Face* by Lucy Grealy, *The Liars' Club* by Mary Karr, *The Blue Suit* by Richard Rayner, and *Moving Violations* by John Hockenberry. Among earlier works paving this path are Edmund Gosse's *Father and Son*, J. R. Ackerley's *My Dog Tulip*, Kate Simon's

Bronx Primitive, and Frank Conroy's *Stop-Time.* These authors retrieve themselves through language, lofting out of the murk of closeted secrets with the ordering instrument of candor.

Most memoirs fail as literature because their authors mistake
their experience for a story rather than search out the story in their
experience. It's not enough that creepy things have happened, since
everyone's life, prodded enough, looks like a crime scene with chalk
outlines. What matters in the memoir, as in fiction, is the degree
of insight and drama. Post-therapeutic memoirists place themselves
at some personal risk to reveal their tales—but at greater psychological risk to conceal them. They are vulnerable on the page, dig-
ging at their actions and emotions. They incorporate the insights
of psychoanalysis, but their writing is not, itself, an instrument for
catharsis, healing, revenge, or self-justification.

The genre shuttles between victim stories and shame narratives. Victim stories can be history and sociology and even literature if, like some memoirs of torture and terrorism, they are detailed,
eloquent, and self-scrutinizing, but the teller is in a whirlpool, without bearings or recourse, not necessarily passive but at the mercy of
larger, meaner forces. Survival can depend on quick wits or accident, but the tale, even bled of self-pity, is told by a target and the
psychology revealed: how to cope. The victim narratives that re-
shape the category—among them *Moving Violations*—show how
victims are also actors in their dramas.

Shame stories are about what we do to ourselves and the
world, inscribing deeds consequential enough to startle into consciousness that we *have* acted. Such a saga, of course, can come off
a couch rant if the teller wants merely to drain sewage and flash
the sooty glamour of falling into bed or injecting sense-altering
substances under the skin. The challenge is to write about shame
from a post-shame point of view, to enter an ego-free zone, cleared
of mirror-worship and whining, to walk out naked and speak inti-
mately, so the teller isn't inside deviousness, selfishness, and the
other drives and appetites that exhaust our puny human restraints
with their animal insistence; rather the teller sets up the self as a
lab rat and mounts folly and error as exhibits that can be surrounded,
poked. The project is to winnow romance and vanity from the way

others see the self so that, guided by a ranging, meditative mind, the story becomes an emblem of how we live now. With self-scrutiny the teller transforms blunders into the only shapely and reliably honorable offering that can be made of such materials: art.

Though post-therapeutic memoirists are devoted to truth, self-display is part of their incentive, the frisson of going public with secrets, shameful emotions, all the linty unmentionables stuffed in the back of the sock drawer. Perhaps every story worth telling— whether fiction or autobiography—is a dare, a kind of pornography, composed of whatever we think we're not supposed to say, for fear of being drummed out, found out, pointed at.

Post-therapeutic memoirists know that portraying damage and shame doesn't dispel them. These writers don't believe they can be reborn, cleansed, honed down to a recovered nubbin, and they don't want to be. They are interested in their layers, their ambivalences, their irresolvably mixed feelings. Their eyes are trained not on the prize of release but on measuring limitation: the myths with which we flatter and comfort ourselves, the encoded scripts that won't quit. You can hear this understanding in their first sentences. All the rage, self-pity, and self-importance have been spent, all the shrinkage accomplished. What's left is a voice that may once have told its story as a weeper but now knows, ineluctably, it is threaded with comedy.

Victim and shame narratives break down into four main categories: books about identity; books about illness and disability; books about family trauma, incest, and other domestic abuse; and books about compulsion, addiction, and limits.

Identity memoirs burrow into race, sexuality, ethnicity, et cetera, often the voices piping up from the margins and stripping the armor and camouflage off otherness. Veronica Chambers's *Mama's Girl* records growing up as a black kid in a family where Dad leaves. It's a book as attuned to the romance of loving Mom as it is to the family's deprivations. Japanese American David Mura's *Where the Body Meets Memory* is a seductive meditation on whiteness, sexual trancing, and pornography—the crossroads of shame, eros, and what lies beneath skin. Bernard Cooper's *Truth Serum* unspools a gay boy who doesn't quite know he's gay, nor does his mother until the afternoon he dons a Day-Glo shirt and catches her astonished recognition—an intensity in her eyes that makes him feel "beautiful, if not quite human."

Memoirs of the hurt body are often the most gallant. In *First Comes Love*, Marion Winick writes of a crazy infatuation with a man she knows is gay—she's a boundary-basher with a heroin habit and a freshly broken heart. But the romance is remodeled into intimacy, family life, and a leavetaking from Tony, who dies of AIDS. At age nine, Lucy Grealy was diagnosed with Ewing's sarcoma, a deadly form of cancer from which she was cured but which, as a result of radiation treatments, destroyed her jaw. *Autobiography of a Face* is a brilliantly detached rendering of the thirty operations she endured to reconstruct her damaged jaw and a searching contemplation of being seen. In *Moving Violations*, John Hockenberry, rendered paraplegic in a car accident at nineteen, wheels beyond his anxieties about being an exceptional marginal and pushes us past our fears of imperfection and loss of control.

Among family stories, few equal the complexity of Art Spiegelman's *Maus*, a memoir of his parents' survival of the Holocaust and his own journey from a barbarous childhood—years spent pinned beneath the hairy paw of his tyrannical father. *Maus* is a wondrously spare, fanciful, and profound work that takes as accurate a measure of private anguish as of global nightmare. Like Spiegelman, Mary Karr could easily have gone down in the *Titanic* of her childhood. But instead of becoming vague and passive, she remained wide-eyed, storing the impressions that propel *The Liars' Club*. Karr's mother, Charlie, and father, Pete, were hard-drinking and reckless. Following the death of her mother, Charlie went nuts, burning the family's possessions and capping off the horror show by brandishing a butcher knife over Mary (eight) and her sister Lecia (ten). Karr evokes the glamour of her parents' wildness without softpedaling their abusiveness. Events cascade through the watchful scope of a child at risk; she's aware she lacks safety and freedom, yet she's juiced on imperilment—a hot zone against which other experiences pale.

Among compulsion lit, Claudia Shear's exuberant *Blown Sideways through Life* mines clarity from fat, depression, and sixty-five jobs that floated her above destitution while sucking her blood. She dramatizes all entrapment in which we conspire (the way we hunker down in passivity and armpit smell) but her specific morass is the service job: the kitchen/desk/counter/telephone reality of rubber gloves, filthy floor mats, fatigue, and insults, about which she is deliriously specific and ingeniously panoramic. Richard Rayner's unsparing and tender *The Blue Suit* shadows the author (now forty-one) during his teens and twenties when he stole compulsively: mainly books, everything from used paperbacks to rare first editions. There were break-ins too and stints passing stolen checks and credit cards. Feeling robbed of stability—both parents cut out on him—he contrives to remain dangling, getting hard doing crime: trancing out, manically pumped, acting harebrained, feeling scared but more nettled by any sort of fear.

For *Close to the Bone*, I solicited writers energized by the new wave of candor and willing to cut as deep. As far as specific subject matter was concerned, I didn't want to be prescriptive. Everyone's pornography is their own. At the same time, I was looking for material relatively unexplored in literature. The collection mixes daylit tales and fringescapes, tosses a salad of the celebrated authors Lois Gould and Phillip Lopate together with the first-time published, seventeen-year-old wunderkind who goes by the name Terminator. The other authors: Jane Creighton, Peter Trachtenberg, Jerry Stahl, Catherine Texier, and myself generally write fiction and memoiristic literature.

Each of the stories grabbed me by the lapels and demanded I listen, though the writers speak in a range of voices, from Gould's icy detachment, to Trachtenberg's mordant noir pastiche, to Stahl's crack-addled, hyper-real blow-by-blow. Creighton eyeballs her erotic feelings for her brother with such calm comprehension we feel on level ground and wonder only why this household taboo remains so closeted. On the other hand, Lopate, recording visits to his tottering dad in a nursing home, finds in this commonplace an opportunity for self-understanding so startling the trip feels like travel to an unexplored planet.

Terminator, who hails from a born-again background and has lived for periods on the streets, tells a story about loving an unreliable mom that is nearest in emotional timbre to Gould's piece about her remote father, a man who, when he saw his daughter at all, waltzed her through New York's haute bourgeoistopia. Whether raised in France, as was Texier, or in Pittsburgh, as was Stahl, whether speaking from the beginning of a career or from the perspective of major achievement, whether male or female, gay or straight, these writers leave soul prints with remarkably consistent components: sex, the family, aloneness, the city, addiction, illness—most trenchantly AIDS.

The stories are ordered like pieces in a music program: varying tempos, amplifying themes, catching echoes through juxtaposition. Jane Creighton's tale may be the most musical by itself, a song of longing for her brother that refuses to fit into her notions of pathology. In this beautifully written, dreamy collage, brother and sister are caught in glimpses during car rides ferrying Jane to some new location as she leaves a lover. She is always leaving someone, and she thinks that need to fly, maybe that is her stuck needle. She wonders if anyone can inspire what she felt in childhood.

Her brother had an immune deficiency, and maybe that wound made him gentler and more needy than other older brothers would have been to a younger sister. To touch wasn't scary or painful. It never was. "How does it start?" she wonders. "You're making me laugh so hard I'm crying. You make your penis jump like a puppet, and you make it talk. . . . You invite me to touch it and I do touch it. It bobs up and down and I am delighted." Without turning the sexual adventurer into a hero of transgression and without romanticizing drives, Creighton rescues the incestuous desire of siblings from the abuse police, allowing us to regard its pleasures as disturbing but perhaps not ineluctably damaging.

I was introduced to Terminator through the novelist Bruce Benderson, who in turn had been informed about him by novelist Dennis Cooper. At fourteen, having read hungrily since early childhood, Terminator began writing stories for his therapist and, once he started, felt an urgency like sex, the erotics of reading and writing kicking in early, as did his brilliance and skill. Every so often —but truly rarely—a talent comes along that seems fully blown, though it's not as if the writing is unworked. It is astonishingly accomplished: the sense of drama, the descriptive nuances, the shuffling of time.

"Baby Doll" is saturated in suffering the writer allows us to behold without sinking into it. He knows what he is telling us about eroticized revisits to early pain. He feels such an exuberant urge to share, the energy proves he wasn't defeated. Remaining conscious and collecting details mean survival, and he practices turning himself into an instrument of his own will—lest he bleed into the demands of others: "Usually when I'm alone and not allowed out, I walk around the narrow trailer and turn on the TV and all the radios as loud as I can take. I sit somewhere between the sounds and let the voices and music come at me and compete for my attention. I enjoy deciding which appliance will win me over. I'm proud of my ability to concentrate totally on whatever I choose to hear, and tune out what I don't."

His mother is a child herself when she has him; and by the time we meet her, she is drowning. Abused by her evangelical father, she in turn metes out punishment as a way to control and connect with her son. To thwart her, become her, annihilate her, incorporate her, the little boy—called Jeremiah in the narrative— seduces his mother's current boyfriend and suffers an impaling crucifixion that feels like justice, victory, and love. Terminator writes from inside the battered child who ordinarily does not survive childhood. It is as if he is giving voice to kids like Lisa Steinberg, murdered by her father Joel Steinberg, whose very brilliance and vitality are a red flag to rampaging bulls.

In a Manhattan far from Terminator's Virginia dirt roads, Lois Gould recaptures her father, whom she encapsulates as Businessman, but a similar child-eyed perspective marks her pages.

Gould's father is as mysterious and emotionally unsteady as is Terminator's mother, not completely withdrawn but more tantalizing, dangling affection only to snatch it away. A proper sadist but in the dark. While Terminator is all trembling sensibility, Gould's voice is even, an archeologist picking up shards and antiquities at the hole of her life's history. What's this? Oh, that's father in his perennial striped pajamas, installed in front of the TV stock quotes, about to dial the current woman in his life he calls Red—they all have to dye their hair that color so he can use this nickname.

With dry minimalism, Gould informs us that her father was with the original Red the night her mother gave birth to her. Invoking him, she is trying to see a kind of love she feels for absences, but in doing so can't help outing his lack of feeling for others, the way he exhales the word "women," "like bad air," the way he enlists her in his infidelities to her mother so they can both betray her. Gould's mother, a famous dress designer, is aloof too, but hers is a coldness installed, a presence that's rejecting but still there.

With a delicacy compelled by the frightened child still alive in her, Gould lifts the lid on her father's contempt for women, showing it's his dependency on them and the softness in himself he hates, his lack of character. Without lording it over her parents, Gould shows how she survived them. Unable to oppose them directly, she left writing for that, but she's in control of the need to retaliate, for what comes across isn't dislike but infatuation for her parents that kept her porous. The lively tension in this piece ripples from its tough voice revealing the author's vulnerability.

Nailing another shadowy father—those stubbly ghosts of the family—is Phillip Lopate's mission, too, but "The Story of My Father" is more acutely a self-portrait, the artist carving autobiography less through direct self-scrutiny than by the way he sees. Lopate judges this piece his best, and it is indeed a model of the form: exhaustive, fearless, and funny. "We spend most of our adulthoods trying to grasp the meanings of our parents' lives; and how we shape and answer these questions largely turns us into who we are," he says, stating terms—with his trademark elegant simplicity—that frame not only his story but the collection.

There is a literature of writer sons grappling with defeated fathers—Spiegelman and Philip Roth come to mind—the fathers' shoulders sloping under the weight of their mismanaged lives, the sons twitching in the discomfort that they might have stolen their fathers' dicks. Lopate makes mischievous common cause not by competition but by identification. Lopate senior is so solipsistic he can't respond to the Holocaust because it didn't affect him personally. He didn't talk to his children, buy them birthday presents, show them affection, or even go to the hospital when they were born. Yet Phillip, out of at least in part a perverse need to oppose the other members of his family, defends his pop, finding a mirror lest he become his father and see nothing.

"I feel my father's vagueness, shlumpiness, and mania for withdrawal inhabit me like a flu when no one is looking," he confides and elsewhere observes, "My tendency is to adjust to an environment passively, like my father, until such time as it occurs to me to do what a considerate Normal Person (which I am decidedly not, I am a Martian) would do in these same circumstances: shut the window, cut up the old man's meat. . . . He too approaches all matter as obdurate and mystifying." Phillip sees as maverick his father's refusal to conform to conventions: like romance, even hygiene. He knows the enlarging view is a tactic to rescue his own humanity. Of course by copping to this, he proves how far he is from duplicating his father's methods. Lopate turns the survivor guilt of the successful son into an act of retrieval, giving his father a nuanced, detailed life on the page—noticing him rather than ignoring him—a corporeality that, in his own hands, he didn't achieve.

Peter Trachtenberg shares Lopate's slouchy rectitude and wryness, a voice whose first notes convey: There is nothing you can say about me I haven't thought about myself. Trachtenberg's obduracy is focused on love, with a belief that desire—his for a woman and hers for him—will reduce him to a husk. Love, or sex—or love that can't take a form other than sex—is a blood sucker. He wouldn't have it any other way, but he can't take it. For Trachtenberg love is always a noir scenario: kill or be killed. He prefers not to.

Still, inevitably, loneliness draws him out, and in "I Kiss Her Goodbye" he explains the origin of a tattoo on his wrist: a circlet of stick figures copied from a girlfriend's design. "I got it less out of hope than out of pessimism, for the same reason I break my neck looking for souvenirs when I'm leaving a place I love and suspect I won't be visiting again." Prepared to think that fate is only a euphemism for his own bad character, Trachtenberg, a former junkie, is credible presenting his unreliability. Introspection has become his devotion, and though at times callous, mournful, and weak, he catches himself in lies. His is writing with a complete absence of special pleading.

The narrative jolts along on the tension between his energy to tell and his subject: his deficient appetite for connection. Of all the authors in *Close to the Bone*, Trachtenberg best earns the epithet bard of aloneness. He sounds like a late-night radio talker, like a phone sex worker—albeit a literate one—his rap lewd and pungent, its clarity more exciting than its flights. "In time," he writes, citing the chief benefit of prolonged isolation, "you will know yourself so thoroughly that you finally realize what all those people had against you."

He dumps a girlfriend who wants him to beat her harder than he likes to, and she stalks him. Cringing in his apartment, he gets so lonely he weeps into the fur of his cats. Lured out again by Tara—a former prostitute and addict who shags her hair with nail scissors and aspires to write—he is at first attracted to the combination in her stories of porn and transcendence. "I got the bloody meat of sex, sex with bruises and coat hangers and crumpled ten-dollar bills, and the pristine Wedgwood of literature, or at least something that was trying to be literature, stringent and pitiless in its control." A reluctant top who has to be led kicking and screaming to edge play, he is an equally gingerly guide to the lower depths that beckon as soon as he walks out the door—dives that play "chattering dance music that makes you want to drop acid, butcher your parents, and write PIGS on the wall in their gore."

In the people who want him he sees a reflection of his own worst feelings about himself, and he thinks that his desire, in turn, is more of an insult to them than a compliment. With other people's needs and expectations withering him, he rejects them with a Bartlebian firmness, an anorexic preference for abstinence. Every time he gets what he wants, he feels a sense of defeat.

With Trachtenberg, we seesaw between attraction to the writer for uncloseting his feelings and aversion to what's revealed. The same can be said about my offering, "Hump," and Jerry Stahl's "Pipe to the Head." We are the compulsive portion of your dining pleasure.

In "Hump," I am craning to see parts of myself you can usually glimpse only in dressing room mirrors. I am in the middle of my life, inventorying damage, a lurch triggered when I run into a writer who is talented, famous, and pregnant out to here. I think about the reasons I didn't have a child, not so much wanting to be a parent but regretting that it wasn't really a decision I made but one made for me while my psyche was running errands. I measure myself against two women: my friend Natalie, whose twin daughters—the loves of her life—died in their twenties; and my mother, Toby, who admits she didn't really want kids. I am mesmerized by the pleasure Natalie takes in mothering and equally fixed on the mutual aversion my mother and I feel toward each other. Insufficiently loved, I am inadequately loving.

My mother doesn't welcome my will or mind any more than my body, but it is the body I glom onto, the body, whose acceptance by men, I think can repair the hurt. In sex I don't have to think about the fact that nothing is repaired. In sex I feel okay instead of disgusting, even when I am doing disgusting things. I prowl, feeling the autoerotic urgency of sexual hunger, the capacity, at the flick of a neuron, to find everyone arousing, the landscape morphing into a mirror of my restlessness, objects of desire, even if they are loved, becoming instrumental to my will.

Measuring another willed plunge, longtime heroin addict Jerry Stahl, in his memoir *Permanent Midnight*, guides us through circles of personal hell that revolve back on each other. But he turns repetition into a subject, filling each story of drug use with increasing revelation. The book is a great, funny progress of self-understanding, its comedy not minimizing pain but earned from it.

"Pipe to the Head" too is a drug yarn—an outtake from *Permanent Midnight*, when Stahl, on vacation from smack, spent a week sliming with LA crack dealers. The teller's voice is a rollicking mix of self-deprecation, pulp idioms, and couch smarts, though he never twelve-Stepfords himself. "I had no veins that hadn't caved," he explains. "I'd burned out my neck, my legs, my feet, my arms, and the backs of my hands. There was a good vein in my dick, but the one time I tried it, my fingers shook so much, in the grips of some junked-out stop-and-go palsy, I missed by a mile and my balls swelled up like distended apricots."

"Gaunt as a med school skeleton and puke green," he plays wheelman to a pair of bad dudes—one so fresh out of jail he's still wearing his wristband—while they rob other dealers and marks. He feels like an impostor, but no more so than as a yuppie, husband, and sitcom writer. His idea, observed in retrospect, is to go native with black criminals, thinking their lives less chosen and therefore less ambiguous, seeing them as ultimate outsiders with no visa for getting back to safety since it was never made available to them. He wants to be a bad guy instead of a fucked-up one, thinking crime "sexier than angst."

What he means is that crime is active and anguish passive: crime a dick activity, self-loathing a pussy state. What makes his story unconventional is that Stahl scopes his passivity, knows it is the desired drug he needs the other drugs to get to. He's open on the page, wanting, really, so little to be erect, rather to slug-crawl into a womb hole where other people and the claims of his own humanity will leave him alone. Drugs and the crime he gets into here figure even in his semicomatose brain as lame expressions of rebellion. What's gutsy is the clarity maintained in the fog, the undead pleasure he feels in seeing.

The working dick in him is in his brain, his ability to formulate, to leave his body and recognize what others observe. "I was, at this point, one of *those people* you see in the street, not quite scabbed and drooling but not, you know, 'normal' either. The kind you look at, as you edge to the other side of the pavement, and wonder: *How did he get that way? What the fuck happened to him?*" The pride that sneaks into Stahl's aria is unavoidable. He has gone to Mars and returned—well, not Mars but some ricocheting junk planet exploded off an environmental disaster, a place fetid, miasmic, and afloat with viscous, unidentifiable fluids. You've got to grant the guy amazement that instead of returning an oozing hulk sans gray matter he can type on a keyboard. Limbo lower: He didn't snap his spine. His escape from decency and middle-class entitlement is the kind only a kid from the bourgeoisie would have to fabricate. Stahl knows that.

Catherine Texier's "My Father's Picture" mixes ingredients of all the pieces with a lush idiom and meditative intensity all its own. It's partly a noir, in that Texier hunts for secrets about her life, secrets involving sex and her mother's past, and the McGuffin, in this case, is her father. He is missing from her life. She grows up with her mother and her mother's parents—really the grandparents boss and protect both females, so it is as if Texier's mother remains a big, rebellious girl. When Texier is five, her mother shows her a picture of a man, spitting, *"ton père."* When she is in her forties— a successful writer with two kids and a long marriage—she decides to track him down, and they meet, finally, over lunch in the South of France.

Like Gould, Texier has a missing father, but Texier is more focused on the parent who remained, a mother whose explosive sexuality taunts her parents and enslaves her child. The little girl is enraptured and invaded, the boundary between her body and her mother's never quite established. Like Creighton, Texier pokes around in blood-tie spaces, gazing up at the Brobdingnagian dimensions before her: "When she gets up to soap herself, water drips from her in big gushes, drips from her curly, black bush, cascades from her hips, way above me. When I look up, I see droplets balanced at the tip of her nipples. Again I want to turn away, but I can't help staring at her. She lifts a leg and balances her foot on the edge of the bathtub. She runs the soap between her legs. I see far under her thigh, too far."

While blitzed by her mother, she is kept in the dark about her origins, her birth a secret that, like conspiracy theory and thoughts conjured while listening at the bedroom door, are sexy. When Texier confronts the actual man in his flesh, she's unsatisfied, having to exchange long-held wishes for a finite reality. A bit morose, he makes her feel sorry for him, an emotion that turns to anger, because, unbeknownst to herself until this moment, she has come wanting a father—a father to enfold her—and she resents being the stronger one. Until she sees that he has given her his vulnerability, a piece of himself that is real, which she cannot do—keeping up a front of well-being and contentment—and she sees this is his strength.

It is her power, too, as a writer. Refusing to keep family secrets is what releases her imagination and catapults her into the world. The same can be said for all the writers here, their disinhibition inspiring, even if their actions are sometimes repulsive. In memoir, the strip-show element, the sideshow frisson isn't transcended but remains. It's sexy. I'll show you mine if you show me yours.

These writers do not ask for love or understanding, offer no apologies, just steer narratives as thoughtful as they are madcap. The pieces create an atmosphere in which knowledge and arousal don't eclipse each other but oscillate, where understanding—even of the shabby origins of excitement and the melancholy theaters we erect for it—rather than draining fantasy of its erotic juice still admits pleasure. The retrieval of desire, they show, is an underground activity: bucking repression, turning disadvantage into victory, flipping emotional deprivation into a kind of gratification. *Close to the Bone* draws fuel from the erotics of knowledge: The more we know about what makes us tick, the freer we can be to cop whatever joy we find.

Close to the Bone

Memoirs of Hurt, Rage, and Desire

Brother

JANE CREIGHTON

THE HOUSE ON A DIRT ROAD, A STREAM RUNNING BY IT.

In the dream I am always fighting to stay. Someone tries to move me out, an ex-love, someone who thinks my things should remain in boxes, someone who would knock down a wall, make guest rooms, "brighten the place up a bit."

Of course, I would never want to live there again.

Dogs, cats, us children, we had white ducks. The mother duck was nasty and once stuck her bill into Aunt Greta's skinny back while Aunt Greta was sitting on the wooden foot bridge. Sent her screaming into the creek.

Pearl and Allan, sister and brother. We call her Pearl, sometimes Pearlie-pie, which she hates, loves, hates. Too much giddiness in the house. We call him Bub, Bubby, and by the time I reach my teens, Bro, Brother. Brother, come here.

We are driving this time, 1988, in my car. You are accompanying me on my current move, five days from San Francisco to Houston, and I am relieved to have you with me. Outside Fresno I pull up to a gas station and make a quick call back to San Francisco, some last thing I have forgotten. It's 9 A.M. and August in the dun-colored valley, and while the phone rings on the other end, I toe the asphalt to see if it will give, not hot enough yet, and glance at you waiting patiently in the passenger seat. You've done this before, waited for me while I was stringing out a series of last-ditch reasons why I should stay in touch, not leave, hold the fort.

3

—There's so much we . . .
—Yeah, there's . . .
—a lot we could talk about.
—Uh huh.

The house on a dirt road, a stream running by it, nestled at the base of a valley a mile or so long. The stream is named Log Run, after the logging industry that flourished in these hills in the eighteenth century, a point of history I use at school to construct a personal mythology for myself. We are, I think, rugged country people. In July 1967, we are moving out. Dad is two years dead. Mom and I can no longer take care of the house and grounds. You are a college student, only home summers, and Pearl is off in New York. You and I have rolled up the rug in the living room and we can't stop laughing. I can't. You're making me laugh so hard I'm crying, and I tell myself I am doing the same for you but when I look you are busying yourself, tending to the lamps. What are you doing? I can never remember your jokes. Where's Mom? running an errand, perhaps cleaning the kitchen floor in the new red house in town. That's why we're running the hi-fi full blast, bellowing out "The Bells of Rhymney" on the Judy Collins album you gave me last Christmas. I sing loud because the living room looks so peculiar without the rug.

This is not unlike sex, I think to myself, letting up on the accelerator. A figure in dark clothes cutting across a snow-blanketed field, getting closer and closer. Who is it?

Often, when I am with you, I see us in that house stomping around on the bare floors, giddy with loss. We are ragging each other with puns, well uh uh, not quite. You are five years older than I, and it seems to me you've always led in wordplay, generously inviting me in, in fact, creating—as I suspect most older brothers don't—enormous room for me to dance and spin around you. You talk. I repeat what you say as if it were my own, you roll on the floor, I jump on you, you laugh at my jokes but they're your jokes, my, your, my body. Yours.

My towel, your towel. A game he played with you that I don't remember. Nor could you until it came up for you in a gathering of men who were trying to understand their rather complex relation to their own bodies. I don't remember but I can see it as you tell me. Our handsome, healthy, robust father on his knees leaning over to bathe your—well, I can see him but I can't quite see you at three, four, five? Your soft flesh. Not mine. The game starts with the sound of the water gurgling into the drain, you are standing up, unsteady on your chubby legs and Daddy has the towel. Soft, luxurious, the anticipation of being wrapped and wiped, his strong hands sweeping across your body with the towel, rubbing between your legs and around your buttocks where the dripping water is just now beginning to cool. "Is this—my towel? Or your towel?" He holds it up, pulls it to his chest, thrusts it toward you, and pulls it back. You look at the towel and look at him. His face is rosy, his blue eyes sparkle with the pleasure he takes in you. "My towel? Your towel?" You teeter a little, your lips damp and slightly open, eyes darting from the towel to his face and back again. You're ready to burst. When you do, you are like a little pot boiling over. He sweeps you up from the tub and rubs you silly.

Didn't he? Isn't this a game he played with me?

You roll up the rug in the living room and we arrange it next to the neatly stacked boxes, making sure all is ready for the movers. There must have been movers, but I can't remember them. We are being good children, sober in our responsibilities, though you seem much more an adult now, not yet twenty-one.

We decide to take the last hike, up the trail into the woods, past the place where we always cut a tree for Christmas Eve, on up to the fresh spring, a stopping place on the way up and up. I always drink from this spring, no matter how little water there is, because I thrill to my story of our land: that we have a place so wild and untouched it does not have to be mediated by questions about its purity, unlike the sullen creek it falls to that sometimes gives us earaches when we swim it in the summer. The spring bubbles at the base of a ravine. I love to tear down the slope through the gnarling pines, to leap with accumulating speed over downed branches, twisted and rotting trunks, always seeing myself in a race, a pack leader, the best of my girlfriends, a challenge to my brother, or me and the dog out prowling, wild and loosely ripping up the forest floor on our way to a headfirst dive into that crack of damp and puddling earth.

We embrace this last hike soberly. We are two good soldiers about to be relieved of duty, making a last tribute to our father who ritually took this trip with us during a full moon. The route forms a great circle that takes us bushwhacking through to a trail that leads up one side of the hills to the very top of the valley, and on back down following Log Run to the road and home. By day we walk carefully, stopping often to check the view behind us. Still there. Lycoming Creek drifts along the cliffs out below the grove of pines he planted long before I was born. Up the other side of the ravine we follow old electrical wires along the path of tree stumps.

I used to jump on each stump, turn toward my father and sing out in a mad prepubescent chant, "Ladies and gentlemen, take my advice: I now pronounce you man and wife. You may now kiss the bride!" By the fourth stump I was besotted with myself; my rendition of a televangelist-cum-commercial announcer opened the way for whatever laughable thing was meant by the coming together of men and women. Swinging up the path, my father, his plaid flannel shirt settling loosely across his broad chest, would whistle and clap.

Goodbye, we say. Goodbye, goodbye. Trees, old shack deep into the forest of the next hill. Who built it? The boarded-up window hides a hairy monster behind the broken plate glass inside. Agh, no, it's only the reflection of my eye, my lashes peering back at me through the crack. Safe here. I am safe here. Goodbye, the opening into the cornfield at the very top of the valley. The pulling out of the woods, the great gallop across open space toward the single tree at the center where we have arrived, breathless, on top of the world looking down.

* * *

Going the speed limit, I look over. A buzz of landscape profiles the haggard beauty of your face. I know your body without looking. I have just left behind a man in Oakland whom I think I love, whose broad body I held through the night, pursuing its sweep, swimming out to meet the curving, lolling wave of his embrace. I don't know when I'll see him again. You and I joke about how as adults we've only been able to be close when one of us helps the other move. Our daily lives an impediment. I'd been trying to make a go of it with someone else, a man you couldn't like, and neither, finally, could I. Nor could I imagine the home I'd make bright enough to draw you. Two years living across the bay and we saw each other ten times? Maybe twenty? But haven't we always been close?

Sometimes, when I think of you: Congenital immunological deficiency, let him rest now, Janie.

Mommy, is Bubby going to be all right?

Yes, of course, she says brightly. Or she says—does she?— Oh, he's doing the best he can. Her worried face. I can hear her talking, she murmurs to Dad in their bedroom and, every once in a while, he murmurs back.

Once, looking over her shoulder. You are sitting in a chair in your bedroom, wearing boxer shorts and a robe opened and falling away from your body. She sits holding your leg in her lap and doesn't know I am right behind her, but you do. You look up at me and look back down, noncommittal, your chin on your chest, your hands perhaps loosely clasped across your stomach. There is a basin of hot water, a clean towel, gauze, tape. She wraps her fingers around a lump with a tiny hole in it on the inside of your thigh. She squeezes. I must gasp when the pus erupts from the hole because she turns her head sharply, not removing her hands. "No, Janie! Get away!" which is neither a hiss nor a shout, but—do you remember this—a kind of warding off. I retreat and carry with me the way the hole and the red swelling seem to float within your flesh, foreign and invasive, making your leg something different, something other than you.

"My brother gets abscesses," I solemnly learn to say. Otherwise, a mystery. Delicate. Two steps forward, two steps back. Once that sledding accident: a raucous sweep down the hill slams you into a tree. A cut on the forehead and stitches turn to blood poisoning and the air of the house thickens with worry. Somewhere below me a mother and a father move about. I am in bed upstairs, morning light streaming through the frosty window. Pearl's there? You are in the hospital and we wait for you to come back home. I never go there to see you because healthy children aren't allowed.

Warding me off. Do you remember?

I know your body without looking. Mostly unlike mine, except for the ways we carry ourselves, a certain set of the shoulders when walking, the way we gesture with our large hands when we speak, an occasional inclination to mutter during intimate conversations through a hand clamped over mouth and chin.

Some doctor in a hospital years later will come up with a name: Job's Syndrome. Perfect, you'll say. The man plagued with rashes and boils who sits in a corner, cursing his fate, and you'll laugh.

A car, enclosed space, cutting across territory. My home in boxes you helped me pack. Take these books. Leave these. Let's stop for coffee, Bakersfield, cut east through Tehachapi, let's have some country music. Fine. That's fine. What were those things Dad made, we don't have a name for them. The stained wood rectangles he made to fit around the backs of the couch legs, that kept the couch from slamming into the wall when we'd throw ourselves on it? Who else in the world would know, or care, about that?

I know your body. You showed it to me over the period of a year. Two? I was eight, you were fourteen, thereabouts. A mother and a father move about somewhere. We are upstairs in your room, behind the closed door. How does it start? You're making me laugh so hard I'm crying. You make your penis jump like a puppet, and you make it talk. "Hey you, little girl!" it says. "What's your name?" Penis, is that what we call it? You invite me to touch it and I do touch it. It bobs up and down and I am delighted. Your penis is always erect whenever you show it to me. I think this must be its natural state until I catch you sleeping naked one afternoon and see it curled in a small heap. I am startled but say nothing, don't wake you. Later, you seem to be fine.

Later, you come to know my body. You begin to touch and probe. I know it's a game, like being tickled, only better. I don't have to scream to make you stop. I enjoy myself. You have been my brother and my friend all my life. You have read all of *Johnny Tremain* to me and stopped to explain the part where Johnny injures his hand. You yourself have big hands and you showed me just how the wound kept Johnny from using all his fingers, kept him from practicing his trade so that he had to find another way to survive and, because of injury, become heroic. That's how I remember it.

We take turns applying our hands to each other's bodies. Much laughter. Perhaps, occasional silence. Uncertainty? A moment of uneasiness, looking at you while you finger me. What comes later? There must be stories we make up to go with this too, but I can't remember them. I don't know the word "sexual," and this has so little to do with the climax and release that I will learn through practice years down the road, the earnest and passionate rituals I'll perform, using my body to familiarize strangers and, at times, make strangers of friends. Because this is you. And me. Riding a first wave, *my own, my own*, before I teach myself a physical language of possession that dictates, also, the probability of loss. You are jocular, intent. We never finish what we've started, but remain circling.

After a while, the parents figure it out.

You come into your room, or I come into your room, always your room, and one of us closes the door. You sit me down and tell me in a sober voice that we can't play this way anymore. Mom and Dad have taken you aside and explained to you that what you are doing is a very bad thing. I laugh that off, suggest a way to fool them. "Let's just pretend we're playing a game called 'Rip' where we rip each other's clothes. And, uh, the person who rips off the most clothes wins!"

"No," you say. No, we can't.

We do. Don't we? Not that game, and not a game any longer. Outside now, without regularity, almost random. When we catch each other. Once in the barn, where the Crosley has been put to rest. You have become more instructive with your body, yet more obscure in what you say. My own voice trails into muteness. I am less certain of your face, the hurried way you tell me what to do. We take our clothes all the way off and you tell me to lie down on the Crosley's back seat. You get in and slowly lower yourself over me until your penis barely, just barely touches the lips of my vagina. We are trembling. I see your body up there, hovering over me, the pink flush and the pallidness of it all mixed. I'm excited and appalled. Your body and my own stretch away as if we both now belong to something else, as if our names are being stripped from us and, the dust-moted air and the roof of the car and the dark wooden beams beyond the open car door breaking the slants of light pouring through the barn walls, all, all of it wheeling away from us before we stop, we stop there.

A figure in dark clothes cutting across a snow-blanketed field. Who is it?

Sometimes I have thought unkindly: Well. He's certainly made a career out of that story.

In the late seventies we are both drawn to the movement against violence against women. I stay there for several years, then move on to U.S. foreign policy. You commit, become an activist, build an organization of men who raise consciousness about the male proclivity for dominance, and the resolution of gender conflict through aggression and violence. You counsel sex offenders, have developed programs for working with teenagers meant to allow them the sense of their own bodily integrity, their own voices, and also meant to teach them how to tangle with the abuses of the adult world. In adult public workshops you sometimes refer to your own experiences, how you lived in the country, a special—a "bright"— boy from the middle class among the working-class families strung up and down our road, how you were isolated from your classmates because you were too smart and perhaps too sickly on occasion. How you had in late adolescence a few trysts with girls across class lines, girls you would not be seen with about town, girls to whom you told yourself you were benevolent, unthreatening, that you were differ-

ent from other men in the way you intended to get sex. Sometimes
you talk about me.

You tell me about a peculiar thing that happened to you as a
consequence of your work. An irate mother, a psychologist, has
called you up. She thinks you have been manipulating her daughter. You were making a videotape with high-school students who
were writing and acting out scripts meant to teach them how to
protect themselves against sexual violence. Her daughter scripted
and acted a story about being molested by a "cousin," who turned
out to be her brother. The psychologist, to whom this was news,
denies it and has threatened legal action. On the phone she has
accused you of being a known child molester. She says you are guilty
of once, over a period of time, abusing your own sister.

I laugh that off, puzzled at the direction the story has taken.
Then annoyed. What happened to the part, I think, about us, about
me? The pleasure I took, safe in my knowledge of you?

Sometimes, when your friends meet me: Oh, you're Allan's
sister. I've heard so much about you.

A house on a dirt road. Two cars, trees, dogs, cats, the angry
duck. A mother and a father move about somewhere. I know so
much about you. Once, 1974, I am out of college and working as a
landscaper on a construction crew in your town, Colorado. I have
been reading *Lesbian Nation* and sharing it with another woman on
the crew because I think, *maybe*, and, *well, what if?* You are miserable in graduate school and living with a woman whom you suppose you love and who supposes she loves you, but all that will
change. You and I have been to see Bergman's *Cries and Whispers*
and have gone for several pitchers of beer because we are so wrought
up. How I remember: Three sisters, one of them dying, and a maidservant. The two healthy sisters cannot minister to the third, will
not touch her. They circle in separate agonies, falling back from
the deathbed, always upright and fiercely cold in each other's presence, but once alone, disintegrating. A glass shard and blood, a
sexual wound, self-inflicted.

We drink glass after glass.

Circling in the snow white landscape, the deep reds and black
of the interior.

I am obsessed with the maidservant, how she climbs into bed with the dying woman, opens her breasts to her, gets behind her, and holds her with all of her body. How the woman dies that way, a full embrace.

You are my brother across the table. I think you know everything about me. We are drunk when I walk with you back to your house, a circuitous route toward mine. Years I've spent tailing you on woody trails, or out following the weave and kick of your body threading creek water. The informing and surreptitious pleasures of your room. Would you have known me, tracing my hand across your sheets when you weren't there, repelled for an instant by the spots of blood crusting the fabric? How ashamed I was and didn't tell anyone, afraid I couldn't love you enough for the solitary days and nights you spent, your body in torment? You lean against a tree in front of your house and I lean into you, take you in my arms and kiss you, keep kissing you, losing myself in your mouth. There is so much personal pain. Some of it has made me special. You stop me. We stop there.

You referred to this once as "that time you wanted to screw."

Warding me off. Do you remember?

You tell me she was always so "chipper." Everything's going to be all right. So that, when you were feverish, in terrible pain, you felt you had to pretend for her, you had to protect her from how badly you were hurting. "I remember doing that when I was five years old," you tell me, when you are forty-two. What you say to me the times I've come worried but cheerful to visit you in the hospital: "I'm fine." I never know what to do. When have I strayed too far or come too close, trying to fill you up with myself?

Always, as these things happened between us, it was the both of us. Never just you, and never just me. A mother and a father somewhere.

On top of the world looking down. Enclosed space. Cutting across territory. You were the last to see her alive. One minute talking to her in the hospital bed. The nurse, you said, called her E-*liz*-abeth, musically, as if she were a little girl. She could barely speak and you were there to watch over her, be cheerful. Then she seized up, her body arched in the bed. I try to see it, be there. The last thing, as they push you back, pulling the curtains around her. They tear off her shirt, eclipse her head, face. The large failing breasts. Pump frantically at her heart.

Going the speed limit.

The haggard beauty of your face, years in the making. I see us there always now side by side, profiled, gazing into the world. I see this at odd moments when I am struck by a longing that spreads far beyond my ability to say what it is I want or need, right then, right now. I reach for bodies, a father and a mother alive, caressing voices, the chatter of children growing out of themselves and into something else against the terrifying weightlessness the dead leave behind. Inside that longing, you arrive. A brother and a sister who tease and parry, investigate desire, love what they love. Which is, in each other, how alive we are still, how alert to the fragile weight of our bodies.

Going the speed limit.

The haggard beauty of your face.

Baby Doll
TERMINATOR

MY MOM'S NEW BOYFRIEND, JACKSON, IS BORN AGAIN, SO WE SCOUR the dirt like gold panners for the fingernail-sized rocks with crosses naturally formed on them. Angel tears. Supposedly when Jesus died the angels cried and their tears turned to stones. We try to escape from the busload of Baptists giving praises and hallelujahs, which echo loudly all through the forest of Fairy Stone Park, Virginia.

I always find the best ones, with clearly defined crosses rising out of the brown stones, not the broken, crumbly ones my mom finds.

"You find 'em like an old horse finds glue, don't ya?" Her eyes squeeze up all jealous-like, her nostrils widening.

"Lord smiling on you today, son." I look up into Jackson's big face, long and black-bearded, exactly like Paul Bunyan, smiling down at me, with the emerald treetops shifting the light above his head in glints and glimmers like a halo.

He reaches down and takes the cross stone from my outstretched palm. "Have to show this one at services." He nods. "Let the Lord guide you to more, son." He pats my ass as I turn away. I catch my mom's jagged glare and my smile folds. We continue to hunt, bent over the dark peaty moist earth in silence.

"Look at this one, Jackson!" My mom rushes over to him. She holds out her hand like I did, her other hand pushing her yellow hair back against her skull, repeatedly. He leans over her palm, she shifts back and forth, he turns it over and shakes his head.

"Not as good as his, baby doll." He nods toward me. I look away grinning. I hear her throw it into the bushes.

"I found another one!" I yell, and raise up my arm, holding another perfectly formed tear of an angel.

"You're my baby."

I raise my head silently from my pillow. There's only a thin divider that doesn't reach up to the trailer roof anyway.

"My sweet little girl." He half whispers, and I hear blankets moving and sticky skin noises.

"Yes I am." Her voice sounds too high and babyish.

"What are you, darlin'?"

"Daddy's little girl," she answers right away.

"Daddy needs his little girl." I hear the patting of flesh and I lay my head back down. She makes purring noises.

"Tell me you're Daddy's good girl," he growls. She says it.

I reach under my blanket.

"Ya want Daddy to fuck ya?"

She says yes, says "Daddy" twice.

I reach between my legs.

"C'mon baby girl, c'mon, give it to your daddy." His voice rises. "C'mon. Good girl, good girl."

I take my thing and push it backward between my legs, and I feel the trailer swaying. I rub the smooth skin where my thing was, in time to the rocking.

"Good girl, good girl, Daddy loves you." I close my eyes.

I watch her from the side in the morning, leaning into the tiny mirror over the kitchen sink, smoothing tan foundation over her face with a small triangular white sponge. She dabs it on heavily over her nose and cheeks, covering the spray of freckles that she hates. The same ones on my face I hate, too.

"Make mine disappear?" I ask her suddenly. She turns to me in surprise that I'm even there. I step back. She smiles.

"Pull over a chair." I drag one of the red metal folding chairs over.

"Climb up." I stand on top and see our faces in the mirror.

"Let's get rid of those." I nod my head and watch her dab the sponge into some beige liquid foundation that's open with the rest of her makeup above the sink ledge.

"Here." She rubs it over my nose and cheeks, not gently like she did to herself; but my freckles are darker. I enjoy her touching me.

"There! Look." I stand on my tiptoes and lean into the mirror. They're gone. I smile up at her.

"We gotta do something about your nose." I look at hers: delicate, upturned, thin.

"Somebody fucked their nigger slave, and you got the nose to prove it."

I look at mine: short, turned up like hers, but with thick nostrils, wider and almost flattened.

"Nigger—nigger nose!" She laughs.

"Fix it? Please?" I don't want to cry.

"Sure, nigger nose!" She laughs again and I smile, my lip shaking.

"Camouflage it . . . see I learned that in beauty school." I watch her take a small brush and dip it in brownish eye shadow.

"One day I'll go back, I'll get a shop for the models in Hollywood . . ." She sucks the wooden end of the brush. "Or I'll be a model."

"Take me?"

"Hold still." She runs the brush along the sides of my nose like she's dusting.

"Well, we'll see if we can fix this nigger nose."

I try to see in the mirror but her hand's in the way.

"Okay, now I lighten it with concealer." She dabs some creamy stuff onto my nose.

"Blend, okay, now . . . look at me." I look up at her, feeling excited and nervous.

"Can I go with you?"

"Take a look." She pushes my face toward the mirror. My nose has brown-beige strips on its sides like war paint.

"Definitely camouflages!" I nod hard.

"Okay, now your eyes . . . You have my eyes, so you're lucky. Okay, close your eyes." I do and I feel brushes gliding across my lids, her coffee breath warm and moist against my cheek, her hand resting on my forehead.

"Look up, look left . . . right, blink . . . again."

It feels like she's writing on my eyes. I don't want it to stop.

"Look at me!" I do and what happened is freeze-framed in my head forever, her licking her finger and running it gently under my eyes. It reminds me of those nature films of a mother bird regurgitating food into its baby's mouth. I feel so happy I almost hug her.

"Can I look?" My hands flap at my sides.

"No, you ain't half done. Let's see if we can give you lips . . . you ain't too lucky—you got the nose, I got the lips."

I trace my finger across my thin lips with little crowned points. Hers are big, shiny, and red.

"Look here." She holds a rust-red pencil. I pucker my lips.

"Nooo . . . relax 'em," she says, a little irritated.

"You ever see me pucker when I do my lips? I shake my head no.

"Well, course I got lips, even a chicken's got more lips than you." She laughs, I smile.

"Close, just natural like."

The pencil moves around my mouth.

"Okay . . . now . . ." I hear her opening lipsticks.

"Open." I look up at the white corkboard-like ceiling. She dabs lipstick on my lips.

"Hmmm . . ." And then a brush with mushy wet goop sweeps across my lips. I look up at her, so close to me, staring at my mouth, she catches me, I look away fast.

"Here . . ." She holds a toilet paper sheet to my mouth. I open and close on it like I've done a million times, copying her, but now I leave red kiss marks. I laugh and try to turn toward the mirror.

"Not yet!" She grabs my head.

"Blush?" she asks.

"Yeah, yeah," I practically yell. "Please." My eyes flutter as she lightly sweeps a big fuzzy brush across my cheeks and over my face.

"I won't do your nose, don't wanna bring no attention to that, do we niggey nose?"

"Uh uh."

"Okay, now, to set. Close your eyes." She dusts me with translucent powder, her hand over my eyes to protect them, and again I feel overwhelmed with joy.

"Can I look?" She regards me.

"Go ahead." She turns my head toward the mirror. I blink at myself and try to recognize what I see. It's her same eyes, a mottled mix of pale blue-gray-green, painted and outlined, only smaller. My lips are full, almost like hers, and satiny red. I don't even notice my nose.

"Well?" She sounds impatient.

"I, I look pretty," I say quietly.

"See, I told you you were meant to be a girl."

"I know," I mumble, and bite my lip.

"Stop that!" She hits my head, not hard. "Don't mess my lips!"

"Sorry."

"Now, ain't you glad I didn't cut your hair short?" She reaches for the curling iron. I nod yes and realize I've gotten used to it and like it when we go to the shops and the store owners say I'm a pretty girl like my older sister. Sometimes I get free candy. Only once did I correct someone.

"She's my mom and I ain't a girl!" The tall, pimply man behind the meat counter leans forward.

"Pardon?"

Her hand reaches out, grabs the back of my hair, and gives a quick, sharp yank. She laughs.

"Playin' games . . . she always is . . . now say thank you . . ."

She unloads the groceries silently into the trunk. I go to climb into the back where I usually sit when she has a boyfriend, if he's with us or not.

"Sit up front," she says. I watch her start the car and push in the lighter.

"I want a haircut!" I feel strong in my anger. She says nothing, just starts to drive.

"Everyone says I'm a girl. I'm not!" I almost yell. "Even Kevin!" The lighter pops out, and she pushes it back in and starts humming.

"I'm not a girl and I want a haircut, okay!" I'm yelling, my body turned toward her. She pulls onto a dirt road.

"I want a haircut, I want a haircut!" My fist pounds the vinyl seat. "Grandfather would never let my hair be long!" I say spitefully. The car jerks to a stop.

"Wait here," she says really friendly, smiling.

"Huh?"

"Wait here." She puts on lipstick.

"Where you goin'?" I feel my anger draining. I try to hold on to it. "We gettin' my haircut?"

She points wordlessly to the back of the sheriff's tiny brown wooden building. She turns to me with a wide smile, all her teeth showing.

"I'm turning you in. You are too evil and bad."

I swallow hard and try to adjust to her words. She starts to pull open her door.

"No! . . . Please!" The world starts to tilt and melt.

"I've hid you, changed your name, my name, how many times now?"

"Please . . ." My air is choking off.

"'Member when those workers came round last time? I moved and changed everything so they wouldn't get you."

I start to see colors swirling around the windshield, making it hard to see clearly.

"They warned me Satan was entrenched in your soul, that you should be put to the chair and sent to hell to burn forever."

Spit bubbles between my lips. I can't say a word.

"I'll be back with the sheriff in a jiffy." She caps her lip-stick. "They'll cut your hair for you, they'll shave your head for the chair, unless they stone you, or . . ." Her eyes turn from corner to corner, then stare straight back down at me. "I won't be surprised if they don't just lynch you when word gets out who you really are." She adjusts the car mirror to see herself and rubs lip-stick off her teeth.

"Don't go . . ." I'm crying. She doesn't turn.

"They usually take a knife and cut your evil tongue out first and then your eyes—scoop 'em right out, and they laugh and celebrate. They'll be extra pissed 'cause you've tricked 'em all."

"Please . . . please." Spit rolls down my chin.

The lighter pops out. She shoves it back in and gets out of the car.

"I tried to make you good. I see I've failed. Wait here."

The door slams and I squeeze my eyes to try to see past the fireball of reds, blues, and yellows cycloning around me. I can see her cross the street and enter the sheriff's station.

All the voices inside scream at me, and I can't see outside anymore, I can only hear the taunting. I see the huge wooden electric chair, wired, waiting and empty, and the silver-gray switch. I see all the faces laughing and jeering, and the Horned One clutching his blood-soaked pitchfork. And I'm alone, so alone, and I deserve it all, and there is no one to take it away. No one. I lean forward and bang my head on the dashboard. My mom told me that when I was a baby I used to bang my head all day and all night long. She kept me in the top dresser drawer. It drove her nuts, she said. It was Satan fighting for my soul. It would get so loud she'd have to close the drawer.

"Stop it, stop it!" I feel a hand holding me down, pushing me back into my seat, keeping me still. The sheriff's large, hairy hand is reaching through the open window, resting on my shoulder. My mother is standing next to him. I cannot breathe at all.

"See why I can't send her to school?" I can barely hear my mother's voice. "She should be in third grade. Can't attend without causing problems."

"How long you been in town?" he asks, gravelly voiced.

"Month."

"Well, we'll see about some special classes. You livin' with Kevin Rays?"

"Yes, sir," she says sweetly.

"So you wanna get home schoolin', huh? Well, I'll see what I can do."

"Much obliged, sir." His hand releases me.

"Ya'll take care." He walks away. She gets back in the car, and pushes in the popped-out lighter.

"I convinced him not to take you. I'm gonna try to fight Satan for your soul and make you good, do you understand me?"

I nod slowly, stiffly. We're both staring straight ahead at the deserted, tree-lined dirt road.

"You'll have to be punished." I nod again, the colors settling, my vision clearing.

"Or if you don't want that you can go 'cross the street and turn yourself right in."

I shake my head no.

"Very well, then . . . take your thing out." Her voice is calm. My stomach is tight and I hiccup up a little vomit. It burns as I swallow it back down.

"Take your thing out!" The lighter pops out, and she knocks it back in. My hands tremble, and I watch as they pull down my zipper and pull out my thing, small and pink.

"Hands under." I swallow too loudly.

"Do you want to go in there?" She turns toward me and points at the sheriff's. I shake my head and slide my hands under my legs, like I've done other times. Her hands wraps around my thing; I stare straight ahead at a stray dog sniffing for something to eat in the dirt. Her long red nails flash.

She leans over me and whispers in my ear. "Do you think Kevin would let you stay if he knew about this evil thing?" Her hand starts to move slowly, gently. "Mmm, do ya?" She smells like baby powder. I shake my head no.

"Do you think tellin' people I'm your mother and you are a bastard is gonna help any?" I shake my head a small no.

It looks like the skeletal dog has found some food. My thing moves through her fingers. I try to imagine the electric chair and hellfire. I sob.

"Do you really think the butcher would give us free cuts if he knew you weren't no sweet little girl, but had this evil thing?"

Fire burns me alive, stones pound into my flesh, everyone laughs. Her fingers give soft little yanks.

"Let's see how evil and bad you truly are." Her fingers stop their caressing.

"You failed the test," she says gravely.

I look down and see it sticking straight ahead, leading me into hell.

"Do you want to turn yourself in?" I shake my head no. Tears roll down my cheeks.

"Feeling sorry for yourself is further proof of your unrepented evil."

The lighter pops out. Her fingers, red-tipped, pluck it out.

"Well?" She looks at me.

"I want to be good." I whisper. I feel everything close up inside me. I see the coils, red and glowing, disappear down to where her fingers hold my thing. I dig my hands, sweaty and cold, under my thighs. I watch the tip of my thing disappear into the lighter. I don't move, I don't scream, I don't cry. I've learned the hard way that lessons are repeated until learned properly, and silently, and Satan is, even temporarily, exorcised. I stare straight ahead and watch the dog eating its own foot.

I listen to the sizzle of the hot iron wrapped tightly around a lock of my shoulder-length hair.

"My hair used to be white like yours." The iron pulls on my scalp.

"Yours'll get darker, too." She releases it and a tumble of white-blond curls roll back. She slides her fingers through another section of hair. I'm aware of every touch as her hands move through my hair against my scalp.

"You better appreciate this." I nod as she wraps my hair in the iron jaws and rolls it up tight.

"You look so beautiful." She beams and leans down next to me while holding the iron up, her face next to mine in the mirror.

"We're beautiful girls, ain't we?!" The iron is too close to the back of my ear and it's burning it, but I don't dare say a thing. I smile at us, two beautiful girls in the mirror, and ignore the scent of burning flesh.

Usually when I'm alone and not allowed out, I walk around the narrow trailer and turn on the TV and all the radios as loud as I can take. I sit somewhere between the sounds and let the voices and music come at me and compete for my attention. I enjoy deciding which appliance will win me over. I'm proud of my ability to concentrate totally on whatever I choose to hear, and tune out what I don't.

If Jackson or my mom gets home early and catches me, they get pissed.

"How can you hear anything?" Jackson asks, not really wanting an answer. "Only put one thing on at a time," he orders. "Otherwise it's too much, you'll go crazy."

Today, though, I don't need my noise. I stand on the chair staring at the pretty face that really isn't mine anymore but is my mom's. At first all I do is stare and hardly blink, as if a wrong breath could shatter her face like a frozen palette. But slowly I get bolder, and start winking like she does to guys who whistle at her. I practice for at least an hour, that fast wink, quick like a gunfighter who draws and shoots before he's touched his gun. Then I work on the kiss blowing—head tilted slightly, lips barely puckered, and the uplift of the head to properly launch the kiss. Then the combo kiss and wink, wink—wink, wink, kiss, kiss—wink. It takes me all morning. Then I realize she needs to wear something other than a T-shirt and underwear, so I go past the divider into their side of the bedroom and open her drawer. I carefully move aside the strawberry

car air fresheners and dress her in a lacy baby-doll nightie Jackson
just ordered especially for her from Victoria's Secret. It hangs down
to her ankles, though, so I have to pin it up to show her legs. I even
dig out a pair of the panties he got her, white, lacy, with ruffles on
the backside. I accidentally put both legs in one opening. I fix it
and pin it to the front and run to the full-length mirror on the bathroom door.

"You are so beautiful, baby doll!" I giggle, and swirl my nightie
around.

"Thank you, honey." I shake my ass in the mirror, wink, and
blow a perfect Fire Red Temptation gloss kiss. "Daddy's sexy little
girl . . . uh oh." I lift the frilly front of my nightie. "Shit! Why do
you gotta ruin everything?" I reach in her panties and push it back
between my legs. "Go away!" I scream down at it. I keep my baby-
doll raised and run my palm over the smooth, flat crotch.

"How's my baby doll's honey pot?" I wink at the mirror.
"Needin' all your lovin', Jackson." I walk sexily toward the mirror,
and my thing pops out.

"Shit, goddam it!" I punch it hard with my fists. "Owww!" It
starts aching. "Go away! Fuck!"

I close my eyes tightly so the tears won't ruin her makeup.
And then it comes to me. I start to laugh. I run over to the sink and
lift the flowered sheet hanging down, hiding the stuff stowed under
it. I dig past the Windex, Turtle Wax, and Comet, until I find it.
"Why didn't ya think of this before, baby girl?" I hold up the Krazy
Glue and laugh until it hurts.

All the lights are off, leaving just the strobe-light glow of the
TV. Jackson sits in his brown velour easy chair watching the satel-
lite services live from Sermon Mount and sipping steadily on his
fourth beer.

She walks toward him, slow and slinky like a spider doing
the creepy crawl up to its catch.

"C'mere to Daddy." He waves her over, not looking up. She
stands a few feet in front of him spinning in circles, making the white
frilly baby doll he special-ordered from Victoria's Secret glow a
ghostly blue-gray in the twilight TV light of the trailer. Her blond

curls twirl out like cast fishing lines. She twists around and around, weaving her magic love spell that no man can resist.

"What the hell you doin' in Lord's name and creation?" The spinning stops. She blinks at him, winks, blows a kiss.

"Jesus, Lord above, what happened to you?" He's not watching Sermon Mount anymore, he's watching his baby doll: me.

She moves closer, one foot in front of the other as if on a tightrope, in the shiny black leather open-toed, sling-back heels, being careful not to trip. She blows a kiss, fingers held out displaying Red Lust nail paint.

"What the hell . . . ?" He motions with his beer and spills a dark patch on his Day-Glo orange forklift operator's jumpsuit leg.

"Your mother put you up to this?" He wipes the spill with his hand, staring at her, his face narrow and pointy, a perfect triangle from his nose down. It's hard to see both his eyes at once.

"I'm your baby girl." Her voice is shy and sweet, the way he likes it. He laughs, muting out the sounds from the sermon.

"She home early?" He takes a long sip of the beer, smiles, and looks her up and down.

"Sarah!" He leans past me and shouts.

She giggles. "It's me, Daddy . . ." she whispers.

"Jesus." He finishes off his beer and the empty clank of it dropping on the linoleum floor echoes through the trailer. He reaches around for a full one, never turning from her.

"Jesus, you look like your mother . . ." He pops open his beer. "Few years on back, I reckon." He grunts. She puffs out her lips, pouty and hungry, and slowly slides her thumb into her mouth and begins to suck, the way he likes her to do.

"Take that thumb out, you know you ain't to do that." She pulls it out, then slowly slides it back in and out, in and out.

"There is something wrong with you, son." He slowly wipes the foam from his lips. "Or whatever the hell you are. Jesus." He smoothes out his pants lap.

"Lord . . ." he chuckles. "You do look . . ." She turns around, raises up the back of the baby-doll and shakes her ass, making the panty ruffles flutter like wings, the way he likes to see. He gulps more beer.

"Your mama's gonna whip the daylights out of ya." She wiggles her bottom a few more times, then turns to face him, thumb still buried in her mouth.

He always tells her, "Baby doll, I love ya best when you're sucking on that thumb, makes me think you're an angel." When she asks him for money or anything, she puts her thumb right into her mouth; she'll sit on his lap and lean on his chest, and he'll stroke her hair. "Tell Daddy what ya need, baby doll." If she takes out her thumb to speak, he pushes it back in. He doesn't tell her she's too big for acting like a baby, doesn't rub hot peppers on her thumb so she'll quit sucking, doesn't laugh and tease her for it. With her thumb in her mouth she gets what she wants. Always.

She faces him silently, mouth sealed with her thumb, blue eyes wide, and ringed in black, standing in lightning flashes of color splashing from the TV, waiting for recognition. And he stares, his eyes circling like a plane waiting to land. And then he burps, deep and resonant. His gaze turns downward like an ashamed child's. "Pardon," he mumbles. And with his shame she knows she is recognized. She jumps on his lap, into his arms still laying on the arm rests, his nails combing the velour to expose its shiny, silver-brown underbelly.

"Lord help me, what's got into you?" His eyes squint, and his chin doubles as he thrusts his head back like a chicken. His mouth is frozen in a half grin.

"Ain't your baby doll pretty?" she asks with her thumb half pulled out, against his chest. It vibrates, bouncing her delicate, sculpted head with his stiff laugh.

"Ain't your little girl pretty?" she whispers, past her thumb, deep into the padding of the wiry curled hair of his chest. Her other arm is wrapped around his waist tightly, the way he likes her to do.

He says nothing, stares past her to the TV sermon, turns his gaze back to her, then to the TV, back and forth, his eyes shifting like dull metal weights on a balance beam, weighing. A slight frown makes little gullies on the ends of his mouth. She pumps her legs, dangling from the edge of his lap, like on a swing, forcing it higher. One of her oversized shoes flies off and lands with a crash somewhere in the dark silence of the trailer. It makes him jump. She giggles, causing her front teeth to bite down on her red-ringed thumb. He looks down at her legs, wiggling, thin, and shiny, white like sheets of pasta. He clears his throat and lifts his beer.

"Uh, want some?" His voice quivers, while the other hand drums the arm rest. She slides her thumb out slowly as if savoring the last bit of a Popsicle, sucking it, the way he likes her to. She takes the beer and sips it while blinking up at him.

"She, uh, cocktailin' till late, uh, not home early, is she now?" His eyes shift from one armrest to the other. She hands the beer back to him.

"I am your sweet little girl, Daddy." She leans up against his chest in the comfort of a heartbeat outside her own, both arms wrapped around his Day-Glo orange torso. He sits there in the quiet of the trailer's electric hum, not moving, staring intently at the soundless sermon. The beer is empty. He crushes it in one hand and drops it. His breath gets louder. She leans in closer and rubs her fluffy curls against the end of his beard. He shifts his legs. She wiggles on his lap. He clears his throat again. Her hands slide along his sides, thick and solid.

He always tells her, "You're safe in these arms, baby doll. Nobody's ever gonna hurt you again." She reaches her hand out and runs it down his arm like a child sliding down a banister until she hits his fist clutching the remote.

"Play with me," she whispers to him, the way he likes her to say. His fist slowly uncurls.

"Please . . . Daddy?" With a violent pop and flash the light of the TV is sucked back, and it's all dark except for the orange and blue dots of appliances glowing like one-eyed cats.

Whenever she wakes up to the black of the trailer, screaming and flailing, he holds her until it's passed.

"Just a nightmare, my sweet little girl, just a bad dream." He doesn't yell at her for waking everyone up, doesn't spank her for wetting, doesn't laugh at her for crying like a baby. "Let Daddy make you safe," he tells her.

"Hold me . . . Daddy," she whispers, the way he likes her to.

He doesn't give her only quick little pats like a dog, doesn't avoid touching her like she's contagious, doesn't take her on his lap even for a spanking. The ache is severe, pounding, and relentless.

All that's left are the words only she is entitled to say.

Because she's beautiful.

Because she's his baby girl.

"I need your love, Daddy."

She lifts his hand to her waist. The remote clatters at his feet. He stares at the dead TV. His hand, like a paperweight, rests above her jutting hip bone.

"Make me safe," she whispers into his heart.

"My sweet little baby girl," he answers, and his hand starts to move.

"Ungrateful little bitch!"

The water separates into pretty pink pools like Easter egg dye inside the sink.

Something, clock radio? flies across the trailer, its plug streaming like a comet's tail. It crashes and escapes through the window next to me. The white silk folds in the middle of the pastel water like egg drop soup.

"Let fuckin' go of me, you faggot! I'm gonna kill him, let go!"

Things are falling and smashing apart. Sitting in the center of the white, no matter how hard I scrub it, is a red, bleeding, unblinking eye.

"Let me go, you fucker! Let me go!"

I swirl the white silk around and around, like a Chinese dragon chasing its tail, the water spreading pink from its leaking, wounded heart.

"You motherfucker!"

The shoe bouncing off the red metal chair I'm standing on sounds like a gong.

"Let go of me, you fuckin' traitor!" I swirl the now pinkish white silk faster and faster, a cyclone pulling everything down it to its dark hole, including me. She screams with such a guttural force that the trailer vibrates like a tin can and a few loose glass shards from the newly broken window tumble down and shatter. I lay both my hands onto the cool water, stilling it. She screams again but this time it's muted, as if through a hand.

The bloody clump stares up at me, accusing me, claiming me. And the silk is undulating like it's breathing, in the dying waves in the sink.

"Offa my mouth!" she yells, muffled. They're panting heavy and fast as if they're behind the divider, on their bed. I twist my head toward them.

What I can see of her face not covered by his hand is bright red, her hair looks brown from sweat and is stuck all over her face and is twisted up in his curly black beard. Her eyebrows jump up and down as if she's lost control of them. She twists and turns in his grip. His other arm is stretched around her. When she sees me looking, she struggles harder, her hands balled into fists.

He just looks sad and confused, like he's holding a wounded, vicious animal that he doesn't know quite what to do with.

"You better get out of here." He nods at me with his head, looking not at me but at her.

"I didn't get the stain out yet," I sort of whisper.

"You better get out of here," he says again wearily, still holding my mother tightly, his fingers pressing white dents into her arms and cheeks.

I jump down off my chair and reach under the sink for the sacred white jug. "It'll be okay," I tell them.

I climb back up and carefully pour half a gallon of the magic liquid into the water. Its bitter smell reassures me. Bleach is the true holy water, and I know salvation is near.

* * *

"This will help to save you." My grandmother holds me by my right wrist. In her other hand she holds a large mason jar filled with a fluid so clear it's like liquid glass.

"You forgot how we taught you?" She nods her head yes, I shake a no. "Your mother should've taught you, at the very least," she scolds, dropping my wrist and resting the jar on a wooden shelf next to the huge porcelain tub with large lion paws for feet.

"I'm sorry, ma'am," I whisper, and watch a glob of snot and tears fall from my chin. I don't move my right hand to wipe it, I can't trust it, even now.

"I'm sure you are now, Jeremiah." She leans over the tub, her baby-corn colored hair, the same as my mom's, pulled up tight into a bun. Her full-moon face collects little steam drops as she leans over the tub adjusting the chipped silver cross knob.

"I'm very sorry, ma'am," I sniffle, and concentrate hard on holding my right arm still, next to my side. I block out the stinging pain and blink my tears away.

"I can see why she's left you. Not that she's much better, devil's claimed you both, sad to tell," she says into the rising steam, occasionally dipping her hand into the water.

"You mustn't give into dirty temptation," she says, leaning over the swirling tub water.

"Yes'm." I sniffle up some snot. Each time she turns to me, my heart contracts. I see my mother's face in hers, but heavily creased and thicker.

"I hope you are not feelin' one bit sorry for yourself." She shakes her finger at me. I shake my head no and stare down at my bare feet.

"Only the devil would, you got a just whopping and you need to be taught."

It all happened so fast. I'd been at my grandparents' only an hour since the social worker left me there. I'd been in police stations, foster homes, and the hospital for a month, from the time my mother left me on the outskirts of Vegas, until I arrived in West Virginia.

I sat on the straight-back wooden bench in the hall while the social worker and my grandparents spoke. They discussed how my mom left me, how I spit and kicked when they tried to move me. I knew she would be back. They talked about how I had something wrong with me, that I didn't play with other kids or toys, and I didn't answer their questions. I knew they were testing me, to see how bad I was. I kept quiet and stayed to myself. I knew not to touch stuff that wasn't mine. You broke it, you payed, one way or the other.

They heard how I was "disturbed," that I did something bad with a foster father at a home I stayed in before the social workers found out I had grandparents. I knew that if he put his thing in me, he'd let me stay, not throw me out. I was just trying to get it over with because I liked it there. They had a pet pig that came right up to me as soon as I got there and with his snout flipped my hand onto his head to scratch him.

"He likes you," the foster father said.

He found out I was evil, though. He yelled at me to pull up my pants and to be behaving. I tried to tell him it was okay, and I tried to sit on his lap, but he pushed me away so hard I fell. He yelled at his wife to call the social worker. They sent me back.

All the other kids stared at me as I left.

They heard that I'd just been in a hospital for being disturbed because no foster home would keep me. They heard about how I still sucked my thumb and went in my pants. But what made my grandfather clear his throat again and again and my grandmother call for the Lord's assistance was what the social worker, who met me only when I left the hospital and flew to Wheeling, and who hadn't heard more than five words from me, told them.

She told them how I took my thing out in public and played with it. Somebody would tell me to stop and I would be at it again two minutes later. They spoke about that for a while, the social worker and my grandparents, who hadn't seen me since the last time my mom left me, a year or so ago.

"Not in this house of the Lord," I heard his sermon voice boom.

"Lord," my grandmother repeated.

"Good luck," the social worker told them.

They walked out into the hall and faced me sitting on the bench, waiting.

"See what I was talking about," the social worker said to them, pointing at me.

"Good Lord!" my grandmother said, looking like she'd seen a live ghost. My grandfather's hand suddenly slapped my face.

"Cut that out now, Jeremiah!"

"We can hospitalize him if you can't deal with his behavior," the social worker told them.

"Get your hands out of your pants now, Jeremiah!" my grandfather ordered.

The social worker leaned over me, grabbed my right arm, and pulled it out of my underwear and the jeans that I got at a foster home, which were a little too big.

And my feeling of safety, like a blanket wrapped around me, was ripped away. I blinked up at them in surprise. They all stared at me, frowning. She offered to take me to the hospital again. He told her he would cure me.

They started walking to the door with its stained glass panes filtering the hazy November sun. It was nearing Christmas time. She gave them her card. "Call if you change your mind. Good luck," the social worker said.

My mama would come back, she always did. My mama would return because I would be cured. I felt the warmth spread through me again.

"Thanks for your help, God bless you, God bless."

The door shut.

My mama is so proud that I'm cured.

"Lord have mercy!" they said, turning to me.

"I'm cured!" I shouted, and looked straight up at them, my grandparents standing over me.

He reached out, grabbed my right arm out of my pants, and tore my warmth and hope away.

* * *

"I'll cure you, Jeremiah, by the love of Jesus I will." He pulled me into his study where they all were five minutes before. My grandmother closed the carved oak door. I heard her walking down the hall, praying to Him for assistance. He walked around me, but it was as if the sound was turned down; I saw his mouth moving but I couldn't hear him because our breathing was too loud, heavy in my ears, like when a new daddy was behind me, fast, deep, and searching, loud and wet in my ear, holding me, opening his belt like my grandfather was doing now. His mouth poured out hot, heavy breath, and it was warm and comforting and joyful. His hand slapped my face. I knew he'd put his love into me. His belt was off, doubled. His hand slapped me again and its sting echoed inside my head, proof of his love. I knew his love, and it was a blessing, because I was almost cured.

The breathing was deep and needy, and again he pulled my right hand out from the warmth inside, but the heat was permanent now.

He pushed me over his desk and yanked my pants down. I turned my head to look back at him, his face was shiny, red, and shaking. I waited but the belt stayed in his hand, doubled.

I had another chance as the tub filled and I stood there naked next to my grandmother. I held my right hand away from my body and all possibility of evil doings.

"This will burn, Jeremiah." Her lips, full like my mother's, turned down in a frown. "But not one-billionth of what hell's fire will be if you are not saved."

I nodded again, holding my right hand farther out from me, as if it was a contaminated fish.

She lifted the large mason jar and silently unscrewed the lid. The strong chlorine scent filled the bathroom. I breathed in deeply the smell of summer and swimming pools and let the warmth envelop me.

"Jeremiah!" I opened my eyes. She grabbed my right arm away and jerked me toward the tub. "Does he need to whip you again?!"

I stared wide-eyed at her, shaking. "Do you feel the evil creep back into you? Do you even try to fight it?" I just stared at her.

"I want my mama," I moaned, and the tears came so fast I could barely breathe. She sighed and poured the contents of the mason jar into the tub and swirled the water around with her hand.

"She left you, too much for her to take, I believe." She wiped her sweaty brow with her arm. "If you stop giving in to the devil, well, she'll want you again, I believe."

"Like last time?" I asked, wiping my face on my bare shoulder.

"She came and got you, didn't she?" I swallowed some snot.

"But I messed up again."

"Well, you just have to be hard on yourself, Jeremiah, and not give in to the devil so easy." I nodded eagerly. "You can even be an example to her. She needs help, too, I believe."

"I want to, ma'am." She wiped her brow again.

"Good, that's good, Jeremiah. You have to want Jesus' good- ness and love to fill you, and he will, he will. . . . Now let's get you in here."

She placed me closer to the tub and patted the wooden step- ping stool next to it, for me to climb on. I did and looked down into the tub, seeing the water, like a mirror with steam rising off it. I inhaled the chlorine too deeply, expecting comfort, but it only stung my nose, throat, and eyes.

I turned and looked up at her. Her hand patted gently on my shoulder, reassuring me. She nodded to me.

"Hold my arm." She reached it out to me like a steel bar on the seat of a roller coaster.

I leaned over, smelling her kitchen grandmother scent of nutmeg, lemons, and allspice under the heavy bleach fumes.

"I can't, ma'am, it's too far," I whispered, hoping she'd lift me in her arms and put me into the tub like she did when I was last here a year ago.

"Yes you can, Jeremiah." She stepped away and held her arm out to me.

"You're big now."

"Please?"

"Do I need to call him up here?" I grabbed her arm and stretched my left leg up and over the porcelain lip of the tub and pulled myself up until I sat on the edge, my foot curled up tightly above the water like I was dangling over the edge of the world.

"Go ahead." She nudged me. I dipped my foot in and pulled it out immediately.

"It's too hot." Some snot fell from my nose and splashed into the tub.

"Jeremiah, I'm going to call him up here if you're not in this tub by the count of three . . ."

"Okay, okay!"

"One." I put my foot in, steam crawling up my leg. The water had a heavy silky feel to it.

"Two." It landed on the tub bottom. I swung my other leg over and stood in the water up to my thighs.

"It's too hot!" My tears were back, and I jumped up and down, trying to escape the scalding water.

"Not as hot as hellfire! You want to go there? You want to feel hellfire for eternity?"

"Please!" I reached my arms out to her.

"Reverend!" she hollered out.

"Please . . . ma'am . . . please!" I cried so hard I could hardly speak.

"Reverend!" She put her hands on my head and pressed down, keeping me from jumping out. Still, I kept moving as much as I could.

We heard his heavy footsteps marching up the carpeted stairs. As he came closer, she released her weight from my head, and I slowed my bouncing.

He opened the door, and a blast of cool air hit us. She let go of my head and I didn't move. She said nothing to him or me, just turned and left, closing the door behind her. He didn't even look at her, just at me, with his eyes clear and burning like the bleach water I was standing in.

"Sit," he said loudly, the *t* spitting out, echoing off the white porcelain tiles of the bathroom.

I quickly lowered myself until my body was submerged to my neck in the water.

He leaned over me. "Hands," he said sternly.

I reached my arms up to him and he tied a cord hanging over a brass towel rack on the wall behind me to one of my wrists, then the other. He pulled the cord tight so my arms were stretched up and could commit no sin.

"I am right down the hall. I so much as hear a sound from you, Jeremiah, you will regret the day you were born." He turned around and walked out, closing the door halfway. I turned it all off. The welts and sores on my back, ass, and thighs burned like a fire someplace behind me. The scalding water turned my skin bright red, but I'd already left.

I was with my mama in Vegas, winning lots of money. She was so happy she was hugging me, and she kept telling me how good we were, how clean, pure, just like bleach.

I press my hands into the bleached water and rub lightly on the bloodstain, and like invisible ink, it starts to fade.

"Kill you!" my mother screams, still muffled.

"Son, I can't hold her much longer, you best git now." I wish the sink was big enough for me to climb inside of.

"You hear me?" he shouts.

I lift the underwear, the white ones with a ruffled back that he bought especially for her from Victoria's Secret. I spin around and display the panties.

"Look, it's okay! It's out! It's okay!"

Water flows from the sopping underwear onto my feet and down to the chair, ending in a big puddle. We all just stand there staring, the water making ticking noises as it splats onto the floor.

I hold the underwear out to them, up toward the fluorescent light, and there, clearly, is the faded outline of rust-tinged blood. My blood.

My mother screams again, kicks backward in her bare feet at Jackson's shins, and struggles free.

I stand there frozen, her panties spread out between my out-stretched hands like an old lady's knitting, as she barrels toward me. "You're always trying to steal what's mine!" She screams like an oncoming train and grabs a small lamp off the table and hurls it at me.

I watch it flying toward my face in slow motion and some-how I jump off the chair, so the lamp sails straight into the mirror above the sink. Glass shatters and water sprays all over.

I crouch on the floor where I land, like a frog. I look up into my mother's face, covered in red splotches. Jackson's hands cover her mouth again, and her eyes, sparkling blue sapphires in the middle of black streams of mascara, roll wildly like spinning marbles.

"Bleach don't always work," I say quietly.

"Go on," he says, holding my mother, who's rocking back and forth and moaning.

I rise quickly and go past the divider to their bed.

I pull off the white baby-doll that he'd bought for her. I lay it as neatly as I can on the bed, the sleeves crossed in front like a burial gown for a child who has disintegrated away. I go to my side of the room and pull on jeans, a T-shirt, sneakers, but no socks, and grab my jacket from the hook my height that Jackson had put up especially for me.

I walk past them. She's turned toward him now. He's still holding her arms, but her head is against his chest, bobbing up and down with her sobs and moans. They don't say a word.

Jackson motions to the door with his head. I step over a chunk of mirror and I see a face, red and splotched, with black raccoon eyes, lipstick smeared across it like a clown, just like hers. But it's me. It is me. And I have to go.

"Bye," I whisper, and leave.

It's not too cold out, but it feels it. It's still dark. The only light is from our trailer. We're very far away from other trailers. I can see the black dinosaur shapes of the woods of the Blue Ridge Moun-tains rising around me, and I can hear the night sounds of crickets and rustling things. I turn back to our trailer and catch glimpses of movement behind the closed shades. I check to make sure the trailer's still on cinder blocks, not wheels. It is.

In my head I turn daylight on to drive away any wolves or vampires or whatever. It's so sunny I have to squint to see. But I know where I'm going. I walk quickly, cautiously, keeping my sneakers from crunching too much on the loosely packed dirt, so nothing knows I'm here. Some empty lots. Down there's an old doghouse that someone had built and left. It's wooden, with a red, peeling roof and DOG glued on in tarnished gold letters. I go there a lot. To keep the raccoons out, I've put wood from a crate in front of the entrance, like a boarded-up, abandoned building. Inside I keep a pillow, blanket, an overdue library book, and a small flashlight that I stole from a trip with Jackson to Malcom's Auto Supply shop. I slid the thin silver light up my jacket sleeve and prayed to Jesus that no one had seen me. No one had.

Once inside the doghouse I wrap the blanket around my shoulders, with the pillow on the wooden floor under me. I turn the piece of crate sideways, so it still blocks the door but I can see out some. I turn my flashlight on but am careful not to shine it around too much, just enough to see that all the walls are still there and haven't opened to another dimension, like a wardrobe in a book I read did. I'm relieved and disappointed that they haven't. I don't inspect the pointy roof because I know what's up there and I don't need to see the shiny webs and dusty strings. I like to think of the spiders as taking me in as one of their own, ready to swing down, like Tarzan, and attack whatever tries to hurt me. We, the flesh-eating predators of the house of DOG, protect our own.

I breathe in the mustiness of my blankets, mixed with old dog smell and the faint smell of urine I cleaned up as best I could from the last time I had an accident. It's so comforting I decide never to leave; I will wait until a wall finally dissolves away and I escape into another dimension. My mom will really cry then. I lie on my pillow and shine my flashlight on the faded picture on the wood of the crate. I stare at the smiling, freckled, red-haired boy in a large sombrero, climbing a ladder, leaning against a lush tree dripping with plump peaches. He's waving with one hand and reaching for a peach with the other. If I jiggle the flashlight, his hand moves, beckoning me to join him. I lie on my stomach as I always do, resting on the pillow, with my flashlight under my chest, pointing like a spotlight.

I start to rock up and down.

"Come have a peach with me," the boy tells me. "We'll go into my treehouse and eat peaches, just you and me, and we'll go to the other dimension and never come back."

My hands start to reach for my thing.

"You can wear my sombrero," he promises, and stretches his arm out to me.

I open my fly and grope around because it's not there sticking up like a mini–screwdriver handle against my lower stomach. I feel panicky and excited all at once. God has finally cured me, the bleach has worked! I pat my hands on the flat skin of my crotch, terrified to go any lower.

I feel something there, between my legs, but I'm not sure what it is. I sit up fast, the blanket wrapped around me like a tent, and lean against a wall. Holding my breath, I lift my hips and slide my jeans to my knees, and shine my flashlight down. It reflects off the smooth white skin. I think I know what I'll see, just more hard, smooth white, like on a Barbie doll.

I open my eyes and my flashlight shines on my thing, yellowish pink, Krazy Glued backward between my legs. And suddenly I feel pressure on my bladder and I need to piss. I move my shaking hand and pull on my thing; it stretches out slightly like gum stuck on a sidewalk but snaps right back. "Oh God," I say out loud, and my voice sounds foreign and dead inside my doghouse.

I yank again, hard, but it only makes my eyes tear. And then I find a string stuck on the side of my thing and I follow it back with my fingers. It disappears into my asshole. I tug hard and it feels like my bowels are being pressed. I moan from the ache of it.

"Oh Lord's Mercy," I say again and again, the words sounding too big and empty inside the wooden box to have any effect. My heart drums too loudly to ignore, so I lay on my back on the pillow and close my eyes.

I turn off the flashlight and reach under my legs to the string. It's definitely attached to something in my asshole and I can't remember how it got there. I pull again and it's like trying to rip off a thick scab. I tug again but it barely moves, and the tears roll down the sides of my face. I reach again for my thing but it's stuck backward. "It's stuck," I cry into the spider-filled roof. My mouth jerks open in a convulsion of sadness and fear. All that comes out is a high-pitched squeal, like a dump dog shot with a BB gun. The sound surprises and frightens me even more, and I roll over onto my stomach and curl up around my pillow. My body shakes and quivers as if in battle with a high fever. I have to pee badly and I think I still can, but I don't want to go outside. It just drains out of me, spraying backward, between my legs. I hear it hitting the wood wall behind me and bouncing off it. It soaks some of my blanket, but the warm relief only makes me sob harder, my breath moving too quickly, out of control.

Same as Jackson's breath, like a mosquito buzzing violently in my ear. "You're my pretty baby doll, pretty baby girl," he says between gasps and pants in my ear.

His hands run up and down under the white baby-doll quickly, like a dog pawing desperately in the dirt. He covers my face in hard, hungry kisses, coating me in the film of his beer-fogged mouth. He lifts me off his lap, my arms like a rescued princess encircling his neck. He carries me past the divider to their side, to their bed. "Sexy baby, Daddy's hot little girl."

"Am I pretty?" I ask.

"Mmmm hmmm," Jackson says, lying next to me, pulling the silver zipper down the middle of his orange jumpsuit, like he's ripping himself in half. My arms are still wrapped tightly around him. I feel his hands working in the dark, and I hear the snap of his underwear.

"Do you love me?" I ask.

"Ready for Daddy?" He takes hold of my arms and pulls them off his neck.

"Nooo . . ." I reach back, but he pushes them down.

"You're chokin' me, baby doll . . ."

I put my arms out again. He slides on top of me, pinning me down. "Ready for Daddy?" He reaches over to the night stand and I hear the fart noises of a squeezed container.

"I'm your pretty baby girl," I say.

"Uh huh, okay, baby, jus' relax, I'm gonna lube you some."

I feel him searching, down there, his wet and sticky finger inside the white ruffled panties he bought especially for her. "What's this?" he presses on my glued backward thing, ignores it, and moves past.

"Am I good?"

"Okay, baby." His wet finger slides into my asshole.

"Am I good?"

"Oh yeah, nice and wet." Another one slides in. I stare at the shadow his huge head makes on the Swiss cheese ceiling.

"Okay, baby . . . just relax it, okay, baby? Relax . . ."

"I am good, right?"

"There, baby . . . open for Daddy . . . I know you done this before, so open for Daddy."

His thing starts to press in on me. He exhales deeply and quickly, so it's hard for me to get a breath.

"I'm good, right?"

He bends down and kisses me, his beard scratching my face, covering my nose. His tongue gags me as I open my mouth for air. He pulls up onto his elbows, his head is tossed back.

"Stay with me," I whisper, and try to put my arms around him, but I can't move them.

He grunts and pushes himself into me. I feel the tearing and remember the feeling from the last time. He was a cowboy, she was passed out, and I had to get stitches from a local doctor he knew. She still says I owe her the three hundred dollars, even though he paid for half.

I swear I can hear the tearing, hear it filling my ears, over his moans and gasps, and I'm losing him. It's blurry and I can't see him, just a giant burning sun being smothered. I try to tell him not to let me go, that I need to stay with him, to know what he knows, what my mom knows, what that cowboy knows, so after, I can lay in their arms, laugh, and curl up so peacefully I could die. But I'm split apart inside, and it's all I know and all I can find. I stand in the bathroom looking at the stain in the middle of her white ruffled panties, the ones he had special-ordered from Victoria's Secret. Afterward he pulled them back up my legs. He said nothing, I said nothing.

I wad up some toilet paper and wipe at the sore, throbbing wetness. I bring it back damp with blood and mucus-y stuff. I still owe her for the last time, and from bottle collecting, the most I've paid her is twenty-five dollars. "I'm split apart and she's gonna leave me," I say out loud to myself and try not to cry. I hear him turning on the TV and snapping a beer open. I stare at the red stain on the panties again, just like the panties she hand-rinses and hangs over the shower door when it's her time. She bleeds because men are thinking evil thoughts about her, including and, especially, me. So I have to walk to the canteen and buy her Tampax with the plastic applicator to stop the bad thoughts. They sit on the back of the bamboo shelves above the toilet, pink and thin and ready to absorb all evil.

She comes home from cocktailing. She sees me, looking like her, wearing the white baby-doll Jackson bought her from Victoria's Secret, standing on a red metal folding chair, washing the bloodstained white matching panties. She goes looking for Jackson and finds him asleep on their bed laying next to a wet, red splotch on the white nubbly bedspread we got from the Holiday Inn. She screams so loud that Jackson himself wakes up yelling. She screams at him for cheating on her. She screams at him for fucking that little fucking cunt behind her back. She screams at him for letting me wear the special things he bought her, which are now ruined. She sees that I have ruined everything, and she's gonna fucking kill me!

But there are worse things than getting killed.

* * *

I shine my flashlight onto the red-haired, freckled-faced boy waving at me to come and eat peaches. Even though my thing is glued backward and there's a Tampax stuck inside me, he's waving me into his treehouse, where we can hold each other as tightly as possible and be split apart together.

We practice like we usually do on the way to the clinic, driving in Jackson's fire-red pickup truck. My mom's not taking me to the local hospital, instead we're going on a long drive to the backwoods clinic in the Virginia mountains with all the retired doctors that don't like to do paperwork.

"Now, how'd this happen to you?" Mom asks, smoking a cigarette in one hand, driving with the other, and staring straight down the highway, occasionally turning her head to blow smoke out her window.

"Did it to myself," I mumble, my stomach feeling tight and sour. I swallow a gag.

"Louder, gotta be louder! You look 'em right in the eye, too, understand?" She tucks a piece of loose hair into her French braid, her cigarette almost burning her ear.

I nod my head.

"Now what happened?" she asks again.

"Did it to myself," I say louder and look up at the squashed-bug-filled windshield, like it's the evil face of the Inquisitor.

"Anyone child-abusin' you?" Her eyes are still a little swollen, but her fresh makeup covers it. I watch her red, glossy lips clamp down hard on her cigarette. She's wearing little Fairy Stone cross earrings. The tears of angels from when Jesus died. Jackson bought them for her at the Fairy Stone Park gift shop. "Well, did they?" She slaps my thigh.

"No, no, ma'am or . . ." I stare back at the windshield. ". . . or sir . . ." I glance up at her. She nods halfway for me to continue. "Did it all myself, sir or ma'am."

"Say it loud."

"All myself, ma'am . . ." I say louder.

"Why'd you do just a goddamn stupid fuckin' thing."

I turn to her, she's staring straight ahead, blowing smoke, not even out the window like she usually does so she doesn't smell like a barroom slut. "Well?"

"Umm . . . I wanted to be a pretty girl," I mumble.

"No, no, no." She hits the wheel after each no.

"You want them to arrest you? Lock you up in a mental hospital like they did before?" She blows her smoke straight into the windshield. "Or put you in jail?"

"No . . ." I whisper.

"What?"

"No, ma'am . . ."

"You make sure you're not rude to them, you show them I raised you correctly."

"Yes'm."

"Now why you'd do such a goddamned stupid evil fucking thing?"

"'Cause I wanted to know," I say too loudly.

"Know what?" she says louder, and hits the wheel again.

I don't answer.

"Know what?!" She slaps it again, lighter.

"What?!"

"What it feels like to be good."

"What?"

"Ma'am."

"What? I think you need to be locked up in a loony bin for quite some time."

"Stop!" I yell.

"What?" But she pulls over to the side of the two-lane highway. I jump out and dry heave into the dark green ivy growing along the black tar road. There's nothing inside me to come out.

"You about done?" she calls from the truck.

* * *

When everything is over and done, the white-haired nurse shakes her finger at me and says, loudly enough for everyone else in the waiting room to hear, for me not to be doing fool things like I'd done. She give us two orange bottles of pills. One is to keep my stitches from getting infected, the other for pain and discomfort. The nurse gives me one of the second ones, and when we get to the truck my mom swallows two of them.

We say nothing on the ride home. I must fall asleep, because I wake up in my bed, under the blankets. I wonder if my mom has carried me in, or if Jackson has. I wish I'd been awake but only faking sleep when someone held me in their arms and put me to bed. I rub my forehead and check my fingers to see if there are any lipstick marks from when I was tucked in. There aren't. They probably rubbed off already anyway.

My blankets are up around me, and a little pink stuffed bear that Jackson won for me at a fair is next to me. A bigger bear he won for her sits on their bed, but it's too big to be held and is thrown on the floor at night anyway.

They're fighting.

"Please, baby doll," he says again and again.

"I'm sick of you," she tells him.

I'm floating like a frog on a lily pad.

"I'm so sorry, baby doll," he keeps saying.

"You make me sick."

I reach over to the window ledge and pick up the perfect brown angel's tear stones I found in Fairy Stone Park.

"Lookit what I bought ya, sugar, please, honey, it's real pretty." He sounds like he's gonna cry. I know it's hopeless. I know she's going to leave. I hold my stone crosses and pray she takes me with her.

"Please, baby, I'm sorry, please, baby."

I didn't really find the stones in the forest.

"I'll do anything baby, anything."

I stole them from the gift shop where they sell the perfect ones that others have found.

"You can't just leave me, baby!"

I pretended I found them, pretended that only I could find something so perfect, so blessed and special.

"Please, please." He's crying now.

I pull myself up with difficulty, like trying to run fast inside a dream. I lean out the small window over my bed.

"Baby doll, it won't never happen again!"

I inhale deeply the sweet decaying smell of autumn, and look at the yellows and reds spreading down the mountains, like wild fire infecting all the other trees surrounding our trailer.

"I thought he was you, I really did, looked just like you, I swear . . ."

I reach out my balled-up fist and toss my crosses out the window into the dirt.

"He was all over me, talking like you, lookin' like you, baby doll . . ."

I will wait for them to grow, like Jack's magic beans, transformed into a beanstalk, growing up to heaven.

"Let me take care of you, let my lovin' fix it up, baby doll."

It will be a crystal rope of diamond tears, and I'll climb it. I will climb it, even though the raindrop-shaped salt water cuts me like nails driven through.

"You can't do this to me, baby girl! You can't!"

And like the thief on the cross, I'll bleed with Jesus and beg for forgiveness.

"It wasn't my fault!"

The sky will open like slit skin, and the rope will shatter like glass.

"Something ain't right with him, baby, just not right."

And millions and millions of angels' tears will shake and pound the earth and solidify into stone crosses.

"I won't let him get me like that again, baby doll, I swear!"

And they will wait hundreds of years for me to return and reclaim them.

"We'll go away, baby, just you and me, somewhere's nice and fancy."

I will reclaim my tears, petrified by the terror of loss.

Businessman

LOIS GOULD

MY FATHER HAS DECIDED TO DIE; HE WILL DO NOTHING TO HASTEN death, but he will be orderly, his things packed; he will not be taken by surprise. I visit him in his sad brown apartment. Color-blind, he has always chosen brown, believing it to be a pleasing gray-green, the color of morning in the country, of mist on a golf-club fairway. He keeps the television set tuned to a channel that lists stock prices, rolling lines of hieroglyphics. There is no sound. He has very little money now, but he has a history of owning stocks, and he lives there, in that time. The largest brown chair is set squarely in front of the television screen. An old alarm clock, ticking, is placed on top of the set. He is in his office, he is engaged in important matters. He picks his nose absently. When I was a child I hated seeing him do this; he did it in darkened movie theaters or at home, behind his newspaper. It seemed to me that he ceased to do it only during meals, while smoking his cigar, playing golf, or beating my brother. Now he cannot smoke; he has had a pacemaker implanted in his chest. The outlines of it are visible through his skin, as though he has ingested a Walkman.

He wears striped pajamas, a robe, and gleaming leather slippers, a gift from one of the last lady friends. My father was never at a loss for lady friends. He made them all dye their hair red, so he could call them Red, the name he called his first, his truest love, the redhead he was with on the night my dark-haired mother gave birth to me.

He looks up as I come in, nods and smiles, turns back to the screen. Numbers are rolling. He cannot speak while numbers are rolling. I am disturbing him at work.

The nurse, a grim black woman, clatters in the kitchenette preparing his lunch. The clock on the TV indicates that it is lunchtime. My father beckons me to the sofa opposite his chair, leans toward me conspiratorially, without taking his eyes from the rolling numbers. I'm going to fire this one, too, he says. His tone is gleeful. I nod, implying sympathy, approval, assent. He has a need to fire people, even if they are only women. (So long as a man can get rid of a woman, he is still free, he is still a man.)

The nurse has confided that he will not use the bedpan, although it is now very difficult for him to manage the trip to the bathroom without an accident. She does not understand that a bedpan is not an acceptable object for the office of an important businessman. It smacks of infancy, of helplessness, of women in control of one's private life. As long as he lives, my father will go to the bathroom like a businessman.

When he had the pacemaker installed, his doctor advised him to avoid undue excitement. My father immediately gave up bridge, which he loved, and his current lady friend, whom he did not love. Following the stock market on TV was not up for renouncing. That was business.

Dad? I said, after a respectful interval. Mm? he replied, picking his nose, watching the numbers.

Those are nice slippers, I said.

Red gave them to me, he said. Can't stand that woman.

The nurse brought his lunch tray and set it on the table. He would have to relinquish his seat on the exchange.

I handed him his cane and helped him rise out of the brown chair. He seemed so fragile, my father. He was not even small, not even old.

This egg is too soft, he shouted. *Two* minutes, *two*. The nurse set her mouth in a thin line. My father looked at me, triumphant in his rage. You see? he said. They can't even count! None of 'em can count!

I exchanged a glance of sympathy with the woman; quick flicker of the eye, all I dared.

I watched him eat his egg, his spoonful of cottage cheese. A sudden memory of him eating an enormous bowl of some wonderful creamy stuff, mysterious. Little flecks of red-edged, transparent discs peeped from it. I thought it must be dessert, a snowy mountain of sweetness, a fairy-tale food. I begged for a taste. He held his spoon to my mouth, pushed it in; I found myself invaded by sour lumps of wet chalk. Gagging, retching, vomiting on the polished table. How could he betray me, my father? He rose, shouting, furious, his lunch spoiled. Someone came to clean the mess, someone came to take me away. Sobbing. Cottage cheese, sour cream, radishes. I was two.

It was time for his nap. I went to sit beside the bed for a moment, like a hospital visitor. The nurse smoothed his covers, fussed with the pillow. He growled at her to get away, to leave him alone. He folded his hands neatly on the taut sheet over his sunken belly. His fingernails were very clean; I remembered that he used to have a manicurist come to his office. Businessmen did that. Their buffed nails shone like their polished shoes. They had soft dark coats, homburgs. They hid behind newspapers.

Dad? I said.

Women, he said, exhaling the word like bad air.

I'll come back later, I said, rising to kiss him. He did not unclasp his hands; they had been placed exactly where he wanted them. The nap would last forty minutes; then he had to get back to work.

Everything is in order, he said, as I bent over him.

Yes, I said.

I saw him once more. Lying in the same position, hands folded neatly over the neat, tight covers. Dad?

Women ruined the business, he said.

How, Dad? How did they do it?

His eyes were closed. I tiptoed out. The nurse—he had not managed to fire this one after all—shook her head. I didn't ask what she meant by this gesture; I already knew I had heard my father's last words.

The task of clearing his life away fell to me and my sister-in-law. My brother was busy: another businessman. There was little of value among the brown things. A watch, an elegant old watch, white-gold, not his taste, probably a gift from my mother. What shall we do with this? my sister-in-law asked, holding it aloft. I'll take it, I said, surprising us both. And the silk pocket scarves.

Those nurses must have cleaned him out, my brother said. Where were all the cufflinks, the studs? All the gifts from all the redheads, true and false?

My brother and I went to the funeral home together. My father, I said to the rabbi, was a wonderfully handsome man. It was his pride, if not his joy.

Saw action, my father wrote, in a note that he had composed for his own obituary. Saw action in World War I.

A wonderfully handsome man, said the rabbi at the service. My mother nodded. Three redheaded women nodded. It was a good service.

Did you love him? a friend asked me. I thought of the whizzing belt, the hairbrush, my brother's screams. My father never beat me. I lied to him, pretending to fail at school, so that he would think me worthy of beating, too, like my brother. He was whistling when he packed his suitcase. Where you going? I asked. He was whistling; I'm leaving, he said. So long. I was three.

I used to get these letters at camp, neatly typewritten, except for the signature Dad. "Affectionately" (typed), Dad. Underneath, it said JMC/ses. I never knew what "ses" meant. Years later my brother explained: "Ses" was Sylvester, the man who was my father's secretary, who wrote every word of every letter, including the word "affectionately." No one else typed letters to their kids. No one else had a secretary write them. Letters from parents were handwritten. And the last word was not supposed to be "affectionately," it was supposed to be "love."

On the other hand, my mother never wrote at all.

A woman is on trial for child abuse: her daughter is dead, a suicide. The charge is that the mother forced the girl to dance naked in a bar, and used the money she earned to help support them both.

The girl presumably killed herself out of shame or despair. Blame-the-mother. My father taught me how. Who else was there to blame, after all? The father? My father? God, the father? An absurd notion.

He said he never "possessed" my mother. Never possessed that woman, he told me. I didn't understand, of course. I was seven, eight. But I knew she had failed him somehow, hadn't loved him, hadn't wanted me, or my brother, didn't love any of us. Didn't even have a secretary to write to us, affectionately.

But he was the one who left, whistling.

In the Great Depression, it is said, many fathers left. One in five or one in four. Divorce was only for fathers who could afford lawyers; poorer ones just left. My father, I learned, years later, left differently from my cousin's father or the cook's son's father. Differently, too, I imagine, from the father of the dead girl whose mother is on trial.

My father came to visit us, though he didn't help pay our bills. He came to visit, and my mother went out, to a party or the theater, while he and I ate dinner in our dining room. The only times I ate in that room, or ate with any company at all, were the times my father came. I was made to get dressed up in party clothes and allowed to eat at the dining table, instead of alone, in pajamas, on a tray in my room, facing a wall.

My father called these visits "our dates" and joked about how we would go to the movies later, and sit in the balcony, and neck. In fact we did go to the movies, usually to meet Red and her husband. Red laughed a lot and hugged me, and wanted to hear me talk about my mother. I told her all I knew, which wasn't much. My mother was in Europe or she had a gentleman caller, the same one as last month or a different one. She was busy; not a businesswoman, but a famous fashion designer. She dressed up in the morning to go to business. She dressed up again at night. That was all I knew, really. But Red wanted to hear every little thing—what my mother wore, who the company was, when she had company. I liked telling; I liked Red asking me so many questions. I thought she liked me. I thought that was why she asked. No one else ever asked me anything, not even my father.

Once I came home early from the movies and my mother was already home, sitting up in her gray satin bed. She called me, and I went in to say goodnight. She wrinkled her nose up and said you've been with your father, he smoked cigars, I can smell it in your hair.

I was with Red too, and Uncle Charlie, I said.

My mother's face looked dark, and then very white. I don't want him taking you with her, she shouted. You're not to go with them, do you hear me? I didn't mean it! I said, flinching, backing away, running into my own room.

And wash your hair! my mother shouted. Wash that disgusting smell out of your hair!

After that, I didn't go into her room after the movies. She never asked me again if I'd seen Red and Uncle Charlie. I told my father what she had said, and he said, well, better not mention it when we run into them. Don't want to upset your mother.

After the movies, Red and Uncle Charlie and my father and I always stopped for ice-cream sodas at Schrafft's. That was when Red asked me about my mother while my father squeezed Red's knee under the table, and Red's husband, Uncle Charlie, smoked a big cigar that my father gave him. I thought we were all having fun. I thought that was family fun. I slurped my soda and made everyone laugh. I wanted to live with them instead. I said that to Red, lots of times. She really liked hearing it.

At my father's funeral service, Red, the original one, came over to hug me. I would love to see you sometime, she whispered. My mother, holding court, sat on the other side of the room, claiming the funeral, the death, like a widow. They had been divorced forty years; each had remarried once and divorced again. Still, it was true she had survived; my brother and I were the proofs of her claim— not to any tangible thing, only to be here, holding court, wearing an elegant veiled hat, a black suit. People were offering her condolences. Amazing. I would love to see you, Red said again to me, urgently.

Yes, I said. All right. I had not recognized her at first. Shocked to see her grown hugely fat. Still Red, though. The hair dyed now, like all the other imitation Reds.

We met at a coffee shop, a week later. I wanted to ask her about loving my father. Whether she really had; when she had stopped. Why.

I knew—he had told me once, long ago—that he had at last asked her to leave Uncle Charlie and marry him. This was many years after the whistling farewell to me, to my mother. Years and years of movies and ice cream sodas, golf games with Uncle Charlie, and dinners at their house and breakfast at the club and trips to Florida on the train, all of us, him and them, and me, and their son who was almost exactly my age and who looked—everyone whispered—almost exactly like my father.

But when at last my father had asked Red to leave Charlie, leave her marriage for him or else let him go, she had turned him down flat. She had chosen Charlie, fat, dull, bald Charlie, instead. Charlie was dead now; he had been the first to die. Red had not seen my father for years, he would not forgive her. The moment she turned him down he stopped playing golf with Charlie and went off to find himself a new Red, the first of all the other women who would become Reds, to please him.

I am sure she too was pleased by that, the original Red. Even if he had never forgiven her.

You won't believe this, she said to me now, in the coffee shop. I loved Charlie; I came to love him; in the end I realized I had loved him all along.

And my father?

Do you know, she said, your father never gave me anything? Not a flower. Not in twenty years.

I shook my head, as if to signify how terrible; that is terrible.

I often thought of you, she said then. All these years.

Really, I said.

We should see each other again. I know Billy—my son—you remember Billy—would like to know you now.

Billy wrote to me, after this. Things he remembered about my father, who had been Uncle John to him. Unless my father was also, really, *his* father, too. I didn't respond to Billy. I couldn't see Red again. I wanted to, but I couldn't. How could I ask her now, finally, if Billy was my brother, my twin? How could I not ask her? Why hadn't he come to the funeral? Better the deepening silence.

What struck me hardest was the thing she revealed so casually. In twenty years of adulterous passion, never even a flower!

When I was very young, he always sent a nosegay to me on my birthday, with a card signed "Affectionately," *Dad*. Always a tight round bouquet of sweetheart roses in a paper lace collar, trailing slender ribbons of pink and blue satin. "Affectionately," *Dad*. I remembered that on my real birthday, my real birth night, my mother, whose own mother died giving birth to her, labored alone in her terror. My father was with Red, who was awaiting the birth of Billy.

If you didn't have your family, what would you write? my father asked me once. Not a pleasant question. What would any writer write? I retorted, trying not to squirm. He was embarrassed by me; I had embarrassed him! Has anyone actually finished reading this book of yours? he demanded then. He had ploughed through some forty pages. He had telephoned several times over two weeks, reporting his painful progress. Then he had stopped trying. Did he mean to make me feel this bad?

Some people, I said, have read it, have even liked it. Not many, though, I admitted. He shrugged, irritated. The last one you wrote was filth; this one is just boring. This one is just a disgrace to the family.

I'm sorry, I murmured, flinching. A sorry response for a grown woman, a published writer, a person with children of her own. None of which counted. Only the wild storm of baby emotions he had struck with his thunderbolt of displeasure. It was not even anger, only that cold censure I had so coveted each time he came to punish my brother. Coveted! Could anyone but my father ever cause my throat to close with such terror and desire? How I had craved the dark look on his face when he came, summoned by my distraught mother, to administer the formal beating of his son for some grave misdeed, some failure at school, some fresh torment of me. All I ever wished then was for my sins to count, my failures to deserve the belt, the hairbrush, the closed door, the howling screams. The whistling sound of the descending weapon, and the other sound, the sickening smack as buckle sliced into flesh. How I had begged my father for it, hit *me*, not my brother! Me! And how they misunderstood, all of them. They thought I meant to defend my brother. I wanted only my father's wrath, which I mistook for love. And now I had won it. And there was no mistake: It was not love.

My father had a faithful Japanese valet, Tom, who brushed his fine suits and fixed his drink exactly right, scrambled the eggs, squeezed the oranges, and smiled at me when I was brought to visit. Tom was the butt of many jokes between my father and Red and Uncle Charlie. My father found it especially amusing when Tom's father sent Tom a wife all the way from Tokyo. How could Tom consent to marry her? A mail-order bride? Tom stared at my father, uncomprehending. My father knows what is needed, Tom explained. He will choose the best wife for me. As his father chose my mother for him. Tom ended with his soft, self-deprecating chuckle. Japs! said my father, each time he told the story. Everyone understood that the story, this couple, were meant to be a sarcastic comment about his own wife, my mother, about the foolishness of love or of marrying for it.

One day when I visited my father, he greeted me at the door himself. Where's Tom? I asked. My father seemed uncomfortable; the place was in disarray. Gone, he said, brusquely. Tom is gone.

How come? Gone where? Gone for good?

Japs, he muttered, turning his back to me. He went to fix his own drink at his little bar, to open his own jar of peanuts.

I was meant to assume that faithful Tom had walked out on him, just like that. Whistling? Packing his suitcase? Tom, who had served my father since before I was born?

Years later I learned that Tom had in fact been taken away, sent to an internment camp. We were at war with "Japs." My father had turned Tom in, voluntarily, had made no protest when they came for him, made no inquiry about him. Never knew what became of him or his wife, that perfect wife his father had sent to him. People just went away; I understood. Packing their suitcases. Whistling.

Shortly after that, my grandfather died following a sudden heart attack, leaving my grandmother hopelessly, shockingly, in debt to her in-laws, my great-uncles. It was a terrible blow to my father. My grandparents had lived in splendor, in a huge two-story penthouse, on top of a skyscraper. There were immense terraces all around, from which you could see the rivers and the whole park, and the Thanksgiving Day parade. I used to ride the polar bear rug on the living-room floor and whisper in her ear. I used to study the tapestries on the walls, the fancy linens and heavy silver in the pantry, the servants in the servants' rooms. My grandfather's library was paneled in golden oak, with secret compartments that released music and held liquor and cigars. Every day he was driven to his office in a gray Packard limousine, and Harold, his chauffeur, wore a matching gray uniform with shiny black boots and a cap. My father went to the same office, on foot. My mother went to her office in a taxi. My grandmother owned diamonds, chokers, and tiaras; fringed ermine opera capes. She had been a rich man's daughter from Chicago when she married my grandfather, whom she called Dearie. Her fortune was larger than his; it was considered a good match.

The day after my grandfather's funeral, moving men came to take everything away—polar bear, tapestries, Belgian linens, diamonds, chokers, tiaras, and opera capes.

The servants were already gone, and the Packard limousine and Harold and his livery. My grandmother looked like a very old woman. She was only fifty-six, but her life had ended. My father supervised the removal of her things, and then of her, and of his younger brother, who had never married and still lived with her. My father moved them both into a stark two-room efficiency unit in a small residential hotel, almost exactly like his own, in another part of town. My grandmother never smiled again. I have a photograph of her sitting in a high-backed chair in that severe little efficiency unit. A framed photograph of my grandfather—of Dearie—is conspicuously displayed beside her. Years later I learned that he had embezzled a great deal of money from his brothers, his business partners, and lost it betting on "the ponies." He had squandered all my grandmother's money in the same way. The family business was saved from bankruptcy by loans and the sale of my grandparents' home and its contents. My father, no longer a prospective heir, was now a hired hand, running the family business to pay off his father's debts and to support his mother and brother. One by one as his uncles died, my father continued to pay, to his widowed aunts, to his cousins. Women, he would say to me, women. Such a hateful word. I vowed never to be one.

Somehow I always assumed my poor father was also burdened by me and my brother. That my mother supported us entirely out of her earnings was kept a shameful secret, even by her. She would not have it known that she was such a failure. For as she saw it, any woman whose husband leaves her to fend for herself is a failure. If she must fend for children too, she is a drudge, a lower-class person, an outcast. It was one thing to be famous and talented, to travel and dress well, on the fruits of one's talent. It was quite another thing, an unmentionable thing, to work because one needed money; one needed money in order to live. I went to public schools, expensively dressed, and had a governess walk me there and come to plays I was in or conferences with teachers. My mother "went to business"; therefore she never appeared with me in public. It never occurs to children that parents choose the way they are. I knew only that my life didn't matter much to anyone, that nothing I did could alter it.

The ways in which my brother and I tried to make my mother notice us were funny and sad. April Fool's jokes. We spent hours in the penny arcade selecting realistic inkblots, blackening soap, insects, dog-doo, bending forks. My mother would pick these things up, absently, and hand them to the housekeeper to dispose of. Once we pooled our allowances and splurged on a whoopee cushion, and planted it under a guest's seat. Lurking at the doorway, trying desperately not to laugh, feverish with excitement. The guest sat, the cushion emitted its resounding fart; no one reacted. In polite society, no one reacts.

After that my brother took to snapping rubber bands against my bare legs when company came, causing me to run through the house shrieking. This did cause a reaction: Servants were dispatched to lock us in our separate rooms. There was, however, a common bathroom between us, and soon my brother would sneak into my room, to continue his attacks. The weapons varied: rubber bands, BB guns, pillows held over the face, precious toys swiped, hidden, or destroyed. I would wail; someone would come; my brother would be punished; I would be left alone, knowing that he was somewhere else, hating me. The cycle was magic; only his torment was proof that I existed. Only my howls brought people running—to take him away, punish him, pay attention to him. My father's beatings grew more frequent. I was more and more confined to bed. A girl, especially, is better off kept in bed. Long naps, early to sleep, coughs and sniffles, temperatures. The child soon grows accustomed. And adults may safely attend to their business. The boy, meanwhile, may be sent to a play group after school. Outdoors. Scuffling; rough play; shouting. Soon he will confine his aggression, his rage, to the designated areas. The problem was that he lived in a house of women, only one of whom was small enough to kill.

My father and I are dancing at my mother's wedding. She is looking at us, critically, over the shoulder of her new bridegroom, the handsome, mysterious Leland. It is said that Leland has a drinking problem; that he has been married four times before, not twice, as he claims; that he is bisexual, a fortune hunter, and five years younger than the age he declared on the marriage license.

My father is still just as handsome as Leland; a different type. Leland is a mix of Louis Calhern and Fred MacMurray. Craggy, suave, possibly a crook, engaging. In his youth my father was often told he resembled Cary Grant; as a joke he took to striking his chin with the straight of his hand, hoping to develop a cleft.

We are dancing in the square mirrored foyer of my mother's apartment. The mirrors have recently been installed; beneath them lie a series of other dancing figures, huge painted Harlequins and Columbines, executed by a famous French artist when I was very young. The artist, reduced to decorating walls for fashionable

American ladies, enjoyed a vogue for a time. But in this decade, in my mother's world, Harlequins are now passé. Like being single. Mirrors are mounted everywhere, pressing against the fanciful masked, dancing lovers. Now we are dancing before the mirrors, mirroring the movements of those invisible ghosts hidden in the walls. My father and I circle my mother and her bridegroom. She is wearing pale gray, fawn, pearl. Her shoes gleam as she prances; the handsome Leland has pale eyes, dove-gray at his temples; hair cut short, bristling, a military brush. My father's hair is still black, smooth as Cary Grant's. I study my reflection, as though it is not me. Who is that girl dancing with Cary Grant? Such a heavy, awkward girl, with a head that ducks forward on her neck as though it has been snapped. She is out of sync with the music, stepping on her partner's nimble feet. Cary Grant seems not to notice; he is engrossed in the moving picture of his ex-wife and her sudden husband. They look wonderful together. My father, tall and handsome, is noticing that Leland is equally handsome in his different way, and perhaps two inches taller than my father. Does he feel jealousy, anger, regret? My mother has not been his wife for eighteen years.

Two weeks after this wedding my father took his yearly vacation in Florida, found a new lady friend, and married her within ten days. A whirlwind courtship, a dance. She was half his age, slim, blond (not red), a mother of two young children, a boy and a girl. She had a deep Southern accent, and wore boys' button-down shirts, barrettes in her hair. It was said she had been married four times before, not twice, as she claimed—and that she was a fortune hunter. Her name was Nancy; she pronounced it in three syllables: *Nay-un-cy*.

I thought it was significant that my father never persuaded Nay-un-cy to dye her hair red. I never dared ask either of them whether he had tried.

If Nay-un-cy was indeed a fortune hunter, she had miscalculated badly this time. My father had done the same, for in Florida Nay-un-cy had given him the distinct impression that she was a North Carolina belle; that the second of two husbands had died suddenly during their honeymoon, leaving her both pregnant and rich.

Most of this, my father slowly learned, was a Southern regional fiction (doubly ironic in its near-match of my mother's mystery romance). Nevertheless, Nay-un-cy insisted on a large, expensive apartment, furnished with antiques and bric-a-brac. My father reluctantly moved out of his two-room efficiency unit, in the residential hotel, borrowed a great deal of money, bought Nay-un-cy what she wanted, and tried to enjoy married life, as the proud father of two children, a boy and a girl. Ironic, my brother said to me. I said nothing. Within a year Nay-un-cy and my father had ceased to speak to each other. She wanted an expensive divorce. My mother's marriage to Leland lasted a year longer.

Bruno and I, marrying, decide to trade our two cars for one: a red sportscar, British, a Sunbeam Alpine. My father is hurt and angry. A two-seater! he exclaims. How could you, why would you, get a two-seater? Except to demonstrate that you don't want me in your life. Well, then, I have got the message.

I was stunned. My father wished to be in my life? A member of my wedding? My father didn't wish me to marry Bruno? Jealous, possessive?

It had happened once before. I was sixteen. I had a boyfriend whose family owned a small farm in Maryland. I was filled with sudden rural longings. Farm, farming, the country air. My father leapt at once into my fantasy, or upon it. I, *we*, can get a farm; why not? I stared at him. But . . . I would hate that, I said. You? Farm? With me? What an idea. And I shook with the strength of my No, of my revulsion. Reminded, horror-struck, of the references he used to make to necking in the balcony. This stranger, this man who never noticed who I was. He wanted something of me now, that was clear. A consolation prize? For my mother's refusal to be possessed, as he put it? Possessed how? When I was six, seven, he would regale me with tales of her coldness—as if I needed them. I always thought (he would sigh) that she would come around. I thought if she had babies, I thought when I made her have babies, my babies. *Frigid* was the word. Frigid is when you have babies and you don't come around? She got rid of my babies, you know. Three of them. He told me that. Almost killed her to get rid of them, he said. Rid of me is what she meant.

I asked my grandmother, my father's mother, what he could mean. She nodded, laughing. I tried to get rid of them, too, of him. Up and down the stairs I went—jumping and jumping. But I had all three, couldn't shake a one of them loose. Russell, your uncle Russell, can't shake him loose even now.

Uncle Russell, the baby, her last unwanted baby, had had to leave her only once. Drafted into the army, the only soldier anyone knew who couldn't make private first class. When they mustered him out, he swore he had paid enough dues for a lifetime. Either he refused to get a job, or he couldn't secure one, not even in the family business. His brother, my father, wouldn't even let him open the office mail, answer the phone. Uncle Russell stayed home. My grandmother wouldn't give him an allowance, though. He would have to earn his spending money somehow. So Russell took his mustering-out pay and invested in five subway peanut machines. Every week he collected the pennies in a big sack and traded them in for dollar bills. Then he went to his club and played bridge.

He was, as it turned out, pretty good at bridge. At least he won enough to parlay his peanut pennies into a dapper pin-striped suit, a camel's-hair topcoat, a white fedora, and a silver cigar case.

My father's contempt for his brother was boundless. I thought Russell was sort of cute; I didn't dare say so. Perhaps he seemed attractive because he made my father so angry and got away with it. He seemed like a boy me: a family prisoner, despised, no-account. I thought it was swell that he won at cards and wore clothes that made him look like a gangster. I wanted to do that. I wanted to run away to sea, and get tattooed, and burst in on the family while they watched the Thanksgiving Day parade from my grandmother's terrace. Hi, I'd say, strutting my natty sailor suit, flexing the blue anchor—or the shimmying mermaid—on my arm. My mother would raise her voice: What are you gotten up for? But my father, I knew, would react just as he had when I wanted to take up golf: Let women in the game, there goes the game.

A least Uncle Russell rated a personal attack. Not just a ne'er-do-well, that Russell, but a perfectly useless creature. Stupid about 90 percent of the time, wrong about 90 percent of everything. You couldn't even think or do the opposite of what he said, because of that lousy 10 percent. That was what made him useless.

More useless than women? I asked once. He laughed, but I think I stumped him.

A month after my father's funeral, I slipped on that elegant old watch of his. I realized that I had no memory of him ever wearing it. A sleek art deco design, all clean angles and beveled edges, it bore his initials in blue enamel on the gleaming clasp. White gold glows like silver or platinum, only warmer. Somehow it evoked my earliest images of him; it, too, had a wonderfully handsome face. A watch Cary Grant would have worn, teaching me how to meld in gin rummy and win the word game in the evening paper (Can you find forty-six words of at least five letters in *affectionately*? Alone, atone, cleft, natty, notice, action, fatal, finale . . .).

I had the band made smaller, so the watch would circle my wrist lightly, an effortless embrace. I like to think he would notice that I always wear it and would say that it suits me. I like to imagine him nodding. Affectionately.

The Story of My Father

PHILLIP LOPATE

Is it not clearer than day, that we feel within ourselves the indelible marks of excellence, and is it not equally true that we constantly experience the effects of our deplorable condition?—Pascal

1

OLD AGE IS A GREAT LEVELER: THE FRAILER ELDERLY ALL COME TO resemble turtles trapped in curved shells, shrinking, wrinkled and immobile, so that, in a roomful, a terrarium of the old, it is hard to disentangle one solitary individual's karma from the mass fate of aging. Take my father. Vegetating in a nursing home, his character seems both universalized and purified, worn to its bony essence. But, as LSD is said to intensify more than alter one's personality, so old age: My father is what he always was, only more so. People meeting him for the first time ascribe his oddities (the withdrawn silences, sloppy eating habits, boasts and pedantic non sequiturs) to the infirmities of time, little realizing he was like that at thirty.

A man in his thirties who acts the octogenarian is asking for it. But old age has set his insularities in a kinder light—meanwhile drawing to the surface that underlying sweetness that I always suspected was there. Dispassionate to the point where the stoical and stony meet, a hater of sentimentality, he had always been embarrassed by his affections; but now he lacks the strength even to suppress these leakages. I have also changed and am more ready to receive them. These last ten years—ever since he was put away in old-age homes—have witnessed more expressions of fondness than passed between us in all the years before. Now when I visit him, he kisses me on sight and, during the whole time we are together, stares at me greedily, as though with wonder that such a graying cub came from his loins. For my part, I have no choice but to love him. I feel a tenderness welling up, if only at the sight of the wreck he has

64

become. What we were never able to exhibit when he had all his wits about him—that animal bond between father and son—is now the main exchange.

Yet I also suspect sentimentality; and so I ask myself, how valid is this cozy resolution? Am I letting both of us off the hook too quickly? Or trying to corner the market on filial piety, while the rest of my family continues mostly to ignore him? Who is, who was, this loner, Albert Lopate, neglected in a back ward? I look at the pattern of his eighty-five years and wonder what it all adds up to: failure, as he himself claims, or a respectable worker's life for which he has little to be ashamed, as I want to believe? We spend most of our adulthoods trying to grasp the meanings of our parents' lives; and how we shape and answer these questions largely turns us into who we are.

My father's latest idea is that I am a lawyer. The last two times I've visited him in the nursing home, he's expressed variations on this theme. The first time he looked up at me from his wheel-chair and said, "So, you're successful—as a lawyer?" By my family's scraping-by standards, I'm a worldly success; and worldly success, to the mistrustful urban-peasant mind of my father, befogged by geri-atric confusion, can only mean a lawyer.

Lawyers, I should add, are not held in the highest regard in my family. They are considered shysters: smooth, glib, ready to sell you out. You could say the same about writers. In hindsight, one reason I became a writer is that my father wanted to be one. An autodidact who started out in the newspaper trade, then became a factory-worker and, finally, a shipping clerk, he wrote poetry in his spare time, and worshipped Faulkner and Kafka. I enacted his dream, like the good son (or usurped it, like the bad son), which seems not to have made him entirely happy. So he turns me into a lawyer.

Not that my father's substitution is all that far-fetched. I had entered college a prelaw major, planning to specialize in publish-ing law. Secretly I yearned to be a writer, though I did not think I was smart enough. I was right—who is?—but bluff got the better of modesty.

The last time I visited my father, he said: "I know what you want to be. *Abogado.*" He smiled at his ability to call up the Spanish word you see on storefronts in barrios, alongside *notario*. So this time I was not yet the successful attorney, but the teenage son choosing his vocation. Sometimes old people get stuck on a certain moment in the past. Could it be that his mental clock had stopped around 1961, right about the time of his first stroke, when he'd just passed fifty (my present age) and I was seventeen? *Abogado.* It's so characteristic of my father's attachment to language that a single word will swim up from the dark waters of dotage. Even before he became addled, he would peacock his vocabulary, going out of his way to construct sentences with polysyllabic words such as *concomitant* or *prevaricate*. My father fingers words like mahjong tiles, waiting to play a good one.

Lately he has been reverting to Yiddish phrases, which he assumes I understand, though I don't. This return to the mother tongue is not accompanied by any revived interest in Judaism—he still refuses to attend the home's religious services—but is all part of his stirring the pot of language and memories one last time.

I arrive around noon, determined to bring him outside for a meal. My father, as usual, sits in the dining room, a distance apart from everyone else, staring down at his chin. There are a group of old ladies whom he manages to tantalize by neither removing himself entirely from their company nor giving them the benefit of his full attention. Though he has deteriorated badly in recent years, he still remains in better shape than some, hence a "catch." One Irish lady in particular, Sheila, with a twinkle in her cataracted eye, is always telling me what a lovely man my father is. He pays her no attention whatsoever.

It was not always thus. A letter he dictated for my sister Leah in California, when he first came to this home, contained the passage: "There's a woman by the name of Sheila who seems to be attracted to me. She's a heavyset woman, not too bad-looking, she likes me a lot, and is fairly even-tempered. I'm not sure of my feelings toward her. I'm ambivalent." (*Ambivalent* is a favorite Albert Lopate word. Purity of heart is for simpletons.) "Should I pursue this more aggressively, or should I let things go along at a normal pace?" The last line strikes me as particularly funny, given my father's inveterate passivity (what would aggressive pursuit entail for him?) and the shortage of time left to these ancients.

It took me a while to give up the hope that my father would find companionship, or at least casual friendship, in a nursing home. But the chances were slim: This is a man who never had nor made a friend for as long as I can remember. Secondly, *friendship* is a cuddly term that ill describes the Hobbesian enmity and self-centeredness among this tribe of old people.

"Don't push anything out of the window!" yells one old woman to another. "If anything's pushed out the window, it's going to be you!"

"I want to get out of here, I want to forget you, and I won't forget you unless I get out of this room!" yells the second.

"You dirty pig."

"You're one, too."

So speak the relatively sane ones. The ward is divided between two factions: those who, like my father, can still occasionally articulate an intelligent thought, and those with dementia, who scream the same incoherent syllables over and over, kicking their feet and rending the air with clawed hands. The first group cordially detests the second. *Meshugena*, crazy, my father dismisses them with a word. Which is why, desperately trying to stay on the right side of Alzheimer's, he has become panicked by forgetfulness.

Asked how he is, he responds with something like: "It worries me I'm losing my memory. We were discussing the all-star pitcher the Dodgers used to have. Koufax. I couldn't remember Koufax's first name. Ridiculous!" For a man who once had quiz-show recall, such lapses are especially humiliating. He has been making alphabetical lists of big words to retain them. But the mind keeps slipping, bit by bit. I had no idea there could be so many levels of disorientation before coming to rest at senility.

This time, he has forgotten we've made a lunch date, and sits ready to eat the institutional tray offered him. In a way, I prefer his forgetting our date to his response a few years ago, when he would wait outside three hours before my arrival, checking his watch every ten minutes. As usual, he is dressed too warmly, in a mud-colored, torn sweater, for the broiling summer day. (These shabby clothes seem to materialize from nowhere: where does his wardrobe come from, and whatever happened to the better clothes we bought him? Theft is common in these establishments.)

I am in a hurry to wheel him outside today before he becomes too attached to his meal—and before the atmosphere of the nursing home gets to me.

I kiss him on top of his pink head, naked but for a few white hairs, and he looks at me with delight. He is proud of me. I am the lawyer, or the writer—in any case, a man of accomplishment. In another minute, he will start introducing me to the women at the next table, "This is my son," as he has already done a hundred times before, and they will pour on the syrup about what a nice father I have, how nice I am to visit him (which I don't do often enough), and how alike we look. This time I start to wheel him out immediately, hoping to skip the routine, when Sheila croaks in her Irish accent: "Don'tcha say hello to me anymore?" Caught in the act of denying my father the social capital a visitor might bring him, I go over and shmooze a bit.

Meanwhile, the muskrat-faced Miss Mojabi (in the caste division of this institution, the nursing staff is predominantly Pakistani, the attendants mainly black, and the upper management Orthodox Jewish) reminds me that I must "sign the form" to take legal responsibility for our outing. Were Armaggedon to arrive, these nurses would be waiting pen in hand for a release signature. Their harsh, officious manner makes me want to punch them. I temper my rage with the thought that they are adequate if not loving—that it was we, the really unloving, who abandoned him to their boughten care.

My father's nursing home, located in Washington Heights, is perched on the steepest hill in Manhattan. After straining to navigate the wheelchair downhill, fantasizing what would happen if I let the handlebars slip (careening Papa smashing into tree), I bring us to a Chinese-Cuban takeout place on Broadway, a hole in the wall with three Formica tables. It's Sunday, everything else is closed, and there are limits to how far north I am willing to push him in the August heat. My father seems glad to have made it to the outside; he wouldn't mind, I'm sure, being wheeled to Riverdale. Still, he has never cared much about food, and I doubt if the fare's quality will register on him one way or the other.

After asking him what he would like, and getting an inconclusive answer, I order sesame chicken and a beef dish at the counter. He is very clear on one thing: ginger ale. Since they have none, I substitute Mountain Dew. Loud salsa music on the radio makes it hard to hear him; moreover, something is wrong with his false teeth, or he's forgotten to put in the bridge, and he speaks so faintly I have to ask him to repeat each sentence several times. Often I simply nod, pretending to have heard. But it's annoying not to understand, so, as soon as he clears his throat—signaling intent to speak—I put my ear against his mouth, receiving communiqués from him in this misted, intimate manner.

From time to time, he will end his silence with an observation, such as: "The men here are better-looking than the women." I inspect the middle-aged Dominican patrons, indoor picnickers in their Sunday best—the men gray-templed and stout, wearing dark suits or brocaded shirts; the women in skirts, voluptuously rounded, made-up, pretty—and do not share his opinion, but nod agreement anyway. I sense he offers these impressions less to express his notion of reality than to show he can still make comments. Ten minutes later, another mysterious remark arrives, from left field, like the one about *abogado*. I prefer this system of waiting for my father to say something, between long silences, rather than prying conversation out of him. If my wife Cheryl were here, she would be drawing him out, asking him about the latest at the nursing home, whether he had seen any movies on TV, what he thought of the food, if he needed anything. And later, she would consider the effort a success: "Did you see how much better he got, the longer we spoke? He's just rusty because nobody talks to him. But he's still sharp mentally . . ." I'm glad she's not here, to see me failing to keep the conversational shuttlecock aloft.

You must have heard that corny idea: A true test of love is when you can sit silently next to the beloved, without feeling any pressure to talk. I have never been able to accomplish this feat with any woman, howsoever beloved, but I can finally do it with one human being: my father. After fifty years of frustration as this lock-jawed man's son, I no longer look on his uncommunicativeness as problematic or wounding. Quite the contrary: In my book, he has at last earned the right to be as closemouthed as he wants, just as I have earned the right to stare into space around him, indulging my own fly-on-the-wall proclivities.

He eats, engrossed, engaged in the uneven battle between morsel and fork. With the plastic utensils they have given us, it is not easy for a man possessing so little remaining hand-strength to spear chicken chunks. So he wields the fork like a spoon to capture a piece, transport it to his mouth, and crunch down, one half dropping into his lap. Those dark polyester pants, already seasoned, absorb the additional flavor of sesame sauce. He returns to the plate with that morose, myopic glare that is his trademark. My wife, I know, would have helpfully cut up the pieces into smaller bits. Me, I prefer to watch him struggle. I could say in my defense that I am respecting his autonomy more, by letting him work out the problem on his own. Or I could acknowledge some streak of cruelty for allowing him this fiasco. The larger truth is that I have become a fly on the wall, and flies don't use utensils.

Eventually, I too cut up everything on my father's plate. So we both arrive at the same point, my wife and I, but at differing rates. Cheryl sizes up a new situation instantly and sets about eliminating potential problems for others—a draft, a tipsy chair—as though all the world were a baby she needed to protect. My tendency is to adjust to an environment passively, like my father, until such time as it occurs to me to do what a considerate Normal Person (which I am decidedly not, I am a Martian) would do in these same circumstances: shut the window, cut up the old man's meat. My father is also from Mars. We understand each other in this way. He too approaches all matter as obdurate and mystifying.

My father drops some broccoli onto his lap. "Oh Al, how could you?" my mother would have cried out. "You're such a slob!" We can both "hear" her, though she is some eight miles downtown. As ever, he looks up sheepish and abashed, with a strangely innocent expression, like a chimp who knows it is displeasing its master but not why.

It gives me pleasure to spare him the expected familial reproach. "Eat it with your hands, Pop. It's okay," I tell him. Who can object to an old man picking up his food? Certainly not the Dominicans enjoying themselves at the next table. Many African tribes eat with their fingers. The fork is a comparatively recent innovation, from the late Middle Ages; Ethiopians still think that the fork not only harms the food's taste, imposing a metallic distance, but also spoils the sociability of each eater scooping up lentils and meat with soft porridgy bread from the common pot. Mayhap my father is a noble Ethiopian prince, mistransmigrated into the body of an elderly Jew? Too late: the tyranny of the fork has marked him, and he must steal "inadvertent" bits for his fingers' guilty pleasures.

I empathize with that desire to live in one's head, performing an animal's functions with animal absentmindedness. Sometimes I too eat that way when I'm alone, mingling culinary herbs with the brackish taste of my fingers, in rebellious solidarity with his lack of manners. Socially, my older brother Hal and I have striven hard to project ourselves as the opposite of my father—to seem forceful, attentive, active, and seductive. But I feel my father's vagueness, shlumpiness, and mania for withdrawal inhabit me like a flu when no one is looking.

Across the street from the café, a drunken bum about sixty is dancing by himself on a park bench to Latin jazz. He has no shirt on, revealing an alkie's skinny frame, and he seems happy, moving to the beat with that uncanny, delayed rhythm of the stoned. I point him out as a potentially diverting spectacle to my father, who shows no interest. The drunk, in a curious way, reminds me of my dad: They're both functioning in a solipsistic cone.

Surrounded by "that thick wall of personality through which no real voice has ever pierced on its way to us," as Pater phrased it, each of us is, I suppose, to some degree a solipsist. But my father has managed to exist in as complete a state of solipsism as any person I have ever known. When he gets into an elevator, he never moves to the back, although by now he must anticipate that others will soon be joining him. Inconsiderateness? The word implies the willful hurting of others whose existence one is at least aware of.

I once saw an old woman in the nursing home elevator telling him to move back, which he did very reluctantly, and only a step at a time for each repeated command. (Perhaps, I rationalized for him, he has a faulty perception of the amount of space his body takes up.) The old woman turned to her orderly and said: "When you get on in years you have to live with old people. Some of them are nice and some are—peculiar." Meaning my father. When we got off the elevator he said, loudly: "She's such a pain in the ass, that one. Always complaining. I'll give her such a *luk im kopf*" (a smack in the head). His statement showed that he *had* been aware of her, but not enough to oblige her.

My father has always given the impression of someone who could sustain very little intensity of contact before his receptive apparatus shut down. Once, after I hadn't seen him in a year, I hugged him and told him how much I loved him. "Okay, okay. Cut the bullshit," he said. This armor of impatience may have been his defense against what he actually wanted so much that it hurt.

"Okay" is also his transitional marker, indicating he has spent long enough on one item and is ready for new data. If you haven't finished, so much the worse for you.

My sister Molly is the only one who can challenge his solipsism. She pays him the enormous compliment of turning a deaf ear to his self-pity, and assuming that, even in old age, there is still potential for moral growth. Years ago, hospitalized with pneumonia, he was complaining to her that nobody cared enough to visit him, and she shot back: "Do you care about anyone? Are you curious about anyone besides yourself?" She then tried to teach him, as one would a child, how to ask after others' well-being. "When you see them, say: 'How are you? What have you been up to lately? How are you *feeling?*'" And for a while, it took. My father probably said "How are *you?*" more times between the ages of seventy-five and seventy-nine than in all the years preceding. If the question had a mechanical ring, if he speedily lost interest in the person's answer, that ought not to detract from the worthiness of my sister's pedagogy.

My father's solipsism is a matter of both style and substance. When I was writing an essay on the Holocaust, I asked him if he had any memories of refugees returning from the camps. He seemed affronted, as though to say: Why are you bothering me with that crazy business afer all these years? "Ask your mother. She remembers it."

"But I'm asking you," I said. "When did you find out about the concentration camps? What was your reaction?"

"I didn't think about it. That was them and this was me," he said with a shrug.

Here was solipsism indeed: to ignore the greatest tragedy of modern times—of his own people!—because he wasn't personally involved. On the other hand, my father in his eighties is a hardly credible witness for the young man he was. What his reaction does underline is the pride he takes in being taciturn, and in refusing to cough up the conventionally pious response.

As I ask the Chinese waiter for the check, my father starts to fiddle with several napkins in his breast pocket. He has developed a curious relationship to these grubby paper napkins, which he keeps taking out of his pocket and checking. I've never seen him blow his nose with them. I wonder if old people have the equivalent of what clinical psychologists call "transitional objects"—like those pacifiers or teddy bears that children imbue with magical powers—and if these napkins are my father's talismen.

Just to show the internalized superego (God or my wife) that I have made an effort to communicate, I volunteer some news about myself. I tell my father that Cheryl and I are soon to have a baby. His response is: *"C'est la vie."* This is carrying philosophic resignation too far—even good news is greeted stoically. I tell him we have bought a house, and my teaching post is secure. None of these items seems to register, much less impress. Either he doesn't get what I'm saying, or knows it already and is indifferent.

My older brother Hal called him recently with the news that *he* had had his first baby. On being told he was a grandfather, my father's answer was: "Federico Fellini just died." This became an instant family joke, along with his other memorable non sequiturs. (If indeed it was a non sequitur. The translation might be: "What do I care about your new baby when death is staring me in the face?") Though I could sympathize with Hal's viewing it as yet another dig to add to his copious brief against our father, who has always tended to compete with his sons rather than rejoice in our good fortune, this Fellini response seemed to me more an expression of incapacity than insult. The frown on his face nowadays when you tell him something important, the *c'est la vie*, is a confession that he knows he can't focus enough to hold on to what you are saying; he lacks the adhesive cement of affect.

Even sports no longer matter to him. It used to be one of our few common topics: I was guaranteed a half-hour's worth of conversation with my father, working my way through the Knicks, Mets, Rangers, Giants, Jets . . . His replies were curt, yet apt: "They stink. They got no hitting." He it was who taught me that passionate fandom that merges with disenchantment: loyalty to the local team, regardless of the stupid decisions the front office made; never cross a picket line, just stick with the union, for all their corruption; vote Democratic no matter how mediocre this year's slate. I would have thought being a sports fan was part of his invincible core, as much as his addiction to newspapers. He continues to have the *Times* ordered for him, but now it sits on his lap, unopened, like a ship passenger's blanket.

* * *

Back at the home, I bend down and kiss him on the cheek before leaving. He says "I still got more hair than you do." This statement—untrue, as it happens—no longer can provoke me. He shakes my hand, to demonstrate how strong his grip is: it's a stunt he's learned, no indication of his actual strength, but, like the occasional big word, all that is left in his armamentarium of self-esteem.

"Do you need anything, Pop?"

"Well, I do and I don't."

Not knowing what to make of this enigmatic response, I say: "Do you need any money?" I hand him two twenty-dollar bills. He takes them uncertainly and bunches them in his hands without putting them away, which makes me think they will not stay long in his care. My father seems much more solicitous of his old napkins than these greenbacks.

"Do me a favor," he says hoarsely.

"What's that?"

"Try to see me more regularly. Once every few weeks."

This request takes my breath away. He's right, of course.

"I'll try. I *will* try. I was insanely busy this past month, but from now on . . ." I lie. Then, to shift the burden elsewhere, I ask: "Did you get any other visits recently?"

No, he shakes his head. I know this is not true: my brother visited him last Sunday. He gets no brownie points, Pop's already forgotten. Which means he won't remember my visit either by tomorrow.

2

"IF I WROTE MY LIFE DOWN, I WOULD HAVE TO TITLE IT: *THE STORY OF a Failure*." This is, in old age, my father's idée fixe. Ask him for particulars, he will reply tersely: "I was a failure. What else is there to say?" Being a failure apparently grants one the privilege of taciturnity (just as being a success must condemn me to garrulity).

Many times I have argued with him: "What makes you so presumptuous or so arrogant as to judge yourself a failure, when you accomplished no less than ninety-five percent of the rest of humanity?" He will not hear of it. He thinks I am trying to reassure him.

Besides, he seems at times proud to be labeled a failure, to partake in its peculiar romance. Nineteenth-century Russian fiction perfected this defense of the failure as the underground man, the marginal, economically redundant, passive intellectual, for whom superfluousness was a mark of superiority. The less you accomplished, the more you built up your store of latency, and the purer your integrity remained.

About a year ago, my wife and I were driving my father to a midtown restaurant, just to give him an excursion. In the car he was telling us he considered his life a failure.

I had heard this too many times to comment, but Cheryl said: "Why? You worked every day of your life, and you raised four children and they turned out fairly well."

"But I was always doing what I shouldn't have been doing, and not doing what I should have," he replied.

"What do you mean? You were supposed to go to work and you did."

"Yeah, but even though my bosses said I was a good worker, they didn't pay me well."

"Then it's their failure, not yours," said Cheryl. "They failed to do the right thing."

"What do you think you should have been doing?" I interrupted.

"Writing," he said.

"What kind of writing?"

"Fiction."

I never knew he thought of himself as a failed *novelist*. "Fiction?" I demanded.

"Or semifactual," he reconsidered. "I always wanted to be a writer, or something of that sort, and in some aspects you fulfilled my ambition. Vicariously, I am *kvelling* in your success as a writer." He added that lately he had been having "hallucinations" that he wrote a book, or rather stole it from me, and in so doing brought shame and dishonor on us all.

This confusion between his and my writing achievement has been there right from the start. Growing up, I was impressed by my father's large vocabulary, his peculiar, formal, crisp feeling for language. I submitted my first short story (about a gangster shot in a dark alley) to his criticism, and watched as he struck out the unnecessary words and told me, "Write about what you know." Still trusting his infallibility in writing matters, I was graduating from junior high school when my teacher asked me, along with four other students, to compete for valedictorian by writing a speech. Since I had the highest grade average in the school, everyone assumed I would win the contest. But I had no idea what a valedictorian speech was supposed to sound like, and so—oddly enough—I asked my father to write mine for me. He complied, employing his fanciest vocabulary and dwelling on the *parents'* feelings during such an occasion (using words like *vicarious* and *progenitors*). The speech laid an egg, and a chubby girl named Andrea Bravo who expressed herself earnestly if tritely got chosen instead. After that, I was warier about asking for his writing help.

I remember when I told my father back in 1971 that my first book of poems was about to come out. His only response was, "I haven't been writing any poems recently." I was struck then by how little feeling he had for me. Yet my siblings claim that I am my father's favorite—that he brags about me more to strangers, or, to put it another way, that he pays even less attention to them than he does to me.

"The possum," my mother calls him. "He plays dead. It's an act, he thinks the Angel of Death won't notice him if he lays low. The old man's stronger than you think. He'll outlive me, you, everybody."

All my life, it seems, I have been rehearsing prematurely for the death of my father. At eleven years old I woke from a dream in which he had been killed, got up like a sleepwalker, and, as if by dictation, wrote down a poem of grief over the vision of him laid out on a bier. My mother took it to her analyst, Dr. Jonas in the Bronx, and he told her that dreams were wish-fulfillment. She broke the hard news to me: It wasn't that I loved my father so, it was that I wanted him dead in order to marry her. This made little sense at the time, but I have always been willing to believe the worst about myself, and began to accept the possibility of harboring a patricide within.

(*Patricide*, incidentally, was a concept very much in the air when I grew up. My father had no love for his father, and his favorite book was *The Brothers Karamazov*.)

I must say, never for a conscious instant did I wish my father dead. But that may be because he seemed, as long as I can remember, already suffering from a mortal wound. One of the movies that left the deepest impressions on me in my youth was *Odd Man Out*, in which the sympathetic IRA operative, Johnny, played by James Mason, has been shot and spends the rest of the movie trying to stay alive. Somehow you know just by looking at him that he is bleeding to death. James Mason (cerebral, ironic, solitary, drawn) was a sort of idealized version of my father. Wiry and gaunt my father would come home, his job having consumed his stamina, and sit like a zombie, half dozing, letting the cigarette ash grow dangerously, while a ballgame sounded on the radio.

Avoiding pain and love, he withdrew into that dreamy, numbed zone that Schopenhauer (one of his favorites) called "the lost paradise of non-existence." These withdrawals, this maddening, arms-folded passivity of his, infuriated my mother, goading her into ever-stronger provocations. We, his four children, also provoked him, wanting him to notice us. It was like baiting a bear; occasionally he would treat us to a smack, but for the most part he shrugged us off, with a half smile that said: You can't get to me.

I have never known a man who was criticized as severely as my father. You would think he had committed some heinous crime. Hour after hour, he would be told he was uncouth, insensitive, thoughtless, gross. It made no difference in his behavior: he didn't get it, or he didn't want to get it. He continued to do things in what seemed like an alien, oafish manner—not to mention the things he didn't do, such as: talk to us, buy us birthday presents, show us affection, compliment us, even go to the hospital when my mother gave birth. By today's sensitive-male standards, he was certainly a washout. On the other hand, I wonder if he was really so different from many men in his generation.

Just for variety's sake, if nothing else, I would defend him in the family circle. But then he would say something mean to me as well that would catch me up short, and make me realize what hostile bitterness had collected behind that carapace of silence. It was the custom for my father to take us to the museum on Saturdays when he didn't have to work—usually after much badgering by my mother, who wanted some time to herself. One Saturday morning when I was about ten years old, we were all hounding him because he wouldn't take us anywhere; and this time I joined in the assault. Suddenly he lashed out at me with rabid fury: "You! You stay out of it, you're a cold fish." It was as if he were rebuking me for not having attacked him "warmly" enough in the past. I think he liked being attacked, or at least knew how to convert that coin into love, more dependably than direct expressions of affection.

"Cold fish" is an awful judgment to hang on a ten-year-old kid. But give him his due, he could have had a prescient insight: I often think there is something cold and "fishy" about me. Or, perhaps he was really saying: "You're like me, detached, unemotional." An inverted compliment.

So I became a writer.

But this is not about me; I must restrain myself from turning my father into a repository of clues to the genesis of my own development. I must get back on track and try to tell the story of this tight-lipped man's life, attempt to discover its underlying meaning. Why had he gravitated toward death-in-life? What made him throw in his hand so quickly? Or did he, really? There are organisms, such as barnacles, that manifest the most dogged willpower through a strategy that looks initially like weakness or dependency.

Albert Donald Lopate was born on September 2, 1910. He grew up in Jamaica, Queens, with three older half siblings and one full brother. He felt unloved by both his mother and father, with good cause.

My grandmother, Sophie, died before I was born, so I cannot describe her from experience. (I am told that she spent her last years looking out the window spotting car makes, went mad, and died in a mental hospital.) But I remember my grandfather, Samuel Lopate, quite well. He was a *character*, a Jewish Fyodor Karamazov in his appetite for women and money, and his utter indifference to children.

My grandfather was born in Russia; when he was about ten, his parents fled the pogroms, via Turkey, to Palestine. Family legend has it that they were thrown out of Palestine because he pissed on the Wailing Wall. My father says, more conservatively: "He did something that caused the Arabs to expel them. He made fun when the Arabs were praying at the wall, and they were outraged."

The next we hear of my grandfather, he has come to New York and married, for love, a woman who dies in childbirth. Soon after, for economic security, he latches onto an older widow, Sophie —a second cousin of his—with three children and a dry goods store. He goes to work in the store and wrests it from her. He sires two sons, Arthur and Albert.

Sophie was almost fifty when she had my father, and felt so lukewarm toward this child, whom she had tried unsuccessfully to abort, that she would not even look at him. Afterward she used him as her servant, making him wash the floors every Saturday. She favored the offspring from her first husband, the love of *her* life.

My father's parents fought openly. Sophie called Samuel a *trumernik* (loafer, bum, philanderer). My grandfather was, in truth, something of a lady-killer. According to my father, he had one talent that would knock women dead: he could cry at will. The sight of those plump crocodile tears rolling down his émigré cheeks melted many a female heart. (This led my father to the unfortunate conclusion that being emotionally undemonstrative was a mark of sincerity.) All told, Samuel buried three wives, which gave him the reputation of family Bluebeard. The last wife, Esther, I knew as a child. She was sweet, gave us oatmeal cookies, and was a reader (by which I mean she subscribed to the Book of the Month Club). My mother, who despised her lecherous father-in-law, used to say: "He'll drive her into a grave, too, like the others." Sure enough, Esther died, leaving Samuel a chunk of money, and us a box of books, which included Goren's *Contract Bridge*, *Thirty Days to a More Powerful Vocabulary*, and Henry George's tracts on social economy, which I tried to penetrate but could not.

I remember Samuel in his widower dotage: a cranky, cold, bald-headed, fat old man who would sit on his porch in Ozone Park, his bulging pants held up with suspenders. The only time I ever saw him pleased was when he took out a rainbow-speckled Irish Sweepstakes ticket, ornate as a stock certificate, and stared at it. He was convinced he would win, and not have to enter an old-age home; but he didn't, and soon he was complaining from the much smaller confines of half a room in the Rogers Avenue Nursing Home. My father would take us there to visit, perhaps in the hope that his grandparental warmth would be belatedly awakened and he'd leave us something. We were all very conscious that the longer he stayed in that nursing home, the more our possible inheritance was being eaten up.

I tried to encourage Grandpa to go out into the little garden and take a constitutional. He never listened to me, any more than he did to my father. My sister Molly alone knew how to handle Grandpa. Whenever she needed money for the movies, she would pay him an impromptu visit and wheedle a dollar bill out of him. This game he understood; he had played it on women often enough.

But to return to my father's youth. He used to sit in the back of his parents' dry goods store and read for escape. Dumas, Hugo, *The Count of Monte Cristo*. At school he was skipped ahead, and a sympathetic teacher helped him to catch up with the older kids; by the end of the term, he had the highest average in the new class.

The next year, my father, a natural lefty, had a less understanding teacher, who tried to force him to write right-handed. He developed a stammer, and his grades suffered when the teacher couldn't decipher his penmanship. Defiantly, he went back to writing left-handed.

In high school, he continued to read voraciously on his own, meanwhile ignoring the assigned schoolwork. Later in life, he would brag about his scholastic exploits in high school: acing a Latin test he hadn't studied for or frustrating teachers with his nonchalance. "I had a math teacher who would open up the class with a question, 'Lopate, did you do your homework?' And I would say, 'No, ma'am.' And she'd write down a zero in front of my name. Then I got ninety-six on the final, and she gave me a sixty-nine for the course. I said to her, "How could you give me a sixty-nine, when I got ninety-six on the final?" So she showed me all the zeroes and when she averaged them out, I got a thirty-four. I said: 'Why don't you give me a thirty-four, then? What you're doing is dishonest.'"

He was proud of being an intellectual dark horse—a "gifted underachiever," as it would later be called. I asked him once why he took such pleasure in flaunting the teacher's authority, when he must have known he would get punished for it. He said: "I didn't give a good goddamn what she thought, so long as *I* knew I understood the math."

His rebellion extended to rejecting his own family's Orthodox Judaism and Republican politics. They thought him a Socialist, and at least temperamentally he was pointed that way. "I thought of money as evil. I became an intellectual snob. I *eschewed* financial gain," he boasted. He wanted to go on to college, and asked his mother for a loan, and she turned him down, "although she had the dough," and although she had already subsidized his brother Arthur's higher education. He knew enough not to ask Samuel. "My father never treated me with the proper respect." The only one in his family who saw he had a brain, and encouraged him to continue learning, was an older half brother, Charles. But Charles obviously could not foot his tuition bill, so my father went to work, with the notion that eventually he might save enough to pay for his own college education.

He was drawn to newspapers. His first job was taking ads and running the switchboard for the *Long Island Press*. From there, he tried out for a job at a trade magazine, *Editor and Publisher*. Typical of my father's somewhat self-destructive integrity is that he made a point of telling the interviewer he was Jewish (he does not look noticeably so) at a time when discrimination against Jews was widespread. They hired him anyway. After that, he became a reporter for the *Queens Evening News:* his beat was to cover the political clubs and civic organizations in different neighborhoods and drum up stories. Though I find it difficult to imagine my father engaged in anything so extroverted, these cub reporter days were happy times for him. His terse style suited the newspaper format.

Having saved enough money, he enrolled in night school classes in journalism. But, after the long workday, he would fall asleep in class. So he dropped out of college in his freshman year, focusing on reporting instead.

"Then the Depression came, and the paper folded up, and there were no more journalistic jobs to be had." (Whenever my father would say, "Then the Depression came," the historical, capital *D* event always carried an echo of clinical, small *d*.) He took the only job he could get: a stock clerk for six dollars a week. As this was not enough to live on, he augmented his salary by playing poker at night. My father has always disliked gambling, but he was blessed with a poker face and always believed himself smarter than others; so, by cautious, close-to-the-vest playing, he would pocket a few extra dollars.

It was still not enough to make ends meet, so he asked his boss for a raise. "I was told: 'I can replace you with a college graduate who will willingly take your place for the same salary.'" My father answered: "In that case, you can get someone else." Years later he recalled vividly the boss's utter power over him; in that encounter, despite his shaky bravado, he was traumatized by a lifelong fear of unemployment. He reluctantly took the step of going to work for his older brother Arthur, on the assumption that a family member, at least, would never fire him.

At this moment in the story we may pause and note two things: (1) my father's capacity for defiance and self-assertion was still operating; he had not yet joined the legion of the defeated;

(2) his explanation that the Depression had closed down his journalistic options, true as it may be, does not explain why he never
tried to reenter this beloved milieu when the economy improved.
His fatalistic statement, "Then the Depression came," became one
of those family myths that remains to this day sacrosanct, unques-
tioned. On the other hand, I have no business judging him on this
score, never having lived through such an ordeal. The critic Manny
Farber once told a younger man: "You know, I'm not someone who
ever survived the Depression. It's not the sort of experience you ever
really get over."

In any event, my father despised his powerful brother Arthur,
so that to go to work in his ribbon-dyeing factory, Parkside, meant
no small swallowing of pride. The source of this fraternal dislike must
have had roots in childhood, but my father always harps on a later
incident. "When my brother Arthur got married, he started cater-
ing to my mother, he played up to her, and he got a good present
for the wedding. I thought he had prostituted himself to get some
dough, because he didn't give a damn about her. I don't think he
cared at all about her, he didn't have one iota of feeling."

"Did *you* care about your mother?" I asked him.

"Not really. But I wasn't ready to prostitute myself."

As people are rarely entirely unselfish or sincere, I could
never understand my father's enduring shock at this bit of filial
pretense (if it was that). His outrage had something primitive about
it: Arthur had stolen the "blessing" of their mother, through guile,
and he had gotten nothing. Jacob and Esau all over again.

It was also said in my family that Arthur "cheated" my father
by skimping on his salary. I have a feeling he paid him the going
rate, no more, no less. My father liked certain manual labor aspects of the job: lifting hundred-pound bales, going out with the
drivers on delivery. One time, however, the workers struck; my
father was sympathetic to their cause but felt an overriding family loyalty. When the labor trouble was settled, everyone got a raise
except my father, who was not in the union and was treated, conveniently in this instance, as management. To compound the
indignity, Arthur "threw me a few extra dollars from time to time,
to keep me quiet."

If Uncle Arthur had that family knack of treating his brother with insufficient respect, my father also seemed quick to take offense. In recent years, he would tell of running into Arthur at the funeral of a relative. Arthur took him aside and said: "We're the only ones left. Let's stay in touch. Give me your phone number." My father pulled himself up with dignity: "You should know my phone number. It has been in the book for years." He offered this story as proof of Arthur's hypocrisy: "He was phony as a three-dollar bill." Of course, my father could have just as easily phoned Arthur all those years, and didn't.

It strikes me as curious that, though my family has been willing to mock my father at every turn, it has never questioned his judgment of Arthur. In our family myth, Uncle Arthur is the Evil One, the vulgar Capitalist, like the figure of the watch-chained plutocrat in left-wing cartoons. On the few occasions we visited Arthur in his spacious Queens home, usually for his children's Bar Mitzvahs or engagement parties, he struck me as a typical hail-fellow-well-met type. I remember his prosperous, well-fed look, the rosy spots on his cheek—and the well-founded report that he had a mistress.

That he kept a mistress made me like him. I dreamed of attaining the same worldliness as a man. Over the years, in fact, I developed a blasphemous feeling of identification with Uncle Arthur, partly because I did not myself "eschew" financial success, and partly because I took with a grain of salt my impoverished family's self-serving antagonism toward him. Maybe Arthur really was a shithead, maybe he was a decent guy, I have no idea. All I know is the role he played in the family mythology. After he sold the ribbon-dyeing plant, he went into "the oil business." Probably what was meant was some sort of fuel delivery, but I always liked to fancy him an oilman, the Queens equivalent of a Texas millionaire. If I secretly identified with Uncle Arthur, I also suspected my father associated me with his older brother. He had been told when they were growing up that Arthur was the handsome one, and he, not; he has often described me, with mixed pride and rue, as "a good-looking guy." At such moments I feel myself lumped with his nemesis. The glib-tongued charmer. The lawyer.

My father, from the photographic evidence of his young man-
hood, seems to me to have been quite good-looking, in that brood-
ing, sunken-cheeked way of Lincoln, Joseph Wiseman, Jack Palance,
Cesare Pavese, and an Appalachian farmer in a Walker Evans photograph. But what matters is what my father thought; and when my
father met my mother, he thought himself ugly. At twenty-seven,
he had never been in love; he had never slept with a woman who
was not a prostitute. My mother, Frances, was working in a beauty
parlor when they met. She was sexy, she had a voluptuous figure,
and all the guys wanted her, or at least, as she puts it, wanted to
fool around with her. But she was attracted to brains, and, in their
Jamaica, Queens, circle, Albert was the intellectual. He wooed her
with talk about politics, books, art, Bach. He taught her. He saw
in my mother an unformed intelligence—but an intelligence. "All
of Fran's siblings kept saying she was the dummy in the Berlow
family. I took one look at her family, and I said, 'You're not stupid.
They are.'"

Bonding on the resentful basis that they were both insufficiently respected by their families, they married. Many good mar-
riages have been founded on less. In their case, however, it was not
enough.

My father tells it one way, my mother another. The difference is that my mother's version is juicier and more voluble; my
father's, extremely laconic. (I once tape-recorded my mother telling her life story: it took six sessions and twenty-two sides. My
father's took less than an hour.) As long as I can remember, my
mother has been honing and expanding the story of his husbandly
wrongs. According to her, the problems began while they were still
courting; he had laughingly allowed a gibe by Arthur's son ("Gee,
you got a big nose!") to stand, and she never forgave him his lack
of gallantry. My mother had notions of a gentleman's behavior toward women that my father violated at every turn: he did not pay
enough attention to her on their honeymoon, he lacked the proper
romantic approach to lovemaking. Later, back in the city, he would
come home from the factory, reeking with sweat; the odor turned
her off. She would make him take a bath immediately. His personal

hygiene standards she felt left much to be desired; his sexual tech-
nique, likewise.

My father says: "Look, Fran was not a virgin when I married
her. She insisted that I wasn't 'liberated' enough, that we weren't
sexually 'compatible.' Although we managed to have four kids, supposedly we weren't 'compatible.'"

Juxtaposing their testimonies, I can still hear the sound of
two people not listening to each other—that sound that dominated
my childhood.

My mother says now that my father missed out on the joys
of fatherhood by not involving himself in changing diapers, preparing bottles, cradling us, and so on. By his own account, he kept
a distance from child rearing:

"When Hal was born, we used to have a next-door neighbor
named Herman. And Hal would say 'Herman, Herman' before he
said 'Daddy.'"

My father's deadpan voice on the tape betrays only a quiver
of the pain this memory must have caused him. "How come?" I hear
the interlocutor (myself) ask.

"I don't know. Maybe I wasn't exactly a loving father like
most fathers are. And this man paid a lot of attention to the kid,
and the kid reacted to it."

"Do you think it was because you hadn't gotten any example
of love from your own father?"

"Probably. Same thing happened all over again."

By my father's admission, he was ambivalent about having
children. The first one he accepted philosophically. "When we had
the second and third, I became a little leery."

Understandably, since there was never any money, and he
had found himself indentured to the economic burdens of a large
family. He took them on without complaint, working six days a
week. At home, he was both an ineffectual and a scary figure. I remember as a boy being physically frightened of my father. He was
much more prone to hit my older brother than me, being more jealous of Hal, I suppose. And Hal was more willing to trade blows with
him: they would go at it, crashing into furniture, with my mother

in the back, screaming to them to stop. I felt it taboo, unthinkable, to raise my hand against my father. He could have killed me. I kept my distance, knowing he could hurt just as easily through absentmindedness as intention. One time, we were waiting to be served in a bakery, and he accidentally let a cigarette ash drop down my back. For years, I felt that ember on my back with wincing reflex.

By the time I was six, the fighting between my mother and father had become so severe they had almost split up. This is how he tells it:

"Let's get to the nitty-gritty. When I was first married, your mother was unfaithful to me. And I found out. And one day, I found myself choking her. Then in the middle of it, I stopped short. Because I said to myself, 'Why am I doing this? This is not me. I am not a violent person. I'm not a person of action.' And I stopped. That's when your mother had me. Because she had something she could always hold against me, that I tried to choke her."

My father had very consciously set up this experience as the key point in his oral autobiography, although, with his usual self-absorption, he was unaware of the repugnant effect this confession, that he wished he had strangled my mother, might have on me, her son.

"Why didn't you leave her instead?"

"That's the story of my failure. Because I couldn't leave her. I'm not saying this in defense of myself. I *said* I made my mistake: I should have killed her, and it would have ended then and there. I would have been tried and sent to prison, and that would be that. This way I let everything linger on, and solved nothing."

"So your greatest regret in life is that you didn't kill her?"

"Yes. That I didn't stop the thing—the condition."

"And that would have been the only way to stop it?"

"I don't know whether it was the only way, but it was a solution. Whereas what ensued was not."

"How would you characterize what ensued?"

"Years of nothing. Of numbed nonexistence." (I was surprised to hear my father himself acknowledge this death-in-life state.) After a long pause, he said: "I want to amend that. The only encouraging thing was that we engendered four children whom I think in some ways have embellished my life." He paused. "I realize, of course, that Leah is not my kid. But I never told her, and I never acted as if I knew. I acted as fairly as possible because I said to myself, 'This is not her fault, why should I hold it against her?'"

In fact he succeeded, to the degree that he showed more fondness for Leah as a child than for the rest of us. What does it say about this man, that he would dote on the one child that was not his own? Self-hatred? But Leah was also the youngest, she was very winning, she was a girl (hence less threatening to him than his sons), and she was quiet, soft-spoken like him. Whatever the reasons, his decision to treat her as his own, without ever letting her know she had a different father (the truth came out eventually but not through him), seems admirable in retrospect. It may be the most noble, disciplined-heroic thing he ever did. A shame we never gave him sufficient credit for it.

But something is bothering me: "How is it that you and Mother were so sure Leah wasn't your kid?"

"I wasn't that sure until your mother told me . . . Look, it doesn't make any difference, that's the way I felt."

"Still, it's a hard thing to know for sure unless you take blood tests."

"At first she looked a little different than the Lopates. Don't get me wrong, I think Leah is, in her way, a wonderful girl."

He spoke about the summer that had led up to her birth. "We went upstate on vacation, and we lived in a bungalow colony—a *kuchalein*, they called it, because you did your own cooking. At that time I used to play cards. I spent a little more time with cards than I should have. That's when your mother took up with this fellow. Benno. He was supposed to be related to one of the big-shot families in the Israeli government. He was a nice guy. He must have aroused a spark in the old lady. He didn't seem too bright to me.

But that judgment may be qualified by the fact that I resented him. Actually, I spent too much time with cards, and I shouldn't have."

"So you blame yourself partly?"

"Oh, yes. The old lady wasn't entirely wrong."

This responsible, mature perspective somehow manages to coexist with the regret that he did not kill her.

My father's emphasis on the choking incident spooked me because I had already used that episode as the climax of my story "Willy." After the story appeared in my book *Bachelorhood*, my mother informed me that I had exaggerated the ferocity of his beating. "I wasn't afraid of him for one second. If he'd really tried to hurt me," she boasted, "I could have broken him in half." (My mother is a stout woman and, in fact, outweighs him.) My father, on the other hand, was so impressed with the story's dénouement that he seemed to have appropriated it as his central myth. I'm not at all convinced he saw his whole life as leading up to and away from this failed-homicide until he read my story, which could have put the notion into his head.

Around the same period that I tape-recorded him, when he was in his mid-seventies, my sister Molly asked him, point-blank: "When did you decide to become a vegetable?"

He answered her: "When I had my hands around your mother's throat, I was so horrified at the violence this evil woman had provoked in me, when my nature is not violent, that I decided then and there to punish her by becoming passive."

To Molly, this answer confirmed her belief that he had deliberately created a passive persona—out of spite. I remained skeptical. For one thing, it was almost word for word what he'd said to me, and sounded too canned. For another, I could never accept the family's idea that my father had sinisterly willed himself to be a "vegetable." This gave him too much credit for intent; he was trying in the final hours to pretend he had caused the shambles of his life, rather than acknowledging the more common fate of limitation and deterioration.

But Molly took him at his word. Her response was funny if harsh: "If you want to be a vegetable, you gotta be sent to the farm!" (i.e., the nursing home).

* * *

My mother's tendency was always to speak of my father as a needy child. "I got five kids at home, you four and Al. He's the biggest baby of all." Or: "He doesn't want a wife. He wants a mother. A nursemaid," she would say bitterly. She is a large-bosomed woman, and I took her comment to mean she found something infantile about my father's fixation on that part of her anatomy. But what is so unusual about a man looking for nirvana at a woman's breast? Freud argued that fantasy had its origins in an irrecoverable experience of bliss at the mother's breast, and that all later gratifications, including sex, are bound to be incomplete. In my father's case, his own mother had been cold toward him, so his search was all the more imperative, if tinged with the expectation of rejection.

Many of the dozen or so poems my father wrote my mother, in an effort to win her back when she was seeing another man, speak to this pathos of unsatisfied desire, the distance between coitus and possession.

> Dilemma of Love
> I made love to you and you sighed
> And violently clawed my heaving flesh.
> This should have been ecstatic joy,
> But both you and I know that
> Tho I possessed your body, I had
> Penetrated only to your outer shell.
> Deep inside there remained the
> Suppressed mask of discontentment
> The ever-present search for
> I know not what. But not for me.

I make no claims for my father's verse—he was clearly a self-taught, Sunday poet—but what mesmerizes me is the Cavafyan dryness and refusal of consolation that pops up in the last line. Another poem is again about sex; this time he is the onlooker. It begins:

Last night you were entwined with another.
I saw your passionate embrace
And heard your deeply contented sighs,
And I fondly remembered that there
I had once joyously nestled.

Nestled—so fitting a word for the infant at the breast. He then seeks
to recall her to their happy hours together: meanders through Central Park and Coney Island, long conversations on her stairs. The
poem ends:

Even tho you presume not to remember,
And your thoughts are concentred on him,
I can never obliterate them from my mind—
And neither can you.

That menacing last line—no wonder these poems did not do the
trick of winning her over! Reading through them, I am struck by
their narrow range of lament at love's inconstancy. However, as Faiz
once said, "the proper subject of poetry is the loss of the beloved."
Certainly there is something moving about a pain so unbearable it
could find expression only in poetry—and then only once, during
the initial marital crisis.

    That early threat of losing her had elicited, then, two extraor-
dinary responses: the poems and the choking, that violent aggression finally coming to the surface. After that, he was spent, for the
rest of his days, or so he says. But isn't this too pat, too "literary" an
interpretation of a man's life? Are there really such crossroads
of decision in life, like a well-made Chekhov story, after which
the person who has chosen unwisely drags on to the end like a ghost
of himself? Is there such a limited supply of life force in a human
being, that it can be consumed at one go?

    Interestingly, my mother dates his giving up to an earlier
point: the marriage itself. "He didn't read as much after he got
married. He started quoting what he'd already read." Since she had
married him for his brains, this relaxing of mental striving caused

her understandable chagrin. Still, it means he stopped trying to expand his range not from jealous spite but from relief of the sort that follows accomplishing a goal. Supposing this lonely, cerebral young man had yearned for "normalcy," marriage and family, and, having attained this plateau—like the woman who lets her looks go after marriage—he had less need to develop his intellect as a lure.

All the while that he was working at his brother Arthur's factory, my mother was always goading him to improve his situation in life. Among other things, she urged him to become a life insurance salesman. One of her beaux sold insurance and said he would put in a good word for Al. My father went so far as to enroll in a training program. At night he would practice the standard pitch, the euphemisms sticking in his craw ("Should one of your loved ones drop out of the picture . . ."), using his children as audience. But he had such a mournful countenance that one could not imagine him selling anything, much less insurance. When he took the aptitude test, he scored high on the intellectual portion, as expected, then was disqualified by a disastrous personnel interview.

According to my mother, he kept resisting advancement. After he left his brother's plant to work in another factory, he took a test for a foreman's position and scored very high, only to see a man with a lower grade but more seniority hired. "Instead of telling himself, 'Okay, I'll get it on the next opening,' he gave up. He was defeated before he started," she said.

My mother is, if anything, the opposite: She had a lifelong dream to become an entertainer and, after she was fifty, did succeed in getting acting jobs, doing commercials, playing Golda in road productions of *Fiddler on the Roof*. Perhaps she has had so much life force, so much determination, that he has receded before it, feeling that department was already being looked after. He was, in any case, supportive of her efforts to enter show business.

I think another reason for his resistance to climbing the managerial ladder is that he already had an ambition—to write; failing to achieve it, he didn't wish to substitute a less compelling one. All this is speculative; my father himself offers only the murkiest explanations about this area. I asked him once: "Did you *want* to be promoted to manager at the plant?"

"I didn't know what the hell I wanted. I was so confused at the time."

Eventually, he followed my mother into the white-collar side of the textile industry, becoming a shipping clerk in midtown Manhattan. He was an excellent clerk, perfectly suited for the duties of keeping track of numbers and shipments, by virtue of his phenomenal memory. Sometimes he could not resist showing off his intellectual superiority, as when he sent a telex to the North Carolina plant in Latin: *Que usque abutere nostra patientia, O Catalinum?* ("How much longer, O Cataline, will you abuse our patience?") That must have gone over big.

Though my father continued to read, often picking up the novels my brother and I introduced into the household, his main intellectual activity was doing the crossword puzzle. Increasingly, the less respected he felt in the world, the more he took to boasting about his mathematical shortcuts or word power. Or he would go on about how he was the first in our family to appreciate, say, Bessie Smith or Stroheim's *Greed*. Even as a child I was embarrassed by these threadbare boasts, for, if this was all a grown man had to feel good about himself, he was clearly in trouble.

As he grew older, the boasting anecdotes began to substitute for an active, groping memory. He would tell for the thousandth time how he had responded to *Greed* before anyone else knew it was good. "The thing that made it so unusual was that they cast against type. They took Zazu Pitts, who was known as a dizzy comic, and made her play the mean, calculating bitch. Then they got George O'Brien, this romantic lead, and made him play a stupid lunk."

(One time, overcome by impatience at hearing this for the millionth time, I interrupted: "Actually, it was Gibson Gowland who played McTeague, not George O'Brien, and what makes *Greed* so great is the physical detail of the film—the direction, not the casting." He looked miserable. "I don't know, I probably got it confused." Instantly I regretted not having let him ramble on. It was too easy to slay this father.)

Bragging is a Lopate family trait; not only my mother and siblings, but I succumb to it all too often—especially under stress. As soon as I start to brag, though, I hear my father's voice and flinch at the futility of bestowing on oneself the admiration one craves from others.

The other downside of his bragging was that it deepened his obsession with being a failure. Had he not insisted so on his superiority, he might not have been so hard on himself about the way his life turned out.

3

EACH YEAR THE NURSING HOME INVITES FAMILY MEMBERS TO A STAFF meeting discussing the resident's overall condition. I have been to several of these: the psychologist always says, with concern: "Your father seems depressed," as though such a reaction to being locked away in a nursing home were peculiar. Each year I answer: "My father has been depressed all his life." The statement is greeted with meaningful nods but little lasting effect: the training of those in the caring professions seems to obligate them to treat melancholy as a temporary aberration. The psychologist working with my father is a behavior-modification enthusiast who is convinced that if you can get people to frame their statements in a positive form, they will feel better about themselves. The clinical equivalent of a "Smile" face. It is even more futile in this case, given the vanity attached by my father to pessimism. But I appreciate that they are trying their best: the concern and good intentions of the staff are evident. They tell me (first, the good news) that my father is an "attractive," well-liked resident, who makes a strong impression. But (the bad news): "He does not eat. He is losing weight. He shows very little appetite, and he won't even let us feed him." All present look frowningly in the direction of the wheelchaired old man, head sunk on his chest, who, as it happens, has been there throughout his case discussion.

I do my part to scold, as well. "Pop, you're intelligent enough to know that if you don't eat, you'll get sick. Do you want to be sick?"

He's heard it before. Unimpressed. He keeps his counsel: silent, deep, unfathomable.

"Mr. Lopate," asks a social worker sharply, in such a way as to demand an answer: "What do you make of all this?"

"I'm trying to figure out," says my father, "how the hell to get out of here."

When he was in his early fifties, my father had his first stroke. I was still living at home, going to college, and I remember the shrieking in the middle of the night, as my mother tried to restrain him from getting out of bed. "Please, Al, don't move, the ambulance is coming!" He had it in his head that she was trying to kill him, and he had better get up or he would never rise from the bed again.

Tanizaki's novel, *The Key*, which had been making the rounds of our house, lay on his night-table: this perverse story of husband and wife plotting to do each other in may have fueled his suspicion. Then again, my mother had so often declared she wished he was dead that I too watched her uneasily that night.

After the stroke, he never recovered the full strength on his right side. And it threw a fear of death into him that made him even more inert, as though, by doing next to nothing he would conserve strength and live longer: the possum strategy.

On the plus side, he was no longer frightening to me after his stroke. His new harmlessness enabled me to nurture feelings of affection and pity for him: I came to a fondness for the idea of my father, especially in the abstract. I admired his dutiful work ethic, his dry sense of humor, his love of reading, his gentle, long-suffering air, his ethical values, his progressive politics. Moreover, we looked a lot alike—had the same rangy build, shy grin in company and set grim mouth when alone, along with several dozen physical gestures we shared, or, I should say, he had imprinted on me.

After I was set up in my own life, I had a persistent if undeveloped fantasy that I would somehow rescue my father. It seemed to me I was the only one in the family who actually liked and understood him. So I would go out of my way on occasion to be nice to him, or to treat him with the deference and respect to which I imagined a "normal" father might be entitled. These good intentions were fine so long as they stayed largely in the abstract and were not tested by reality.

In the spring of 1969, when I was living in California, I invited him to stay with me for a week. My first marriage had collapsed, I had run away to Berkeley, and I was trying to throw myself into teaching children creative writing, while waiting for the pieces of my shattered ego to reknit. My father arrived and let it soon be known that he was unimpressed with the Bay Area: it had fewer pizza parlors, barber shops, and newsstands than New York. On Saturday afternoon I took him to Candlestick Park to watch a ballgame. His response was lukewarm: too windy. A classically provincial New Yorker, little-traveled, he shielded himself against feelings of unworldiness by making a point of appearing unimpressed with new experiences. I knew this; still, his phlegmatic sourness began wearing me down. After the first few days I left him more and more to himself, especially during the day, while I went off to my teaching job at a private school. At night I would come home bearing excited tales of battles with the school administration, and of the kids' responses to the creative writing assignments I had just cooked up. My father cut off my enthusiasm with the comment: "Those who can, do. Those who can't, teach." At twenty-six, it had not occurred to me, so sure was I that all this pedagogic turmoil would one day be grist for the literary mill (as indeed it was), that in his eyes I was already a failure. Like him.

He continued to work at the textile firm of M. Lowenstein & Sons, rarely missing a day, until he turned sixty-seven and the company forced him to retire. It was retirement that withered him. Without the focused identity that his desk and shipping orders brought, he became hollowed-out. About a year after his retirement, he came down with pneumonia. I visited him in the hospital, where he was hoarding a pile of hospital menus—long green slips with boxes to check off the desired entrées. Disoriented, he thought they were shipping orders, "work" he had to finish while recuperating.

I remember the urgent phone call from my mother at the start of that illness. "Come quickly, he's very ill." I thought: This is it. On my way over, I began preparing for the worst, rehearsing my funeral oration, letting my stomach's churn dredge up the proper words. His death, I secretly hoped, would deepen me. I was always waiting for life to become tragic so that I would merely have to record it to become a powerful and universal writer.

"He's always been such a stoic," my mother said, greeting me at the door. "So when he said he felt a little pain, I knew it must be bad. Poor Pop, it hurt him so much he was doubled over, he couldn't lie down, he had to sleep all night in the chair. I can't bear to see it happening to him. He's like a . . . great tree withering in its branches."

A great tree? My mother, a professional actress, tends to dramatize. Still, I was pleased to hear her invoking this sequoian imagery in his behalf, instead of the usual scorn. We helped him on with his trousers; I kneeled at his feet to strap on leather sandals over phlebitis-swollen ankles, enacting my Cordelia fantasy. There *was* something grand, Lear-like about him that morning, a frail bundled-up survivor lifted into taxis in the freezing cold, to skitter across iced sidewalks.

Once stationed in a ward, however, he became a hospital thing. I visited him two days later: sunk in a bed-wet trough, he was gray-stubbled, bone-protruding thin, his complexion white as celery. Amber traces oscillated on the EEG screen: which will it be, life, death? life, death . . . ?

"If I don't talk, it's not because I'm not happy to see you," he said.

"Please, no need to talk. You can even sleep, I'll still be sitting here." Frankly, I would have preferred he slept; talking was never easy between us. His eyes kept opening and staring at me—accusingly, I thought, though perhaps this was only his myopic stare.

"Don't worry, Pop, tomorrow they'll give you a shave. You'll look a million times better. You want your glasses?" No, he shook his head. "Why don't you put on your glasses?" I repeated. Somehow it seemed to me that everything would be fine if I could just get him to wear his glasses.

"I'm saving my eyes," he said.

"What are you saving them for? A rainy day?" I joked.

The glasses were smudgy with thumbprints; I washed them off with water from the tumbler and placed them on him.

"What are you thinking?" I asked, in the silence.

"I'm thinking, 'Why me?'"

In those days I still hoped for some sort of wisdom from my father, poised at the maw between life and death. "Why me?" was not the illumination I had had in mind. But "Why me?" was a curt summary of what he felt.

"Gimme that thing," he pointed his bony finger toward a plastic bottle which he kept by his side constantly.

I watched, heard him, pee into the bottle.

"Got any pretty nurses?" I asked. "I saw one outside your door, she looked like a cutie."

He stared at me sternly, reproachfully, with sea-green eyes. "Take my word for it, this is the most . . . emasculating experience you could ever have," he said. He swallowed hard, then he rubbed his forehead, looking pained.

"What's wrong, Dad, got a headache?"

No, he shook his head.

"Do you want to hear the news?"

"What difference does it make?"

"What do you think about, lying here all this time?" I tried again.

"Nothing. When you're in pain, that's all you think about."

Again, he was telling me something important, but I didn't know how to listen to it.

4

MY MOTHER AND FATHER HAD ONCE TAKEN A MAGAZINE QUIZ: "DO YOU Know Your Mate?" She had been able to fill out everything about him, from his social security number to his mother's maiden name, whereas the opposite was true for him. "He didn't even remember my mother's maiden name! I realized I was living with a stranger, who didn't care at all about me, as long as I fulfilled his creature comforts." What my mother says is true, up to a point. My father is a stranger to everyone. On the other hand, his not knowing her social security number does not negate the fact that he was completely attached to her and would have undergone any amount of humiliation to keep living in her presence.

Ten years ago, when my father was seventy-four and my mother sixty-eight, she divorced him so that she could put him in a nursing home. She was candid about not wanting to spend her remaining years nursing an old man she didn't love, and it was clear that he could no longer take care of himself. Apparently the nursing home's regulations stated that a prospective lodger could have no other recourse before being taken in: hence, the necessity for divorce.

After the divorce went through, there was an interim period when my parents continued to live together, waiting for an opening at the nursing home. During this time, my father was "on probation," as it were, and if he behaved well, it seemed my mother might reverse herself and allow him to stay with her. In the midst of that limbo period, I was in New York for a few weeks (I had taken a regular teaching job in Houston) and called on them. My mother sent us out to breakfast together so that we could talk "man-to-man." Since he is so laconic and apt to drift into withdrawal, I could only smile at my mother's fantasy of a "father-son powwow." We stopped at the corner stand to buy a newspaper; I was tempted to buy two newspapers, in case we ran out of things to say. It was raining as we walked across the street to the coffee shop, a greasy spoon joint, for breakfast. The breakfast special was $1.55, "Hot Pastrami Omelette." Since he was treating, I had chosen the cheapest place around.

"How's . . ." my father began, then lost his train of thought.

"How's Helen?" I prompted, offering the name of my then-current girlfriend.

"I thought the other one was prettier."

"What other one?" I asked irritably, knowing he meant Kay, a previous flame who had two-timed me, and whose prettiness I did not relish being reminded of at the moment.

"You know, I had a funny dream last night," he changed the subject. "I dreamt I was sick and there were about ten people in the hospital room who came to see me. One of them was Bernie. Now I know my brother's been dead for years. I don't understand the significance of his being there."

"I don't either. What happened in the dream?"

"Nothing. Your sister Leah was in the room, and her friends. That's another thing I couldn't understand. Why wasn't Molly in the dream? Or you and Hal? Your mother would have an interpretation."

"Probably." A long silence fell. "So, you and Mom seem to have made peace with each other."

"You know, your mother and I got divorced."

"I know. Does it feel strange, living together after you're divorced?"

"Yes it feels strange."

"Did you sign the papers too, or—"

"I signed it," he said. "It was a joint divorce. Because your mother was going to go through with it anyway. One of the reasons for the divorce was to get a better tax break. And now they've changed the law, so it wouldn't have made any difference anyway."

"I thought the divorce was so that they wouldn't take Mother's income if she put you in a nursing home."

"Yes. But I don't want to go into a nursing home. My father, my brother, and my sister all went into nursing homes, and I don't have fond memories of them."

I liked the understated way he put it. "What I don't understand is, is it your legal right to stay in the apartment now, or are you there at Mother's sufferance?"

"I think it's the second. Besides, she doesn't want to have me forcibly removed."

"So you're on your best behavior now? And you're getting along?"

"Well . . . there have been some peculiar things lately."

"Like what?"

"We were at a gathering, and your mother was talking as if I had nothing to do with the way you kids turned out," he said, holding his fork in midair and glancing up at me sideways. "She was saying 'My son does this,' and 'my other son does that,' and 'my daughter is such-and-such.' She was taking all the credit, as if I had no influence on you."

"Well that's not true. We all feel you had a big influence on us." For better or worse, I added in my mind.

"I'm not saying I was the only influence. But I did have a little."

"Of course. She was just bragging, Pop. Like you do."

Another long silence, in which I watched the flies buzzing around the Miller beer sign.

"What have you been thinking about lately?" I asked.

"Nothing. I've been slightly depressed," he said.

"About what?"

"Nothing special."

"Your health all right?"

"My health is as good as can be expected for a man my age. I'm actually in good physical shape, except I have emphysema. I haven't smoked for years, but I still have emphysema from all the smoking I used to do."

"Are you still on medication?"

"Just vitamin pills."

"That's great!" I said with false, hearty enthusiasm.

"And half an aspirin a day for my heart."

"You get any exercise at all? Do you walk?"

"No, I don't walk much." He shook his head.

"You used to love walking."

"But now I walk so slowly. I used to walk real fast. Now your mother walks faster than I do, and she gets impatient."

"You can take walks alone."

"But I walk so slowly that it bugs me. Put it this way: My *halcyon* days are over," he said, grinning at his use of the unusual word.

"When were your halcyon days, Pop?" I asked skeptically.

"Before I got my stroke. I thought I was immortal. I was healthy as a horse. I used to work all day and night without stopping. I never even took a sick day. Then I got the stroke and I couldn't get out of bed. I don't know if you could understand unless it happens to you. You try to stand up and you can't. That frightened the hell out of me." Now he was warming up. "And I had this internist. Supposed to be one of the top internists in the city. At least that's what he told me. He prescribed Dilantin and something else. The two medications canceled each other out. Later on someone told me that I could have sued him for malpractice. But someone else said that if he was such a big internist, then I couldn't win. So I didn't sue."

"Just as well."

"He's still practicing. Cut down on his hours, though," he added with a sly grin.

"But that was over twenty years ago. A long time to get over a fright."

"A lot of people at the senior center had strokes. So they understand. That's one good thing about that place. The problem is . . . that the two men I played canasta with, one is sick and the other man . . ." he mumbled.

"I'm sorry, I didn't hear."

"The other man passed on."

"That's too bad. So you have to make new friends."

"It's not easy for me. I'm not the gregarious type."

You could say that again. "Why is that, I wonder?"

"Your mother was the gregarious type, but I wasn't."

"What about when you were younger, before you met Mom?"

A pained look. "I didn't have too many friends."

"Were you shy?"

"Probably I am shy."

"Why is that?"

"I didn't have any confidence in myself."

The truth in a nutshell. Another silence. "Well, you don't have to make friends with the people at the center, you just have to play cards."

"I do. I play rummy. And I find I'm better at rummy than I was at canasta. —Eat slowly. Take your time," he told me. My French toast was so awful that I was trying to get through it as fast as possible.

"Does the center ever go on outings?" I asked.

"They go to Atlantic City. That's not my style. I don't bother going."

"I was once in Atlantic City," I reminisced, "and I enjoyed it. The ocean, the boardwalk."

"The hotels expect you to gamble. I'm not a gambler."

When he was finished he started to get up and reached ever so slowly into his raincoat, which was hanging on the hook behind him, for some money. He found only a dollar. Puzzled. His hand traveled with incredible hesitation across to the other pocket. Nothing in there. A look went across his face, like a child who has accidentally lost something and expects a beating. He put his hand in his shirt pocket. Pulled out a $20 bill. Satisfaction. The check came to $5.60.

"You pay the tip," he said cheerfully.

A week later I asked my mother how Pop was doing. "He fell out of bed again. I didn't help him up, either. He's got to learn to do for himself. What if I go on the road again? It's what I learned when I was working with those retarded kids—same principle. You've got to teach them to be independent."

"It's not very nice to compare him to a retarded kid."

"Don't worry," she sighed, "I'll do what's right. Because I don't want to live with guilt. I've lived with guilt before and it's no fun."

But fighting broke out between my parents constantly. Before I left the city, I visited them again. My mother was telling me about her stocks. Considering how poor we had been, and how she is still living in government-subsidized housing, having stocks, even worthless ones, is a status symbol. "This stock went from fifty cents to four dollars, I didn't sell, and now it's down to a dollar."

"If it reaches four dollars again, you'd better sell," I said cautiously.

"What's the difference? It only cost me a few hundred bucks. If I can't afford to risk that much, forget it."

My father interjected, in his phlegmy growl, something about the Mindanao Mother Lode.

She blew up at him:

"You'll see, you're not getting a cent of that money! Even if the lawyer did say you were entitled to fifty percent of our property after the *divorce*. I'll fix your wagon!"

My father shrank into himself. I was shocked at the venom with which she had yelled at him, even after all these years of hearing it. I asked: "What's this about a Mindanao Mother Lode?"

She said, "Aw, I invested a lousy hundred dollars in this oil drilling outfit in the Pacific a few years ago and never heard a word about it. But from him I never *stop* hearing it! If he keeps rubbing it in, he's the one who's gonna suffer."

Much as I had wanted to protect him in the moment against her temper, after I left them I realized the passive-aggressive cunning of my father in employing just those words that would set her off. (It was the same quiet ability to insert a dig as when he called my previous girlfriend prettier than my current one. For all his solipsism, he was observant enough when he wanted to be, and had a feel for other people's exposed areas of wounded vanity.)

A few months later, the parental truce was shattered. It seemed the toilet had overflowed while my father was using it, and he didn't clean it up. He had phoned my sister Molly to report the toilet had flooded, and she, not having any time that day to stop by, gave him practical advice: Call the maintenance man. He didn't; instead he sat there for eight hours, "with his arms folded," as Molly put it. My mother came home, saw his turds on the floor, the sight of which pushed her over the limit for good.

It was the two women's interpretation that he was not "out of it" at all but had contrived to punish his wife by his passivity, because only by provoking her fury could he get the attention he wanted from her. I suspected geriatric debility to be the greater cause, and was irked at my mother and sister for showing so little understanding of human frailty. On the other hand, most of the burden for taking care of him had fallen on them, not me. It was easy for me to play the compassionate relation at a distance.

My father himself called me in Houston, a rare event, to say that he would not be living at home anymore. My mother was putting him in an adult home near Far Rockaway. I said maybe it was for the best. He said, "Yes, well, in the sense that we weren't getting along."

Desperate for some optimistic note, I added: "And it will be near the beach. That's nice."

"Well, that part doesn't matter to me. I don't swim."

"Still, it's nice to see the ocean." He did not deign to reply to this inanity. "And maybe you can make friends there," I added.

"I didn't make any friends at the senior citizens' club. Although there, the people were walking in off the streets. Maybe here there'll be more people—of substance."

Around the time of the divorce, my family tended to split along gender lines. My brother Hal and I sympathized more with our father's eviction from his home, while the two girls shared my mother's point of view. Molly, a practicing Buddhist, who usually preached compassion, surprised me by her adamance. "Why should I feel guilty for not visiting him regularly? He abandoned the family long ago." She had taken to calling him Mr. Ross because, she explained, if you say Albert Ross quickly, it comes out albatross.

After he was deposited in the home, my mother went around depressed for a while. Hal thought it was guilt; I thought it was being faced with a void. Who would she blame now for her unhappy life? She had never admitted how dependent she might be on him, only the other way around.

My own impulse had been to sympathize more with my father because he seemed the weaker party and because my mother had cheated on him. As a young man, I had taken her infidelity very personally, as though she had somehow betrayed me. Objectively, I could appreciate that it was absolutely necessary for the young woman she was, lost in a miserable marriage, to reach out to other men. Nowadays it isn't her affairs I hold against her so much as that, in justifying herself, she felt compelled to demean my father before his children's eyes. I know, I know, I am being unfair in blaming her for not "allowing" us to venerate him more, as though it were ever possible for her to lie about her intensest feelings—to situate him, by some trompe l'oeil of maternal tact, on the patriarchal throne.

I dropped in at my mother's before leaving New York. She was going on about how he got what he deserved. My mother, for all her psychological astuteness, is someone who speaks and acts out of a righteous wound. Her recognition that she may have hurt someone can proceed only from the perception that she was hurt first.

"Supposing there were two other people you were looking at whose marriage was this bad," I said, "wouldn't you be inclined to assume they were both a little at fault?"

"Yeah, I suppose," she said. "But he blew it."

"If he was so terrible, why did you stay with him so long, then?"

"I wish I knew. That's the sixty-four-thousand-dollar question. He had so much promise! What happened to it? He just didn't have the drive. After he retired, I tried to get him to be interested in things, I took him with me to the community college. But he thought he was smarter than everyone else, and if they didn't appreciate that immediately . . . He dropped out, and I got my degree. To me it was a challenge. To Al, a challenge was already a defeat."

My mother has so much life force, it's hard to imagine what it must have been like to live with her opposite all those years. Vitality like hers, ever on tap, has been a constant delight for me but not a mystery. The mystery has been my father and his deep reserves of inanition.

5

AFTER MY FATHER WAS PUT IN THE NURSING HOME, THE NEXT FAMILY crisis occurred when my mother announced she didn't want him at the Passover seder at her house. I was outraged. Then my friend Max, the soul of kindness, said he sympathized with her. She had suffered for years in an unhappy marriage, and now she was divorced. Why should she be hypocritical and welcome him? Why pretend we were an intact family when we weren't? Each of the children would have to learn how to adjust to this new arrangement; each would have to make a separate deal with our father.

I began going out to the Belle Harbor Adult Home in Far Rockaway. It took forever on the subway; you had to catch a spur train over Broad Channel the last couple of stops. Once off the train, you found a calm residential neighborhood, one- or two-family homes with hedges, an old-fashioned New York lower-middle-class feeling, with quite a few senior citizens' residences and funeral homes in the vicinity. My father didn't like the area because the nearest newsstand was seven blocks away; he was used to a denser city life.

His half of the room contained a bed, a night-table, some pictures of the family, and, I was both flattered and obscurely ashamed to see, my books. His roommate was deaf, a hundred years old, spoke only Yiddish, and was paranoid; when I tried to bring the empty chair near his side of the room over to my father's bed so that we could sit together, he barked at me. No words, just guttural attack-dog sounds.

My father, each visit, would fill me in on the deathwatch. "There's a guy here who dropped dead the other day from a coronary. Fell over into his soup. He seemed in okay health, too."

I wanted to make him feel better. So, one day I took it into my head to buy my father a pair of swimming shorts. Since he lived only a block away from the beach, surely there might come a time, even if he didn't swim, when he'd want to warm his legs in the sand. We walked the seven blocks to the retail street, taking over a half-hour to do so. At the shop, my father wouldn't let me get him swimming trunks but insisted on Bermuda shorts. He went into the dressing room to try them on.

"Do they fit, Pop?"

"Yeah, they fit." This was his highest accolade—the acme of enthusiasm, coming from my father.

On the way home I asked: "Do you think you'll wear them?"

"Not very often," he said, honest to a fault.

* * *

During this time I kept trying to buy my father gifts. First I bought a TV for his room (which he never watched, preferring the common room's), then a half refrigerator for snacks, because he didn't like the food they served. I was doing this partly to lift his depression, and partly to administer a lesson to my family on the right way to treat him—I did not like all their talk about his being an "albatross" or a "vegetable." The problem was, I kept coming up against my own upset at his lack of appreciation. The man had no talent for accepting gifts.

I needed to see my father as a poor, maligned Père Goriot abandoned in old age, who deserved our love as a matter of course and custom, and to dismiss the others' beefs against him as petty. I wanted to start with him on a clean, tender page. But to do so, I had to hide my own scars and keep my buried angers against him in check. And sometimes I could no longer overlook the meaner side of the man, which Molly insisted was holding together the works.

One weekend, I checked him out of the adult home to spend a few days at the loft I was subletting. In a sense, I was trying out my fantasy of what it would be like to have my father move in with me. I had bought us baseball tickets at Shea Stadium so that we could watch Doc Gooden go for his twentieth victory. The morning of our planned outing was drizzly, and Father moped that the game was going to be rained out. Luckily, the weather cleared up long enough for Doc to pitch—and win, but still my father seemed morose. All weekend I had cooked for him, taken him around, arranged dinner at a fancy restaurant, and nothing pleased him: The coffee was too weak, too strong. By the end of the weekend I was completely sympathetic with my mother. Every time he complained about something—say, wanting another radio station on the car radio—I could hear her voice in my thoughts: *Why don't you change it yourself?* Though he didn't know how to drive, he was sure I was going the wrong way, and insisted we ask directions at the gas station. Moreover, he seemed completely uninterested in my life—every few hours asking, "When is Hal coming back from vacation?" Prolonged, continuous exposure to the man was eroding my idealized defense of him, making me see him exactly as the other family members did: infuriatingly passive, selfish, hurtful, uncouth.

Looking back at that weekend, I see now what it might have been like for him. He couldn't give himself over to the pleasures offered when they were so temporary, and when they came at the humiliating price of my expecting his gratitude. If this was indeed a test—a dry run for some possible future living arrangement—he could not afford to be on best behavior. My father would rather disappoint quickly and get the suspense over with.

6

THE TREK OUT TO FAR ROCKAWAY WAS TOO LONG, THE FAMILY MEMBERS were visiting him less and less, and it was agreed that we should try to find a home for him closer to town. My brother was able to relocate him in an ultra-desirable "adult residence" on the Upper West Side, near Lincoln Center. Once again, he could walk to the corner and buy a newspaper. We could take him out to a variety of restaurants, all within a stone's throw of his building. He could look out the window and see Broadway, Citarella's fish store, Fairway's produce stand. He could get himself a haircut. He began perking up again, making observations. One of his repeated *bons mots* was: "When it says 'hair salon' instead of barber shop, that means you're paying extra." Another: "When you see a cloth napkin, that means you're paying extra." This was his peasant, streetwise side letting us know: You can't fool me, it's still the same baloney.

The new residence home seemed, at first, a paradise for seniors. There were classical music concerts, daily video screenings, poetry workshops (to which my father brought his half-century-old poems on onionskin about his wife's defection)—all in a building that felt more like an apartment house than a prison. Each resident had his own separate "apartment" (a room, really), while enjoying the social life of the common parlors. The pretense was that of dignified, autonomous seniors who just happened to need the additional services of a specialized hotel. The problem in such a place was that you could not falter. If you got too sick, too frail, too out-of-it you were told you didn't belong in their establishment but in a nursing home, and were summarily kicked out.

After a while, there was no kidding ourselves: My father was on a slow, inexorable path downward. It was not just that he had cataracts (they could be corrected with surgery) or that he was a loner, acting, by the residence staff's standards, uncommunally. It was that he began to experience "incontinence problems"—in short, wet his pants, making him an undesirable presence in the dining room. The family took a crash course in adult Pampers, rubber diapers, prostate surgery, and behavioral modification training.

Incontinence was the precise metaphorical situation to galvanize family arguments about my father's willpower. "He's doing it on purpose!" said Molly. "He can hold it in if he wants to."

"I don't think so," I said. Meanwhile, my father went around looking utterly hesitant to travel any distance farther than a half block from the nearest bathroom.

I remember one particular night I had planned to take him to a screening at Lincoln Center. When I got there he was so sloppily dressed that I decided to forgo the movie and just have dinner with him across the street at a newly opened Italian restaurant.

We had the usual tepid time of it, neither hostile nor affectionate. The most interesting moment was when Father volunteered this short summary of his marriage: "I felt that I loved your mother more than she loved me." Undoubtedly true, and I realized I had probably contrived my whole romantic life until then so as not to be caught in the same situation.

He also said: "She always attracted dykes. She must have done something for that to happen."

I told my father that Uncle George had died. There was a silence. He finally said: "I have mixed feelings about him."

"Why?"

"Well, I think he played around with her when she was a kid. And then she was madly in love with him, all during the time when we were first married. I couldn't prove anything, but . . ."

It seemed to me he was casting about wildly for rivals, to explain why my mother had come to detest him.

When the meal ended, he tried to get up and couldn't seem to rise, so I gave him a hand and walked him to the men's room, one flight down. He had become very unsteady on his feet, especially managing stairs. "Why do they always put the men's room where you have to go up or down a flight?" he said. I waited outside the toilet door for ten minutes. After a while I thought maybe he had died in there. "Pop, you all right?" I called out. He grunted something in reply, so I knew he was still among the living. "Can I help?" I asked. "No," came his foggy voice uncertainly. Ten more minutes passed. "Pop, what's going on?" Finally I went inside to have a look. "I had an accident," he said. I noticed the tiled floor was smeared with shit. "I made in my pants. I couldn't get them off in time."

"Okay. Let's get outa here." I helped him up the stairs and we left quickly, before the waiters could see the bathroom floor. It was their problem, I thought; I'll never go back to that restaurant anyway.

"I'm sorry," he said, as we crossed the street.

"It's not your fault, Pop. It's old age." I was already thinking ahead to what I would have to do. Get him undressed and into a shower. I was very calm, patient, the way I used to be when I was working with kids. We took the elevator upstairs to his room and he immediately sat on the bed and took off his pants, smearing the bedspread in the process. I helped him off with his shirt and led him into the bathroom across the hall. Two minutes later, I still hadn't heard the sound of running water.

"Pop, what's the matter?" He was standing outside the shower stall, dry and dirty.

"I can't get my socks off."

"Oh for crying out loud!" I said, sounding just like my mother. "The socks can get wet. Just get in the shower!"

I pushed him in.

"I can't get the hot water to work," he said. Now his total helplessness was getting on my nerves. He had turned on the hot water, it would just take a minute to warm up. Didn't he know that, after all these years on the planet? I gave him soap and told him to rinse well and left him there. Back in his room, I threw away his soiled underpants. I stripped the bedspread and bunched it on the floor, hoping his attendant would deal with it tomorrow. And I turned on the Mets game so that he would have something to watch when he returned.

He came back. One of his legs was still covered with shit. I cleaned it off as best I could with water and toilet paper. Wiping off my father's ass wasn't what I'd expected from the evening, but—all in the nature of reality. I tried to tell myself it was good for my spiritual development. As soon as he was lying down comfortably, however, I said goodbye. I could have stayed longer, but I didn't. He could have said thank you but he didn't. He made his usual "okay" grunt. As I fled the building onto Amsterdam Avenue, a junkie was vomiting against the side of the car. What a night!

There was some hope that a prostate operation might improve the incontinence situation. In any event, he had to have one. After it was done, I received a call from the hospital to pick up my father. Molly was also there to help, but she seemed in a foul mood.

"How about if I go down to pay for his TV and phone," I said, "and meanwhile you can see that he gets ready."

"I've got to speak to you," said Molly. Taking me outside the room by the arm, she told me in a fierce whisper: "Look, I didn't get any sleep last night because I have a splitting headache and a cold, and I absolutely don't want to have to dress that old man and touch his body and see his old balls. I can't handle it today."

I was surprised to hear my sister sounding so squeamish, since she is a professional masseuse; but as usual I admired her bluntness. "Fine, I'll take care of it." I went back into the hospital room and found an elderly German-Jewish woman in a white hospital coat, who told me she was the social worker. I started to help my father on with his underwear when she told me: "Don't! He has to do it for himself." She then explained to me that the Amsterdam Residence Home had told her they refused to accept responsibility for him unless he could dress himself and walk. The hospital, for their part, refused to keep him there any longer because "this is not a nursing home" and his operation was over and he'd had a few days' rest. So she would have to determine for herself whether he was capable of dressing himself. If not, the family would have to hire an attendant eight hours a day to take care of him in the residence home.

Molly lost her temper with the woman and yelled: "Why did they tell me yesterday that he could go? Which is it supposed to be, go or stay? Why don't you make up your frigging minds?!" She was carrying on like a street tough, and the social worker, who had probably seen it all (maybe even the camps), was undaunted.

I took Molly aside and told her: "She can't say which it is to be until she ascertains whether Father can take minimal care of himself."

"Oh fine! And he's going to play helpless because he wants to stay here, where they do everything for him."

The woman kept repeating what her responsibilities in the current situation were. Finally I said to her, as calmly as I could: "Look, we're all pretty bright here, we understand what you're saying."

She blinked her eyes and left the room.

I turned to Father and said under my breath: "Pop! Try very hard. Don't give up. It's important that you show her you can dress yourself. Otherwise they won't let you out. So give it your all."

"All right, I'll try," he said. And proceeded to do just that, dressing himself slowly, manfully, with dignity.

Not to be dissuaded by the evidence, Molly started hectoring him from the hallway. "What's the matter, you like it here, so you don't want to try to get out?"

"Sure. I'm crazy about the place," he answered sarcastically. "Show me someone who don't mind staying in a hospital and I'll show you a schmuck."

"You think if you just give up, everyone will wait on you hand and foot—right?" retorted Molly.

"Leave me alone! Stop giving me the business."

I caught my sister winking at me: this was her version of reverse psychology. I realized that the social worker, now nowhere in sight, might not believe he had dressed himself, so I hurried to fetch her. When I spotted her, I explained my errand, adding: "One thing you have to understand: My father has always been the kind of man who becomes more dependent when there are people around to do for him. But he was like that at thirty."

She nodded, with an appearance of understanding. I was trying to establish rapport with her. The stakes were high, we could never afford a full-time attendant. And where would he go if they kicked him out of his residence home?

The social worker returned just in time to see Molly buttoning my father's pants! Molly said: "That's the only thing he couldn't do for himself." But he still didn't have his shoes on. The three of us watched as Father, with agonizing slowness, tried to get his foot into the Velcro-strap sneakers that Hal had bought him. I tried to smooth the way by explaining: "He always has trouble putting his shoes on. Even before the operation."

"I wasn't told that," sniffed the social worker.

"The attendant at the home does it for him every morning," Molly said. Fortunately he got his shoes on by himself, for once, and now the test was his walking ability. He started down the hallway past the nurses' station, the social worker walking alongside to monitor his progress.

"Maybe he needs a cane," she said. "Why does he take such small steps?"

"He always walks like that."

As he approached the nurses' desk he quipped: "She's too old for me. Get me a younger one." The nurses cracked up. They all seemed to like him. (I'm fascinated by the fact that many people do take to my father right away.)

"Your dad has a great sense of humor," a nurse said.

"He's a riot," said the other.

"Goodbye, Mr. Lopate You don't want to stay here with all these sick people, do you?"

He waved to his fan club. We bid adieu to the social worker, who reluctantly agreed that he was ambulatory.

An Academy Award performance. Molly and I got him quickly into a taxi before he could collapse.

Shortly after that, the inevitable happened. He fell down one morning and in consequence was kicked out of the Amsterdam Residence (whose hoity-toity airs I had come to despise) and sent to his present nursing home. This is no doubt the Last Stop. There is nothing he can do here that will disqualify him from the right to sit in the common room with the TV on.

Recently, during a period when he had been feeling too despondent to eat, I visited him there, and wheeled him out to nearby Fort Tryon Park. He noticed a magnificent elm overlooking the Hudson River. "That's a beautiful tree," he said.

"You see, Pop? It's not so bad being alive. Which would you prefer—tell me honestly: to be dead or alive?"

"Alive, of course." He was annoyed to be asked such a childish question.

For the next few minutes, his senescent-poetic mind spliced the word "tree" into different sentences. "They don't brag so much about the trees. Especially since they had that . . . Holocaust."

Later, I tell his social worker that, from my observation, my father likes to be placed in front of ongoing scenes of daily life. Especially activities involving youth: teenagers playing basketball, tots splashing though the fountain, pretty girls walking by.

She says skeptically: "You caught him at a good moment. We took him to the park, there were plenty of children around and he dozed through it all, no interest whatsoever. You know what he wants? He wants you."

I hang my head guiltily.

"But in today's way of life . . ." she adds, that vague, exonerating statement.

I ask myself: Would it be possible to take him in? Where would we put him? The basement? The baby's room? A shed on the roof? We could manage, somehow, couldn't we? In the midst of this deliberation, I know that I will never do it. I take consolation from what a scientist friend tells me: "Societies choose differently what to do with old people. The Eskimos choose the ice floe, we choose the nursing home."

* * *

How much does my father understand? Has his mind become permanently loosed from its logical moorings—like that comment about trees and the Holocaust? At other times, he seems to make perfect sense. During the staff meeting, I had tried to explain the reasons for his depression, adding: "He's also taken a lot of abuse from his family."

My father picked his head up and said, clearly: "I was responsible for the discord."

A final word on failure. I once read an essay by the gifted midwestern writer, Bill Holm, called "The Music of Failure," in which he tried both to argue against the hollow American obsession with success and to redeem failure, to find beauty in it. In effect, Holm was attempting to invert commonplace values and turn failure into a victory, or at least show how it could be better, more human than its opposite. Intriguing as the essay was, I finished it with a sigh, thinking: But there *is* such a thing as failure. There are failed lives, which no amount of rhetorical jujitsu can reclaim as triumphs.

Maybe my father's insistence that he is a failure does not signal the obsessions of senility but grows out of a long, enforced, reluctant meditation at the end of his life, which has obliged him to take responsibility for some of his very real errors. In that sense, there is hope for all of us. I would like to give him the benefit of the doubt.

I Kiss Her Goodbye

PETER TRACHTENBERG

. . . It seemed to me that all the devilment, and meanness, and shiftlessness, and no-account stuff in my life had been pressed out and washed off, and I was ready to start out with her again clean, and do like she said, have a new life.
—James M. Cain, *The Postman Always Rings Twice*

I'VE NEVER BEEN TATTOOED WITH ANYBODY'S NAME. I DOUBT I EVER will be. It would seem like a way of tempting fate, which is most dangerous when it appears tame, though maybe what I'm really thinking of is my own character. The closest I ever came was getting a copy of a girlfriend's tattoo. I got it less out of hope than out of pessimism, for the same reason I break my neck looking for souvenirs when I'm leaving a place I love and suspect I won't be visiting again. I got it not because I thought that Tara and I would stay together but because I knew we wouldn't, couldn't probably. Well, who ever knows what could or couldn't be? Who knows when fate is only the euphemism for a bad character?

With a few changes, we could have been enacting the opening scene from a noir thriller of the 1940s: the sailor and his girl on the night before he ships out for the Pacific. She's played by Gloria Grahame or Susan Hayward, seemingly cast against type—who ever heard of one of those dames playing an ingenue?—he by some juvenile you've never heard of before or since, a boy with a face as vulnerable as an isolated prairie farmhouse. It's San Diego, a seaside amusement park on a warm night. A Ferris wheel's lights climbing through the sky, a crowd of sailors in ice-cream whites, girls in filmy dresses that flutter in the salt breeze. A distant calliope, the hiss of waves. The camera follows the couple into the tattoo parlor. The proprietor wears an undershirt that displays years of needlework, whole menageries and armadas on his arms.

"What'll it be, kid?"

Sailor boy, scared but trying to sound nonchalant: "Oh, give me the usual. An anchor or a battleship. What the hell do I care as long as you put 'Mona' underneath it?" He indicates his girlfriend with a jerk of his thumb. "That's her."

She, laughing: "Oh, Nick, you shouldn't!"

Close-up: Nick and Mona facing each other in profile, so close that we keep waiting for them to kiss. The camera cuts back and forth between their faces but always returns to that establishing shot with its postponed promise of erotic merger.

Nick: "Don't say what I should or shouldn't be doing, baby. There are no *shoulds* in this crazy world anymore. I shouldn't be apart from you. You shouldn't be apart from me. But a couple of hours from now I'm going to be on a tin can heading halfway across the ocean."

Mona: "But you'll come back, Nick. You've got to come back! I don't know what—"

Nick places a finger on her lips: "All I know is that I'm crazy about you, get it? And wherever I'm going, whatever happens to me, I want to take a part of you with me. Something that no one can take away. Even if it's just your name. I want to be able to look at it on those long nights belowdecks, or when I'm standing watch under the stars not knowing if a torpedo with my name on it is coming for me, boring through all that dark water, or when I'm slogging through some godforsaken jungle with a Jap monkey in every palm tree. I want to see your name on me and know you'll be waiting when I come home."

Mona: "I will, Nicky. I promise. No matter what. I'll be there."

Only then do they kiss. But instead of the pro forma fadeout, the last shot is a closeup of the finished tattoo on his right biceps, an anchor with a chain wrapped around it and the name *Mona* written underneath in a finicky Palmer script.

The truth is I was almost twenty years older than that kid, and I wasn't going to war, and the tattoo I got was a simple arrangement of black stick figures that people assume are trees or barbed wire or Nordic runes, though it is none of these. I had it inked on my right wrist, which is where Tara had hers, on a hot September afternoon in a studio off Tompkins Square Park. Through its open windows you could hear the shouts and thuds of a basketball game in the court below and the hollow slap of congas. The place had an altar in its foyer, a folding aluminum table bearing a potted cactus that had been stuck full of tattoo needles—I think they must have been used—and a yellowed dog skull that someone had decorated with feathers. Tara sat beside me through the whole process, as cheerful as though we were picking out engagement rings. She was protective of me and she kept telling the tattooist to go easy with the needle, and I think it pissed him off, since he ended up doing the opposite and leaving me with a thick black biscuit of scab that peeled painfully and unevenly, taking off a good deal of the pigment underneath. Many of the figures came out blotched and prematurely faded. It was a bad tattoo. I had to have it retouched later.

Given a choice, I'd have gone to Slam—she had the taste, imagination, and wrist-control that make for a great tattooist, and by that time I thought of her as my friend. But Slam had fallen in love with a big, dreadlocked woman named Roxy, and they were moving to a lesbian commune in Santa Fe. So I had no choice but to go to Tompkins Square, where the tattooist was a guy named Gareth whom I knew slightly from the New York Tattoo Society circuit. He had a shaved head that was shaped exactly like a light-bulb and tribals by Alex Binnie on both his forearms, and he went at me as though I were a cheap color television he were engraving with his social security number, in case somebody tried to rip it off.

"You're going too deep," Tara complained some ten minutes into the session. "He shouldn't be bleeding that much."

Gareth grunted, "Some people are bleeders."

"I don't usually bleed." I said it as mildly as I could. I didn't want to alienate the guy.

"Maybe it's your attitude." He gazed into my eyes the way certain therapists are wont to do, as though he meant to batter me to death with empathy. "I mean it. You're fighting it. You're tensing up. You're doing it right this minute. You tense up, it dilates the capillaries and shit, pumps all your blood to the surface. You need to chill."

"How's he supposed to chill if you're hurting him?"

"I'm not hurting him. Am I hurting you?" He didn't look at me. "Look, sweetheart. I've been in this business for ten years, you know what I'm saying? I've done work for fashion models and a very well-known actor with his own soap and three guys in D Generation. And not one of them has ever complained about me hurting them. Your *boyfriend* isn't complaining about me hurting him. So it looks like you're the one who's got the problem. No offense, babes, but maybe you should look at that."

I could see the retort quivering in Tara's throat. She resembled a pretty pit bull, small and deep-chested, with a broad, blunt nose and a powerful jaw that would have been ugly if it had been a shade wider. When I'd first met her she'd had a stricken quiet about her; it was one of the reasons I hadn't found her attractive. But over the past year, she'd remembered that God had given her a mouth. She would argue with anybody. She had more or less argued me into going out with her. "I'm okay, sweetie," I said. "Really. It's just blood."

"You sure? I don't want him hurting you. I don't want anybody fucking with my man. You don't know what this means to me."

Most women I've known would have preferred a ring. But Tara and I were at that point in the affair when small gestures count for a lot. She watched raptly while a runny mirror image of her tattoo appeared on my wrist and afterward swung my hand in hers as we walked through those fragrant East Village streets that excited her with their overflowing storefronts of vintage seventies dresses with S&M zippers and used CDs and cheap jewelry. Actually, I *did* buy her a ring at one of these places, a steel band incised with little black spades and diamonds, like something a gambler would wear. "Just don't overinterpret this," I warned her.

"What do you mean?" She didn't sound suspicious, she just wanted to know what "overinterpret" meant, but I was mortified.

"Shit, I'm sorry. It was a bad joke. It means nothing."

Baltimore was where we'd first gotten to know each other, but we hadn't become lovers till later, after my move. She'd driven up a few days before in her used Honda, with twelve changes of clothing in the trunk. And just being together in New York that weekend had the feel of a tryst stolen in a town where everyone is in transit, sailors shipping out for Subic, whores following the fleet, no one rooted, no one committed to anything but these boardwalk days and the nights of panting, valedictory sex, which we dove into later while sirens whooped outside my windows, there was a fire somewhere nearby, clutching and gnawing as greedily as children, as wholly inside and around each other as we could get through our layers of spermicidally dusted latex. Once I whispered, "Lick my tattoo. I want to feel your tongue against it."

She eased away from me in the dark. I could hear sheets crackle like cellophane. "I can't do that, baby. You know I can't. It's not safe."

Speaking of ports and sailors, I want to tell you a little bit more about that movie. What happens next in that movie is that Nick sails out for Truk or Bougainville and about a year later his ship goes down. Zeroes shrieking across the firmament, pillars of oily smoke, the night sea a broken mirror with flames glaring in every shard. Almost everyone on board is drowned. The kid makes it out alive but badly maimed. Just how badly is left to your imagination, since this is a film from the days before directors and special-effects technicians succumbed to the pornographic compulsion to show *everything*. The next we know he's lying in a navy hospital bed, mummified in gauze whose whiteness is an ironic echo of the uniform he wore earlier. An offscreen voice: "We did our best, but even his own mother wouldn't recognize him now." When the bandages finally come off, he looks exactly like John Garfield, John Garfield or Robert Ryan, handsome in a crooked way, but no charm boy. His is a *traveled* face, an odometer that measures how close its owner came to dying.

Back Stateside Nick tries to get in touch with his girl, but when he knocks at her door a stranger answers. "Oh, Mona moved out months ago. I don't know where she lives these days, but maybe you can find her at Corrente's. You know Corrente's? It's a club down in La Jolla." Corrente's has a discreet bouncer at the door and banquettes like submarine grottoes. It's a place where you can pack a gun, if you're a regular, but where showing it will get you blackballed if not worse. Mona comes in wearing an expensive, lowcut number and enough diamonds to give an insurance adjuster nightmares. Gone is the skittish ingenue of the opening scene. The actress, Susan or Gloria or whoever, has shucked off her innocence the way she might shuck off a tight girdle and you can see how relieved she is to be rid of it. If Nick's experience is gouged into his face, Mona's is recorded in her eyes and in the avidity of her breathing. With each breath her breasts rise and her nostrils dilate as though she were trying to inhale the entire room. Nick strikes up a conversation with her at the bar. "Excuse me, I don't want to sound like I'm throwing you a line, but don't I know you?"

Mona: "Not unless you're a regular."

Nick: "These days I'm not a regular anywhere. I thought I might have seen you a couple times around ———" He mentions the place where they grew up. "You ever been there?"

Mona: "Yeah, once." She looks at him sharply, but his face is unrecognizable. A perfect stranger's.

Nick: "What were you doing there?"

Mona: "Being dumb. I left when I wised up. I never went back."

Nick: "You're a little young to have memories, aren't you?"

Mona: "Mister, I've got memories in every town in this crummy state."

They are two dry sticks rubbing together on a bed of sawdust, and the sawdust is soaked in gasoline. A man comes up behind them, places proprietary hands on their shoulders. "Friend of yours, Mona?" Picture the top-heavy bulk and sharkish good cheer of the young Jack Carson.

Mona: "No, Ray. He's just a guy from— you know, my hometown."

Ray: "He's a long way from home. What's the matter, did he get lost?"

Nick: "I was just telling your lady friend that it's been a long time since I've been back. I was wondering if she'd heard anything about the old crowd."

Ray: "This isn't my 'lady-friend,' pal. This is my wife. Mrs. Ray Corrente. Or didn't she tell you that?"

"Sure, I told him," Mona says. Too quickly. "But we might as well make it official. This is my husband, Ray Corrente. He's the owner of this establishment. And this is—"

Nick: "Dillon. Alex Dillon. I'm pleased to meet you."

In most noir films men and women are fatally matched. He is a wounded loner who's picked up his cynicism on breadlines and in foxholes. His greed is the kind that comes from standing too long in the cold watching bigshots ride past in limousines; his callousness is what kept him from going crazy after he wiped his buddy's brains off his fatigues. These things are the scar tissue that has formed around the ragged hole at his center: the hole made by history. The woman was born bad. The films posit no other origin or explanation. Evil goes with her sex; it lies at the root of her attractiveness, as though her cunt secreted a poison that makes a man kill for another taste before it kills him, too. In *Double Indemnity* Phyllis Dietrichson describes herself as "rotten to the heart." The story of *Double Indemnity* or *The Postman Always Rings Twice*, of *Criss-Cross* or *The File on Thelma Jordan* is the story of a marriage made in hell, of an evil woman homing in on a weak man and making him her accomplice in crimes that neither of them could commit alone. He needs her to give him ruthlessness; she needs him to pull the trigger.

On the surface this seems like a remarkably fair arrangement, especially when you consider the general state of marriage in the early postwar years. The noir couple eerily anticipates the democratic partnerships we strive for in the 1990s: "Honey, can you come here and help me a minute? I need to haul this body out of the Lexus." "Oh, all right. But only if you promise to help me write that blackmail letter afterward. I'm having some trouble with the *tone*." But the equality is only superficial. As bad as Walter Neff is, in the end he remains Phyllis Dietrichson's patsy: weak where she is strong, merely venal where she is rampantly malign. The sexual politics of these films is a throwback to the politics of Genesis, where a woman initiates the sin that will banish our kind from Paradise, while Adam, that poor sap, just goes along for the ride. In noir, feminine evil is a virus that invades a passive male host and replicates itself inside him. The ordinary logic of reproduction is inverted: she impregnates him with her rottenness, and often childbirth is fatal to them both.

Have I ever met a woman who was my match? I mean in that slit-eyed, drive-ninety-miles-an-hour-to-the-edge-of-the-cliff-with-a-cigarette-burning-between-your-teeth-and-a-box-of-nitro-at-your-feet sense? When I was with Catherine, her sullenness unnerved me so much that I'd do anything to appease it: answer her phone calls; pick up her clothing from the dry cleaner's; go out on freezing Sunday mornings to cop Valium for her cramps. We had a larcenous routine we practiced whenever we were out visiting. One of us would keep the hosts occupied in the living room while the other foraged through the bathroom medicine cabinet for likely mood-alterants. Once we were lucky enough to get a dinner invitation from a friend whose mother had just died miserably of bone cancer: all through dinner I practically hugged myself, picturing the look on Catherine's face when we got home and I presented her with a handful of Dilaudids. "Oh, honey, you shouldn't have! You've made me the happiest woman in the whole world."

I think of Dinah, who so overpowered me with fear and yearning that I'm reminded of a novel I once read in which a woman tells a man she loves him and he asks her how much and she answers, "Enough to let you cut me open and fuck my heart." How do you protect yourself when you are willing to let your lover slit you open like a fish? When you are ready to issue her an open invitation? I know all about the gay leather scene and have been to clubs where potentates of commerce paid good money to be trussed like smaller cousins of the marbled carcasses that were hanging in the packing houses down the block and thrashed with buggy whips while they squirmed in hog-tied rapture. But my own masochism scares the shit out of me. What I felt for Dinah—what I knew I felt for her—was a kind of unsexing. Somewhere in the back of my mind it is written, "Real men don't wear ball-gags." And when Dinah asked me why I left her I said, "Don't you see? Because I'd do anything for you."

I once knew a woman I'll call Pauline who liked to be whipped when we made love—though "making love" seems a misnomer for what we were doing—and I found myself getting into it, falling dreamily into a sexual wind tunnel whose suction tore us into so many flailing parts, an arm, a hand, a folded strap, a reddening, welted ass, sweat flying like shrapnel, cries that might have been hers or mine, "No!" or "More!" I stopped seeing her when she told me she wanted me to beat her—I mean with my fists. Her response was to start stalking me. I thought it was a gentlemanly breakup, as breakups go, but no sooner had Pauline left my house than she was calling me. Every thirty seconds. I'd pick up the phone—out of the moronic reflex that tells me that I *must* because the person on the other end may be dying or offering me a Publishers Clearing House check for ten million dollars—and I'd hear a voice on the other end, a voice I used to love. Sometimes it said, "Oh, come on, Peter! What's so bad about a little edge play? You want to. You know you want to." Sometimes it said, "How can you do this to me? *How can you do this to me!?* Don't you know I *love* you?" And once, at around two o'clock in the morning, it whispered, "Call your friends and say goodbye to them. Say goodbye to them forever."

I had my number changed, but for months afterward she kept following me. She'd be posted across the street when I left my house in the morning, a perfectly ordinary-looking woman who had the power to strike terror into my heart. On bright days her wire-framed glasses threw the sunlight back in blinding darts, as though she were about to vaporize me with her stare. She'd glide up behind me at the Fells Point Festival, an untouched ice-cream cone dripping down her fingers. For a long time, neither of us said anything to the other: I was too scared and what could Pauline say that would top "Say goodbye to them forever"? I finally lost it one day at my neighborhood smoke shop when I felt something feather the hairs on my neck and turned to see her standing behind me, gazing at me with the blandness of the truly crazy. "Will you give it a break?" I snapped. My voice quivered. "What do you want from me?"

"I want you to suffer." She said it the way someone else might say "I want a pack of Mores."

I'm sorry to say that I started crying. The cashier gawked at me. The other customers gawked at me. *"Well, I am suffering! Look at me, for Christ's sake!"*

Pauline was suddenly solicitous. "You look awful, sweetheart. You haven't been eating. You must have lost twenty pounds."

"Well, whose fault is that?" I sobbed. "Huh? How am I supposed to eat with you skulking after me all the time!"

"Well, you've got to cut that out. There's no need for you to be so dramatic. I mean it, sweetheart, you're going to make yourself sick."

She walked out without buying anything, favoring the cashier with a cheery wave. It was the last time I ever saw her. It was also the last time I went into that smoke shop.

But these stories are exceptions. I tell them mostly because it gives me the chance to feel sorry for myself. The fact is I've usually been the top in my relationships, even in the ones whose sadomasochistic architecture was hidden beneath all sorts of Victorian gingerbread. What made me the top wasn't my aptitude with a belt or my ability to say the cruelest thing at the most vulnerable moment, all those things I tried so hard to give up and finally did only to discover that my nature was still the same. S&M is not so much about pain as it is about power, and in sexual relationships power resides with the one who is willing to leave.

Back when I was a bad boy, I walked because there was always someone to walk *to*, someone I was boffing, or flirting with, or just fantasizing about, a woman-shaped future that made it possible for me to turn my back on the present. I used to arrange it that way, like a crook who never pulls a bank job until he's rented a safe house in another city, with a Magnum and a roll of C-notes stashed beneath the floorboards. But after I became merely a troubled man, with rampaging scruples in place of a rampant prick, I left because it was what I knew how to do (think of Lauren Bacall's famous line in *To Have and Have Not:* "You know how to leave, don't you? All you have to do is open the door and walk"). I left because I had gotten used to being alone. And I left because whatever I felt afterward—the loss, the guilt, the unrequited straining toward a vanished other in a bed as vast as a desert—was still preferable to what I felt each day I remained with a woman I had stopped loving or still loved but no longer trusted or loved so much that I no longer trusted myself not to yield to her completely, not to become her chump, her patsy, her stooge, her pussy-whipped gunsel (a word that originally meant "sissy" but that Dashiell Hammett fobbed off on his readers as a synonym for "hit man"), the abject bottom kneeling at her feet, hands cuffed behind him, tongue extended, with his eyes raised to catch the flicker of permission that must occur before he can begin to adore her boot.

Actually, when I try to imagine just what that submission would amount to, what comes bubbling up is the last scene in *A Hell of a Woman*, where Jim Thompson's schitzed-out narrator allows his wife to castrate him:

> "You deceived me," she said. "You're no different from the rest, Fred. And you'll have to pay like the rest. . . . You won't feel a thing, and when you wake up it will all be over. There'll be nothing more to worry about. Won't that be wonderful, Fred, don't you want me to, darling." I nodded and she began unfastening and fumbling and then, then, she lowered the shears. She began to use the shears, and then she was smiling again and letting me see. "There," she said, "that's much better, isn't it?"

Back to my movie. Let's call it *Riptide* or *The Undertow* or, my personal favorite, *The Mark*, which has the further advantage of being a double entendre. Nick/Alex knows he should stay away from Mona. She's thrown him over; she's married to an obvious gangster. We could throw in a scene where Nick pays a visit to the one person who knows his true identity, an old buddy who's now a police lieutenant: "Sure, everybody knows Ray Corrente," he says, leafing through a bulging dossier. "A little gambling, a little graft, a little hijacking. And maybe a little murder. People who get on Corrente's bad side suddenly turn accident-prone. We've been trying to put him away for years, but every time we find someone who's willing to testify, the guy somehow ends up cleaning a shotgun he didn't know was loaded or falling asleep in the car without remembering to shut off the ignition. It's the damnedest thing." The buddy returns the folder to a file cabinet, slams the door shut. "Don't go looking for accidents, Nick. You're supposed to be dead already. Give her up."

But Nick can't get Mona out of his mind; he can't forget the way she looked at him in that cocktail lounge or the gardenia smell of her perfume. "I couldn't forget the night, it seemed so long ago and not so long ago at all, when we held hands in a tattoo parlor on the midway and I promised to come back to her and she promised to be waiting when I did." We hear him in voice-over as he dresses in his rented room, like a teenager dressing for his prom date. The camera cuts to a close-up of the tattoo. "How could I forget her, when her name was right there on my skin? I couldn't look at my arm without seeing it. It was like a wedding band I could never take off. I was wrapped around her the way that chain was wrapped around that anchor. And even then I knew I couldn't get loose. I didn't want to get loose. Not even if she took me straight to the bottom."

He drives back out to Corrente's, waits in the sun-baked parking lot until he sees Mona pull up. He greets her. She's excited but wary, unsure of him, afraid of being caught.

Mona: "What're you doing back here? You get lost again?"

Nick: "Maybe I'm looking for someone to find me."

Mona: "We're not in the habit of picking up strays around here, Mr. Dillon. My husband takes them straight to the pound."

Nick: "What happens if one of them bites him?"

Mona: "He bites back. Nobody bites as hard as Ray."

Nick: "Actually, Mrs. Corrente—" He's about to tell her who he is, but just then a third car pulls into the lot and Mona starts in alarm. The man who gets out is just a stranger, but the raw spectacle of her fear turns Nick's anger to pity. "Let's get out of here," she says. He follows her down some stairs that lead to a marina at the foot of the bluff. Pleasure boats bob against the pilings.

Nick: "Actually, I was going to ask your husband for a job. Maybe he could use another bartender. I've been having a run of hard luck since I got back from Iwo. A Purple Heart doesn't cut any ice with the personnel boys."

Mona: "You poor kid. It must be rough. Don't you have any family who can help you? A girl?"

Nick: "My folks passed away a while ago. I had a girl before I enlisted. But it looks like she changed her mind about me."

Mona: "Maybe she had it changed for her."

Nick: "What's that supposed to mean?"

Mona: "I mean maybe she just didn't have a choice." She speaks more quickly, although her voice never gets any louder. She's explaining herself, not so much to the stranger standing beside her as to the man she betrayed, not realizing that the two are the same. "Let me tell you something. I loved a boy once. Sweet kid, just out of college. He thought the sun rose and set on me, and I guess I thought the world of him, too. But we were young. You know how it is when you're young. And foolish." Her face softens. Her eyes go as dreamy as an opium-eater's. The camera pans over her shoulder to the jetty, where waves shatter amid gusts of spray. "You think love is something solid, that it lasts forever, just like those rocks out there. You know how that song goes. You think it's something you can count on." Cut back to Mona's face in the instant that it sets into its familiar brittleness. "But love isn't anybody's rock. You know what love is? Love is a ship moored in a harbor. It looks solid. On a calm day you can barely feel the deck roll under your feet. But sooner or later that ship will sail. It raises anchor and it doesn't come back. And if you're not on board when it leaves, well, you're just out of luck."

Nick: "What happened to the boy?"

Mona: "The boy? He went off to war, the way boys do. And then one day I heard that his ship had gone down. I guess it was a different kind of ship."

Nick: "Maybe he made it out."

Mona: "Maybe he did, but how would I know? I never heard from him."

Nick: "Maybe something happened to him, something bad. Maybe he was afraid to write you. Maybe—"

Mona (angry): "Who's telling this story anyway? I told you, I never heard from him again! Maybe he died, maybe he just forgot about me. What does it matter? *That ship has sailed.* And I had to find another one. A girl can't afford to be left ashore when all the ships have gone."

Nick: "So, what kind of ship did you end up with?"

Mona: "A destroyer with a lot of cannon and an extra-large cargo hold. Come on, sailor, I'll take you to him. We'll see about getting you that job."

After Pauline, I was celibate for close to three years. I think it took that long for my balls to peep back out of my inguinal cavity, where they'd retreated in sheer terror while she was stalking me. I swore I wouldn't even go on a fucking date unless the prospect could pass one of those multiple-choice exams you find in *Cosmopolitan*: When my partner hurts my feelings, I (a) confront him assertively and calmly, (b) sulk silently, (c) pretend nothing happened, or (d) sneak into the homes of his friends and family and slit their throats. But I also felt that Pauline had been my just punishment, the thunderbolt God had sent my way as belated payback for a decade and a half of prickery with the opposite sex. I could just see Him peering down from His throne and muttering, "The schmuck wants to play rough? *I'll* give him someone to play rough with!" And I was pretty sure that my penance wasn't over, that one way or another I was supposed to stay alone for a while and savor the bad taste my past relationships had left in my mouth.

I'll tell you the benefits of being alone and celibate.

You can read all night and no one will nag you to turn off the light.

You can go off to Borneo on the spur of the moment without anyone wanting to know when you'll be back.

You can prepare meals so disgusting you'd be ashamed to eat them in company: grill a slice of bologna till it curls up at the edges; fill the cup with baked beans; then top with a slice of Kraft American cheese and broil till melted. Serve with dill pickle and sliced tomato.

You can fart to your heart's content without having to say "Excuse me," though you may grow so accustomed to this that you find yourself doing it in public places—on the line at your savings bank, for instance—and getting nasty looks from strangers.

You can entertain religious delusions.

You can spend your fury at the world by playing Einsturzende Neubauten and Nine Inch Nails at bone-splintering volumes and dancing along, vaulting and twitching and torquing as though electrocuted while shouting the lyrics you've improvised because you can't make out the real ones: "I gave you no permission!!/I give you no remission!/Newt Gingrich, burn in Hell/Jesse Helms, burn in Hell/Larry Wildmon, burn in Hell/I'll know where to find you when I come callin'/In the row next to Hitler and old Joe Stalin." Only do this at reasonable hours.

You can fall asleep with a stack of books next to you on the bed, and if you're a heavy sleeper you won't even wake when you knock them to the floor.

You may come to know freedom from the tyranny of your penis, which thus dethroned becomes only a benign little tube for the expulsion of urine.

In time you will know yourself so thoroughly that you finally realize what all those people had against you.

You will pray wholeheartedly to be changed. "Make me good," you'll call at night, down on your knees in a bedroom that is used only for sleeping, that smells of nothing but your cigarettes and the dust baking beneath the radiator. "Please, God, just make me good."

On bad nights you can scoop up your cats and cuddle them shamelessly, even kissing them on the nose, though they usually dislike this and will try to shove you away with their paws. If worst comes to worst, you can press your face against their bodies and weep copiously into their fur.

I hadn't reached the cat-weeping stage when I met Tara. She was a friend of friends in Baltimore, a quiet, sulky punk girl who cut her hair with nail scissors and dyed it an arctic blonde that didn't go with her dark complexion. She hadn't been clean all that long. In warm weather you could see the tracks on her arms, only partly hidden by a slipshod tribal tattoo that looked like splashed-on paint. Once she complimented me on the piece on my collarbone, and because I couldn't very well say the same about her arm job, I pointed to the tattoo on her wrist. "That's interesting. Where'd you get it?"

"From Kylie at Dragon Moon. You know Kylie? I bet you can't guess what they are."

"I don't know. Runes?"

"No, silly!" It was such an odd, ingenuous thing for her to say. She smiled hugely, baring small crooked teeth. "They're *people*! *Dancing* people! See their arms?" And it's true that if you looked closely at Tara's tattoo—if you look closely at my copy of it—you'll see a line of stick figures with their arms lifted above knobby heads. They might be dancers, the kind you used to see at Grateful Dead concerts, swaying with the boneless languor of sea anemones. But they might also be people who've been reunited with their loved ones after a long parting, flinging up their arms in the prelude to an embrace so fierce, so greedy, that it could be an act of violence.

It was the most we ever said to each other. As I said, I didn't find Tara attractive. She was a good twelve or thirteen years younger than me, and she had a jealous boyfriend. He was an ex–dope smuggler who now made his living as a bail bondsman. There was a story going around that he paid some of his clients to follow Tara and rough up any man who tried to get too close to her. At about the time I was moving back to New York, she came up to me at a party and said, "You're a writer, aren't you?" I said yes.

"I am, too," she said. "I mean, I want to be."

"That's nice." I could imagine the kind of things she wrote, poems with titles like "I Piss on Your Values" and "Yes, I Have Tattoos."

"I was wondering," Tara said. She stared down at her shoes. "I mean, if I ever sent you something, some writing, I mean, would you read it? And tell me if it's any good?"

And like a schmuck, I said "sure."

A month later I got a package from her in New York. I opened it with dread. It was a short story; the title was "All Tomorrow's Parties," the same as the old Velvet Underground song. It began:

> The first thing I did when I got back from Myron's was inspect myself for damage. Well, actually, it wasn't the first thing; the first thing I did was to get off in the bathroom, with my coat still on, one sleeve rolled up above my forearm. But that scarcely counted. There was a big purple bruise on my right thigh, the color of crushed grapes, and some welts on my buttocks from where he'd used the coat hanger. But all in all, Myron had been decent to me. He was a freak, but a trustworthy freak. He always announced what he was going to do before he did it. "I'm gonna wail away at that little ass of yours," he'd warn me. "That's it, I promise. Just your ass, and maybe your thighs. Is it okay if I do your thighs?" "That's fine, honey," I'd tell him. "Just stay away from my face."

The power of Tara's writing came from its utter lack of special pleading, from the author's refusal to ask for sympathy for the "I" who told the story. This is very hard to do. Anyone who writes in the first person is in a sense writing an autobiography, from sheer habit if nothing else. You may be a white woman doctoral candidate in your twenties and your narrator may be a Chinese male dentist in his sixties and everything that happens may be the purest fabrication, but just by using that "I," that monopole of English grammar, you are automatically re-creating all the stories you ever told about yourself: you are telling them all over again. And why do you tell these stories, why did you ever tell them, if not to sell yourself? You want your readers to understand you, to admire you, to pity you, to absolve you. You want them to love you. And, of course, the moment you give in to this self-congratulatory impulse your writing goes down the toilet: that flushing sound is still ringing in my ears. But to resist it is like swimming the Hellespont while holding your breath. Byron is supposed to have swum the Hellespont, clubfoot and all, but even he admitted that "I have all my life been trying to make someone love me."

I wrote Tara back and told her that she'd done something heroic. I scribbled red exclamation points next to the phrases I liked, and I gave her some suggestions that might make the story a little better. The one thing I didn't do was ask her the question that is asked so often of anyone who writes that it has to be counted among the seven stupid questions of the world: Did this really happen to you? You can write a story in which the narrator pedals up to Mars on a Schwinn three-speed and people will still ask, "Did this really happen to you?"

The next story Tara sent me was also written in the first person. The narrator was an ex-prostitute, newly sober after years of addiction. Now she's living with an older guy who's scooped her up out of detox. He's a criminal lawyer who's only a hair less shady than his clients, and he's fanatically jealous. Wherever this girl goes, she's followed by some lowlife he's sprung from the city jail: he's got an entire fleet of purse-snatchers and B&E men and thick-booted biker crank-dealers he's paying to dog her around town and terrorize any guy who comes near her. In the course of the story she goes from paranoia to fury to an odd sense of comfort. "When I was a kid," she remembers,

> I used to have trouble sleeping. There were too many sounds coming from my parents' room. Every cry pierced the walls between us; every fall made the floorboards shake. I used to watch the shadows the trees cast on the white screen of my bedroom wall. In winter, leafless, their shapes were scary, like so many grasping claws. I turned them into guardians: giant grandmothers bending over my bed, death

to anyone who tried to hurt me. I do the same thing now.
In time, whatever thing you feared most becomes the safest
thing of all.

She'd attached a short note to the story: "I had to book kind of suddenly from Walt's, for reasons I can't go into right now, so please
use this post box number if you write back. I don't think Walt will
try to get in touch with you—he probably doesn't even remember
us talking—but if he does, do me a favor and say you haven't heard
from me. Thanks a mil. Love ya."

By this time I was weeping into my cats on a regular basis.
Moving back to New York after all those years had done it to me.
In Baltimore, solitude had been a protective mechanism, like those
sterile, climate-controlled bubbles in which they seal people with
no immune systems. In New York my aloneness became the plate-
glass window of a shop whose merchandise made me dizzy with want,
a shop I would never be allowed to enter. In these circumstances it
was easy for me to become fixated. I had a friend who was spending
hundreds of bucks each month on a phone-sex line because he'd
fallen in love with one of the—do you call them operators or pros-
titutes? I was more high-minded. It wasn't enough for someone to
talk dirty to me: She had to talk dirty with class. In Tara's stories
I got the bloody meat of sex, sex with bruises and coat hangers
and crumpled ten-dollar bills, and the pristine Wedgwood of
literature, or at least something that was trying to be literature, stringent and pitiless in its control. It had the same appeal as S&M,
where Dionysiac abandon turns into Apollonian discipline and then
back into an abandon that is wilder still because no one writhes more
fiercely than someone in a straitjacket, and the hoarsest cries are
the ones that come from the mouths of the gagged.

I had enough sense not to look Tara up when I went down
to Baltimore, which I did pretty often in those days. But one evening
I ran into her by accident, in the back room of a coffee shop on the
waterfront. I ducked in to smoke a cigarette, and she was sitting at
a table with another woman, playing cards. She'd let her hair grow
back to its natural dark brown and wore it slicked back, so that her

head had the shapely sleekness of a seal's. She'd lost some of the
weight people put on in their first months off drugs, when sugar is
the only white powder left to them and they go after it as though
it could somehow give them the same high as the others. I was
about to leave without saying anything, but just then Tara looked
up. Her face burst into the same reckless smile I remembered from
before.

"What are you doing here?"

"I'm on the Nostalgia Tour."

She didn't ask me why I hadn't looked her up. But she must
have sensed my awkwardness and it made her awkward, too, talk-
ative the way people get when they are trying to keep from saying
what they mean and say everything else instead. Without my asking, she started telling me a baroque story about Walt: She'd left
him; he'd tried to get her back, pleading, threatening, finally offering her some coke he'd scored from one of his retainers, only Tara
had turned it down and he'd ended up doing it himself and swan
diving back into his habit and losing everything, business, license,
Mazda, home, friends, he'd sold his dentures for a couple bags, it
was pathetic. I didn't want to hear any of it; I didn't want to hear
her gloating about her escape and her boyfriend's ruin, even if he
was a prick, which of course he was, but I preferred to think of Tara
as a stoic victim instead of a human being with a capacity for spite
and smugness and petty sadism. I didn't want to know where her
stories came from. And I didn't want to look at her broad unfurrowed
forehead, at her smoke-colored eyelids, at her wide mouth with its
lazy hammock of underlip, at the perfect, white-topped breasts that
made me glance away whenever she leaned forward, because I
wanted to kiss them: I wanted to kiss every part of her. I realized it
only now, and realizing it made me sick with anger and shame. I'd
prided myself on the notion that I was acting as this girl's mentor
out of pure good faith, and here was my dick again, as insolent
and unbanishable as Freddy Krueger in the *Nightmare on Elm Street*
movies. I could practically hear it sneering in my pants: "Didja
miss me?"

"I've got to go," I said. "I've got a ride waiting."

"No, don't." I almost shuddered when she touched my sleeve. "Listen, would it be okay if I came up to visit you sometime? I've never been in New York."

"I don't know. Let's talk about it later." Her face fell. For the hundred-thousandth time in my life, I tried to unhurt someone's feelings, even though ninety-nine thousand of such attempts have led only to worse hurts down the line: "Look, it's just my apartment's only one room, you know what I'm saying? I mean, you're a very attractive woman and I wouldn't want to be tempted to abuse your friendship. You may not have any problem with the man-woman thing. But I do."

Let's get back to *The Mark*. Mona puts in a good word for Nick, whom she knows as Alex, and Corrente takes him on as a bartender. At first he keeps a close eye on him, suspecting *something*. ("I didn't get where I was by trusting people. I ain't about to start now.") One night a customer tries some rough stuff. A gun is pulled. Close-ups of the gaping barrel, the goggle eyes of the gunman, a clueless punk who lost his temper and is just now realizing the unstoppability of what he's started; the eyes of Corrente, every broken capillary pulsing with the electricity of murder; the eyes of his thugs, as hard and shiny and immobile as bits of garnet. The last eyes we see are Nick's. They are unreadable. Is he frightened or expectant? Does he want Ray to get blown away or sent up on a murder rap? He begins to talk to the hothead, calmly, the way any bartender would talk to a drunk who's had too many. A moment later, he disarms him. Before Ray or his boys can inflict punishment, the cops burst in. Nick's friend, the lieutenant, is at their head. He looks sharply at Nick but says nothing to indicate that he knows him.

After they leave, Corrente tells Nick: "You handled yourself good back there, friend. I had you wrong, all wrong. Tell you the truth, I thought you were playing Mona. You know Mona. She's a good kid, but she's a sucker for anybody with a hard-luck story. She can't judge a guy's character. I can. You didn't lose your head.

I can use a guy who doesn't lose his head. You plan to spend the rest of your life mixing sidecars or do you want to go someplace?"

Nick: "Depends what kind of place it is."

Ray: "The place where they keep the money."

When Nick closes up for the night, the lieutenant is waiting for him in the parking lot. Again, he tries to warn Nick away: "You think you can get her back? You think you wait long enough, she's going to leave the guy who buys her diamonds? You think even if she does, Corrente's going to let her go?"

Nick: "Leave me alone. I don't know what I think."

Lieutenant: "That's your whole problem, Nick. You don't ever know what you think."

He drives back to his rooming house. Someone is standing on the porch. Nick's headlights sweep over her, then click off. It's Mona. She's wearing a trench coat belted at the waist. Her eyes are slitted. Her skin seems feverish. "I hear you were a hero tonight," she says when he steps up to her. "Ray's practically in love with you."

Nick: "Too bad I'm not interested."

Mona: "I didn't think you were. That's why I was surprised. Would it shock you if I told you I was disappointed?"

Nick: "I don't shock that easy. Unfortunately, I was working for your husband. The guy pays me a decent salary, I figured the least I could do was keep him from getting shot up."

Mona: "It could have been so simple. Just one squeeze on a trigger and it would've been all over. Isn't that what you do? Squeeze it?"

Nick (sardonic): "Am I to understand that you and Mr. Corrente are having marital trouble?"

Mona: "I'm the only one who's got trouble." She flings the trench coat open. There's a black bruise on her upper right arm, exactly where Nick has his tattoo. "*He* did this to me, Alex. Ray did!! Sometimes he uses a belt, but tonight it was just his fists. All in all, I think I prefer the belt. At least that way I don't have to feel him touch me." It's only when she shudders that Nick embraces her. She draws him closer and they kiss.

Nick: "I'm crazy about you, Mona."

Mona: "I'm wild for you, too, baby." She hesitates. "I'm just scared."

Nick: "Of Ray?"

Mona: "Yeah, of Ray. He'll kill us both if he finds out. But I'm also scared of myself. You don't know me, Alex. There's something wild in me, something selfish and cruel. Why do you think I ended up with a guy like Ray?"

Nick: "You said so yourself. He was the last ship on the dock."

Mona: "But also because he's my kind. We're bad in the same way. We see something we want and we take it, no matter who gets hurt. Maybe we're both rotten. And you're not." She runs a finger across his eyelids, down the corners of his mouth, in a gesture that's at once erotic and scientific, as though she could read Nick's face the way a fortune-teller would read a palm. Will she suddenly discern the face that lies beneath the one she touches? "No," she says finally. "You're good. A good man. I just worry that I'm not a good woman."

Nick: "You're good enough for me, baby." He kisses her again, and she opens her mouth to him. When he clutches her bruised arm, she whimpers. "I'm sorry, baby. I didn't mean to hurt you."

Mona: "Go ahead and hurt me. I don't mind being hurt. Not if it's by the right guy. Oh, yes, hold me, Alex. Hold me close. It feels so good just to be held!"

Nick: "I'll hold you as long as you want. I'll hold you all night. Just tell me, Mona. Tell me what you want. I'll do anything you want."

Mona pulls back and gazes up at him. Her lips twitch in what might be a smile or a grimace of resignation. "You know what I want, Alex."

Blackout.

There was a package from Tara in my mailbox a few weeks later: another story, no note attached. It was called "Why Don't You Do Right?" It began:

I never found goodness attractive in a man. It made me
think of the johns who showed me pictures of their wives
and kids, then came inside me with a guilty sputter. They

were the ones who'd ask, "Why are you doing this, a nice kid like you?" as they mopped the sperm off their matted bellies with a washcloth, always a little pissed that I wasn't doing it for them. I always wanted to answer, "Because of guys like you."

I struck out the last sentence with a red pencil.

The story was about a young woman who leaves prostitution and a C-a-day smack habit and decides to become a writer. She meets another writer, older, successful, an ex-junkie like herself, though his addiction seems very far away. Somehow he has learned how to be good: "good" was the word Tara used. I put a question mark beside it. From the beginning the narrator is slightly in awe of him. He doesn't come on to her and seems oblivious when she flirts with him, which she does out of habit because for years it has been her livelihood to make men want her, and because her self-esteem is such a spindly thing that she can't imagine him reading her stories unless he does. He agrees to read them anyway. She supposes he is being kind. When she first sends them to him she is sick with the fear that he'll hate them, that he'll judge the life contained in them. But he likes the stories. He takes their flaws seriously. The odd thing is he never asks her if they're true. At first she's grateful for this. But over time it makes her angry. It's as though his refusal to peer beneath the polished lid of her fiction were a tactful but personal rejection, a refusal to see *her*:

> Sometimes I wanted to write something that would rip through his detachment, something he couldn't answer with a sincere, congratulatory note. I thought of typing it in capitals with double underlining, scrawling it in crayon in letters ragged as a child's: THIS ISN'T JUST A STORY, ASSHOLE. THIS IS MY HEART I'M GIVING YOU. WHY DON'T YOU STOP TELLING ME HOW ADMIRABLE IT IS? WHY DON'T YOU JUST TAKE IT?

I'd barely finished reading when my phone rang.

"I'm sorry. I couldn't wait. Did you get it? You must have gotten it by now. Oh. This is Tara."

"I know who it is. Yeah, I got it. I just finished reading it."

"So? What did you think?"

"You were wrong about the guy."

I could hear her breath catch. "Wrong how?"

"He isn't good. Nobody's ever going to buy such romantic bullshit. He's just scared."

"What would he have to be scared of?"

"Maybe he doesn't know what to do with beautiful young women. Especially ones with talent. Maybe he's scared of wanting someone who would never want him."

"But she does want him. Didn't I make that clear?"

"Then maybe the age difference bothers him. Maybe he doesn't want to be like Woody Allen, slobbering after a nineteen-year-old."

"She's twenty-five. And Woody Allen's an old man."

"Okay, maybe he worries that she's confused. That she's mixing up gratitude with attraction. He's not looking to get laid because of somebody's sense of obligation."

"My narrator isn't confused. She knows exactly what she wants."

"What is it she wants?"

She yelled, "Do I have to spell everything out? I want you to love me!"

"Oh God," I groaned. "Not that word. Listen to me, Tara. I'm trying to tell you something about this . . . this *character* you made up. Because I know him better than you do. And what I'm trying to say is that he has a problem with follow-through. He admires you, he desires you, he may even fantasize about how nice it would be to love you. But he has questions about his ability."

"Stop talking about 'he.' This isn't a story anymore. I want you to love me. I want you to try. That's all. I want you to try. Are you so burned out you can't even try?"

"No," I said. "I can try. I can't promise anything else, but I can try."

"You know what I love about you?" Tara said. "Your enthusiasm."

* * *

Nick's affair with Mona is doubly furtive: Even as they hide from Ray, Nick must also hide from her. Since *The Mark* would have been made when the Hays code was still in effect, we're spared the machinations whereby Nick keeps his tattoo concealed during the roughhouse of love. There's a scene on the beach at night, down the bluffs from the club, where the lovers are clinching and Mona tries to pull off Nick's shirt. He warns her that he's got an ugly wound he doesn't want her to see, but she persists, half playful, half brutal, eyes glazed with the pleasure of inverted rape. At the last minute he hisses, "Someone's coming!" and plunges half dressed into the surf while Mona flees. When he comes up for air, Ray is standing at the water's edge, fastidiously pinching his trouser legs so as not to get sand in the cuffs. During the conversation that follows, Nick stays submerged to the shoulders, as coy as Doris Day in a bubble bath with Rock Hudson leering at her from the doorway.

Ray: "Thought I might find you out here. Turn around." Nick hesitates. "What's the matter with you? You act like I'm about to plug you."

Nick's POV. Off on the horizon we see a thin strand of lights against the starless sky. "See those lights out there? That's the *Dorada*. The 'Golden Girl.' It's a gambling ship. Belongs to a git named Thurlow, used to do business for the boys in Los Angeles before he went semilegit. He keeps it moored just outside the three-mile limit. I run their protection."

Nick (still nervous): "What do you protect them from?"

Ray: "Just losers don't know enough to pay their debts on time. It's a cream puff job. I'm like Thurlow's alarm clock. I tell people when their time is up."

Nick: "Must be good money."

Ray: "Not good enough. You have any idea what the *Dorada* takes in on a good Saturday night? Try half a million. I was thinking you and me might try for a bigger piece of that." The plan is for Ray to work the ship as usual, while Nick and some other men wait in a power launch nearby. When the last suckers go ashore, Ray will signal them to board, and they will overpower the crew, plunder the safe, and make off with the weekend's take.

Nick: "Don't you worry about what Thurlow'll do when he realizes you're in on this? You aren't the only muscle he can hire."

Ray: "He ain't *gonna* realize it! You're gonna knock me out."

The camera cuts to Mona. She stands pressed against the cliff, listening. It cuts back to Nick and at that moment, in his eyes, or really in the space *behind* them, we see the thought that trips his conscience like a lead slug dropped on a jeweler's scale. "I've got a better idea. I'm going to shoot you."

Ray holds up his hands: "Hey, down, boy! Don't get carried away. I want to live long enough to spend that half a mil."

Nick: "You'll live, you lug. The gun's going to be filled with blanks. Only Thurlow isn't gonna know that. I shoot, you fall down, *boom*. We give you the heave-ho over the side, you swim out to the launch. Thurlow will never hear you: he'll be doing everything he can not to faint. Two months later you and Mona'll be ordering room service in the best hotel in Rio."

Ray: "I like the way your mind works, kid. Nobody'll ever suspect me."

Nick: "That's right, Ray. No one ever suspects a dead man."

In the shadows Mona smiles.

I'm afraid I'm too squeamish to say much about the sex. Somewhere beneath the artifice and disguises there's a real woman whom I loved or tried to love, someone who proved so unsettling to me that I had to tell a story about her. Stories are the way we tell the truth and the way we change it into something bearable, encasing the original irritant in the pearly layers of narrative. I've given my irritant another name and another past. I've put words in her mouth. I've done everything I can to hide her. But I'm afraid you might meet her one day—not Tara, but the woman who is her seed or armature—and in spite of all my efforts recognize her. There's still that tattoo: you can see my copy of it when I hold up my wrist, and the likeness is pretty faithful. So don't expect me to tell you about the shape of her breasts or the clasp of her sex or about the way her face looked when I entered her. I mean to keep her decent.

There was the problem of viruses, for which we were both at risk and which I had been tested for and Tara hadn't. Given her history, she thought there was a chance she might be infected. So we took more than the usual precautions and we undressed only to dress again, in all the stretchy gear that industry has devised to reconcile our longing for the little death with our dread of the big one. You can fetishize latex all you want, but there are some things that can't be eroticized: the jerking stops and starts that recall nothing so much as learning how to drive a stick shift; the litter of foil packets that crunch beneath you and whose sharp edges prick your skin, the machine oil tang of nonoxynol-9, the fear of thrusting too hard, of going too deep, of putting your tongue in the wrong place. These things turned the bed we shared into a bomb factory: the last thing we could afford to do there was lose ourselves.

"This isn't very good for you, is it?" she asked me once. We'd been lovers for about a month.

"No. It's perfect. You're perfect."

"You're a terrible liar. What kind of junkie did you make?"

"It's just the technology. It's sort of daunting."

"We can do other things. There's nothing I wouldn't do with you."

I knew this was true. Tara was a generous person. But I couldn't forget her stories. And while the past she revealed in them didn't bother me—if I'm honest, I have to say it excited me in a queasy way—I didn't want to take her back there. "You know what I'd like to do?" I told her. "Read to you."

Here are some of the books I read to Tara in the time we were together: *Bleak House*, *The Third Policeman*, *Mildred Pierce*, *Bad Behavior*. *Bad Behavior* made Tara sick with envy. We'd make love until exhaustion overtook us, and then she'd arrange herself like a cat, coiled half on top of me, her head on my chest, as I read. In this way we'd fall asleep. Often I'd wake with a start to see that the light was still on, her head still pillowed on me, her breath stirring the hairs on my chest. All my life before her I'd fallen asleep with a dizzy sensation of floating. The feeling scared me. I thought that if I surrendered to it fully I'd actually levitate out the window and drift endlessly up into the night. In Tara I told myself that at last I had an anchor. But the feeling of being anchored can be frightening in its own way: really, there's not much difference between floating and sinking.

On one of her visits Tara and I went to the Clit Club, where Slam and Roxy had invited us to a combination commitment ceremony and farewell party: they were leaving for New Mexico in another week. It turned out to be more of a performance piece. We got there late and the upstairs room was already hot with bodies. The audience was mostly female: wiry little dykes with stubble cuts and surgical steel septum rings; big lush lipstick lesbians in spandex dresses. Everybody was tattooed. I found myself childishly eager for a glimpse of another straight couple, but the only one I saw consisted of a woman in a white vinyl cat suit and a huge, unwieldy guy wearing a blindfold, dog collar, and studded leather jockstrap: with his soft, hairless belly and dimpled knees, he looked like a baby afflicted with some freakish accelerated growth disorder. His mistress led him in on a chain leash, then parked him against one of the heavy concrete beams. I watched her thread some monofilament fishing line through his nipple rings and lash him to the beam with it. He remained as docile as a well-trained Newfoundland. "Now, I'm gonna leave you alone for a while," she cooed. "Are you gonna be good?" He nodded. She slapped him across the cheek, then yanked down his codpiece and slapped his penis so hard I winced in sympathy. "I hope so. I don't want to hear any bad reports about you."

Tara said, "I bet you anything that guy's got a corner office. Every slave I ever met was some kind of executive."

They'd been playing that furious, chattering dance music that makes you want to drop acid, butcher your parents, and write PIGS on the wall in their gore. Now the sound was cut. Slam and Roxy walked onto the low stage at the front of the room. The crowd cheered. In the years I'd known her Slam had all but vanished beneath encrustations of tattoos and facial jewelry, but she'd never managed to efface her nature, which was that of a cheerful, hearty big sister from one of the American suburbs' two hundred functional families. "You like me! You *really* like me!" she cried. Gratitude made her tongue-tied. She didn't know how to thank her friends for their kindness or her clients for their loyalty or Roxy for her love, that thing that defies thanks. "And so," she concluded, "Roxy and I worked up this little ceremony to show you what you mean to us, and what we mean to each other and—oh shit, let's just do it."

The lights went down and someone put on a tape of organ music. It was ultra-Gothic: I could feel the low notes vibrate through the floor beneath my feet. A pair of spots formed dusty white cones in the air. Roxy stood in one of them, her broad back to the audience. She was naked to the waist. Beneath the other spot Slam pulled on a pair of surgical gloves, snapping them smartly at the wrist. She stepped out of the light and an instant later reappeared beside her girlfriend, holding a small bottle and a scalpel: the glinting blade seemed oddly decorative, like something you'd see in a jeweler's display case. I watched her daub Roxy's shoulder with an antiseptic, Betadine probably: it left that familiar rusty stain. Then she began to cut. A shudder rolled through me, a wavelike disturbance that might have been revulsion or arousal, the twitch of blood in the microsecond before it plunges toward the groin. The first stroke was a long downward one that took a moment to begin bleeding. The incisions that followed were smaller. Slam's hand moved as swiftly as though she were crosshatching a charcoal sketch. Roxy never budged. Only her ribs pulsed into relief as she drew in breath. Beside me I heard Tara hiss. "You all right?" I asked. She squeezed my hand but said nothing.

When Slam was done, she rubbed the cuts with ink, then blotted the excess with a piece of gauze before returning to the vacant beam of light. With her back turned to us she undressed, shedding layers of leather and denim and cotton until there was nothing but skin and ink: she had a pair of black snakes—really, they were the *suggestions* of snakes, the design was so simple—tattooed along her spine, their coils winding between the vertebrae. Roxy joined her. She gathered Slam's hair in one hand and bound it in a chignon. It was the kind of thing a mother might do for her small daughter. When she began to use the scalpel, I could see her breasts bounce. At first I was afraid that she didn't know what she was doing: that her hand would shake, leaving only some ragged scars that someone, someday might take for the marks of a bizarre accident. But she was careful; she was careful with her lover's body. The design that materialized in blood on Slam's shoulder and then vanished as the blood streamed downward was a perfect trident, the same design Slam had carved into Roxy.

Afterward the two women greeted well-wishers like newlyweds outside a church, bare-breasted and gleaming with sweat.

I'd worried that Tara would be revolted, reminded of razor-wielding pimps who slice their initials in their hos' asses, but she said she'd found the ritual beautiful. I wondered what would happen if Slam and Roxy ever broke up. She slapped my wrist. "Shame on you!! The way you think! They're not going to break up. And even if they do, it wouldn't matter. Not really. Not after tonight. For the rest of their lives each of them will be marked with the other. No matter where they go or who they're with, they'll always know there's someone else who's wounded in the same way. Like a twin. You never lose your twin."

The next day I had Tara's stick figures tattooed on my wrist. We sleepwalked home in a gnat-cloud of endorphins, then made riskless love in the air-conditioner's chilly blast. Afterward she said, "I want to please you," and I said, "You already do," but she brushed it aside. "You know what I mean," she said. "You want to hurt me."

I recoiled. "That's bullshit!"

She gazed at me steadily. "You don't have to pretend. I can see it in you. It's how you're wired. People are wired in all sorts of different ways. And I'm saying it's okay. I want you to."

I protested some more, indignantly, coyly, feebly, and finally submitted to my desires. At least I tried. I got as far as handcuffing Tara with the pair I kept in my closet, the way one keeps suits that were outgrown long ago. But I couldn't get her past out of my mind. I kept imagining her in a room that rented by the hour, naked and shivering with the onset of her jones and consenting to be bound and beaten by men who looked as anonymously ugly as all men must when they're stripped of everything but their wants and the power of the money in their wallets. I told myself that it might not have been as horrible as I imagined, no more horrible, maybe, than having to wipe the piss off a stranger's toilet seat in a Red Roof Inn, and certainly better compensated. I told myself I had no way of knowing how much of it had ever really happened. We tried reversing roles: I had her straddle me and twist my nipples, but all it did was hurt. And the words she barked at me might as well have been in Polish for all the conviction she put in them. Tara wasn't much of an actress.

I broke up with her a few weeks later, this woman who'd wanted nothing more than to give me pleasure. It lasted hours, the two of us weeping and yelling like idiots, faces mushy with grief. "What the fuck is wrong with you!?" she cried, over and over. None of my explanations satisfied her. "I'm sorry," I said. "It's just the way I'm wired." I excused myself to the end.

The Mark too ends in betrayal. The heist goes off as planned. Scenes click past like the numbers on a roulette wheel: the power boat roaring seaward with its foaming comet's tail, Nick at the helm; the strained wait beneath the moon; the sounds of piano chords, laughter, the clatter of dice and ice cubes drifting across the water. Then we're on board the *Dorada*, following Ray in his white suit. He waves at the regulars, but his eyes are cheerless. The last boat ferries off the night's last losers. On the deserted deck Ray releases the rope ladder. The three raiders clamber up and vault over the side. Nick presses a gun to Corrente's spine and walks him forward into the glare of the casino. Croupiers freeze at their green baize tables. The man called Thurlow drops his highball glass; it bounces on the Persian rug. Nick's voice is quiet: "Give it up." Ray mutters to him: "Make this look good."

"Don't worry, buddy. I will." His finger tightens on the trigger.

Twenty years later Ray's death would have been filmed in slow motion, the camera tracking every jetting platelet and plunging into an exit wound the size of a dinner plate. But in *The Mark*, as in all true noir, murder is a psychological phenomenon. What matters is not Ray's blood but the look in his eyes as the bullet spins him in a flailing pirouette: it's the look of the con-man who finally realizes he's been conned.

After this everything moves faster: money stuffed in a seaman's ditty bag; Ray's body plunging overboard with a detonation of spray. Nick is the first man down the ladder. The moment he sets foot in the launch, he turns and shoots the accomplices who cling helplessly overhead. As he speeds off toward the lights of La Jolla, we hear him in voice-over:

"It was all behind me now: the lying and the killing. That's what I told myself. I told myself we could make a clean start, Mona and me. Love would wash us clean. But sometimes love only makes you dirty, like the water around a sinking ship. When my ship went down near Midway, I came up covered with oil. It was as black as tattoo ink, and I stank of it for days. Sometimes I thought I could still smell it on me. And here's the thing I still can't figure: Was it love for Mona that turned me into a murderer? Or did Mona just show me what I always was: a killer from the beginning?"

The scene dissolves to Mona's bedroom, where Mona paces, a cigarette clamped between her lips. Nick enters.

Mona: "You did it?"

Nick: "He's deader than last week's bluefish."

Mona: "What about the money?"

He drops the bag at her feet. "Five hundred thousand, just like the man said." Their embrace is almost mechanical. "You'd better start packing. The cops'll be onto us pretty quick."

Mona: "What's the rush? Let me get you a drink." They go downstairs to the darkened lounge. Mona steps behind the bar and turns on a light, takes out glasses and a bottle. She reaches into the ice tray. "What'll it be, stranger?"

Nick: "We don't have time for this, baby. I told you, the cops—"

Mona (she is holding a gun): "The cops wi̸ find the man who robbed the *Dorada* and murdered my husband. The man who came here meaning to kill me."

Nick: "You've got it all sewn up, don't you, Mona? I guess you were just playing me all along."

Mona: "Don't be a dope, Alex. I hated Ray. And I loved you. I still do. I loved you so much I almost forgot what Nick taught me. Nick was the boy I told you about, remember? You remind me of him sometimes. You've got the same eyes, only yours are meaner. Anyway, Nick taught me always to keep an eye out for the next ship, the one that won't sail off without you. And you want to know something? It turns out the only ship you can ever count on is the one that's just got room enough for you."

Nick: "You and half a million dollars."

Mona: "A girl doesn't want to get too lonely."

Nick: "Ever wonder what happened to Nick, baby? The guy who left you stranded? Let me show you."

He starts to pull up his shirtsleeve and Mona fires: maybe she thought he was reaching for a gun of his own. Nick staggers backward. The look on his face is not shock but bitter amusement, as though he'd expected this all along and were perversely pleased to be proved right. "Don't be scared, baby. I was just trying to show you something." With shaking hands he finishes what he started. Mona stares at him in horror. Her eyes are wet. "Remember when I got this tattoo? Remember what I told you? I said I wanted to take you with me wherever I went. I guess I did. Or maybe it was the other way around. That tattoo dragged me all the way back to you. I couldn't fight it. And I guess you were telling the truth, too, weren't you, baby? You said you'd be waiting for me. And look, here we are."

He collapses. Mona kneels beside him, cradles his head in her lap as sirens keen in the distance, coming closer. The last shot is a close-up of the tattoo.

* * *

What else can I tell you? A few months after we split, Tara met a guy who turned out to be steadier than I was. They're married now, with two kids, and I hear that they're happy. I think of her every time my eye falls on my tattoo. It's the one I see most often: I am looking at it as I write this. After a while its spotty nakedness became unbearable, and I went all the way back to Amsterdam to get it touched up. Aesthetics aside, those stick figures kept me thinking about the question Tara asked me the night I left. I'm still trying to find an answer to it: "What is wrong with you?" I could blame it on my childhood or on Tara's past or on my inability to come to terms with my own cruelty. But these are just stories I tell myself. They are entertaining and even, sometimes, consoling, and mostly true. But it doesn't pay to take your stories too seriously.

I used to like falling in love. I liked the gratitude that went with it, the ridiculous gratitude for the dime-store present and the late-night phone call. Tara used to call me late at night, and for a while it made me happy. You can tell you're falling out of love when the gratitude ceases, when those gifts feel like shameless bribes and the ring on the telephone makes you mutter, "What does she want from me now?" I suppose falling in love is good for the character and falling out of it harmful. The one makes you trusting, generous, expansive; the other pinched, suspicious, jealous of your prerogatives. Or maybe what happens is that love offers you an exit from the seedy hotel room of the self. You meet someone, and she calls you away from the narrow bed whose mattress might be stuffed with iron filings, the yellowed linoleum, the single, fly-soiled lightbulb, the windows with their film of soot that give onto nothing but an airshaft. You walk out of the room and you join her in the bright air outside, and if you're lucky you get to stay there with her. But some of us, you know, are agoraphobes. We can't take the raw, unfiltered light, the hurtling distances. They make us anxious. And sooner or later we turn on the one who coaxed us out, we blame her for overturning our lives, and we go back to the old hotel, where our old room is always waiting for us.

Hump

LAURIE STONE

I WENT TO A PARTY FOR A FAMOUS WRITER. THE PLACE WAS POSH AND jumping, lots of celebrities, the kind you don't usually see at book parties. There was a handsome actor I think was John Shea, and Carly Simon was sitting at a little table, as if cordoned off by velvet ropes. I stared at her. No one else was staring. Waiters passed around tiny food: dime-sized blinis, miniature pizzas, Lilliputian slices of beef. I hugged a wall, and the trays kept coming. I got full, and it was consoling, until I minded being comforted by food.

Across the room was a man I meet only at book parties, but I couldn't remember his name. I could picture his last book in its alphabetical slot on my bookshelf, so I could have figured out his second initial, but I was too alarmed by the lapse of memory. Alzheimer's? NutraSweet? The man was standing in a circle, everyone holding glasses, no one lunging for food.

In another part of the room posed a prolific novelist I slightly knew. She was reed-thin, tall, and raven-haired, and she was laughing with the guest of honor. Her last novel was now an artful movie, which everyone liked, including me, but I hated her—hated her so much it made me thirsty.

As I moved toward the bar, who should I run into but a woman who was even more illustrious and achieved than the raven-haired wonder. Call her Lucy. Lucy was ten years younger than me and pregnant out to here. She said my name, smiling. I said hi without moving my mouth. I hadn't known she was pregnant, hadn't known I would see her and feel like burying myself in dirt.

I gripped a bowl of peanuts. I would remain at the bar until the waiters cleared the glasses and napkins, until the cloak room was left with one dangling cloak, mine. I would join the kitchen staff and prepare small food.

But two friends appeared, and one of them, Sheila, described an article she was writing about therapists who induced false memories of childhood abuse in their patients. I wondered what was in it for the patients. Why believe you had suffered more than the usual amount of damage? I had a thought: People craved something large and definitive to blame the mess of their lives on. One unassailable explanation, and whisk, whisk whisk, wash your hands of further probes. It had its allure.

My mother, Toby, has an expression in Yiddish: "No one can see their own hump."

Toby and I are widows. My father died twelve years ago, and my lover Gardner, three. Sometimes Toby and I don't see each other for long periods, but we are in a thaw phase, sitting in the Joe Bar when she says, "I regret you didn't marry and have a family. If you had married Nathan at twenty-five instead of nineteen, you would have stayed with him."

Toby is saying, "I think I'm not normal, because I raised a daughter who isn't normal." That is her hump.

"I'm glad I didn't have children," I lie. I recently met a man who was thirty-seven and had had a vasectomy. He said he didn't want to bring more children into the world. He said he would adopt if he decided to care for another kid. He was the stepfather of his wife's son but acknowledged it wasn't the same as his own flesh and blood. Did I think he was a failure because he hadn't reproduced? No. Do I think other childless women are misfits? No. But me, yes, I think my childless state is a consequence of my damage, and maybe it is.

Toby: "But you wanted a child for a while."

"For a while I did, but now I don't."

She stares off. "I never wanted children, not really, not if anyone had asked me, which they didn't, and I wouldn't have known

what to say if they had, because who knew what I wanted?" Toby
says she has no interest in food or sex, never did, insisting that her
mother forced her to eat and marry. She sips coffee. "I wanted to be
a WAC."

"Then why didn't you enlist?" I say, knowing what she will
answer.

"Get out of here. Nobody enlisted. *Nobody*. My mother would
have killed me."

I can't take my eyes off Natalie, who says she has no ambivalence
about motherhood. I don't question this, me who questions everything. She worships her daughters, who are dead, loves them, loves
them to pieces, never has a harsh word to say about them, a tainted
memory, nothing. I go into a trance thinking about a mother who
loved her girls this way. I don't get to see this love because the daughters are dead, but I get to imagine it, and Natalie, who is beautiful,
is affectionate to me in a maternal way.

Soon after we met, I began losing my hair. I thought about
hair all the time. It took a year and a half for the problem to be
controlled—with minoxidil and estrogen. During that time I con-
sulted seven doctors, some in remote parts of New Jersey. Natalie
drove me to the appointments, helped me as no one else. Our connection is erotic, in that, when I'm with her, I don't miss men.

Natalie had four children: Will, Mark, and the twins Dana
and Jill, who were born with an immune deficiency and lived to be
twenty-three and twenty-five. I crossed paths with Natalie when
we were volunteers at God's Love We Deliver—the organization
that feeds homebound people with AIDS. We were cutting onions
when I told her about Gardner, who had recently died of bone
marrow cancer. She spoke about her daughters, tears spilling, not
from the onions. It had been five years since Dana's death and three
since Jill's. Natalie said, "They were the loves of my life." I thought
about the people who were left: her sons, her husband, her friends.
They would never measure up. Natalie didn't touch others readily,

nor offer her body easily. Her most unbridled desire was for the two dead girls.

She seldom evoked them in the presence of her family, but she would tell me stories in her car, reliving the pain, details that had firmed into a litany. Dana had suffered from corneal herpes for most of her life. The condition would erupt twice a year, requiring hospitalizations and causing ulcers that had to be cauterized and that left scar tissue. Eventually she lost the sight in one eye and feared she might become blind.

Both children were subject to bronchial infections, but Jill's were more severe, progressing to pneumonia at least half a dozen times. Twice a day the girls required postural drainage, meaning their lungs were pounded, so they could cough up phlegm. Natalie: "I hated the sound. I would hear it even when no one was home."

Natalie recalled Dana in the hospital as a baby: "The herpes treatments were painful, and she would cry. I would hold her, unable to give her comfort. Once I walked into her room, and her head was swollen to twice its size. An IV needle had slipped from a vein in her temple, and fluid had infiltrated. I threw a fit."

When Dana was seventeen, her nose began to deteriorate. The condition started with a lesion, a spot that Natalie thought was another herpes sore—like ones that would flare from time to time on Dana's chin. Instead the sore grew, and no diagnosis could be found. That summer Dana went to camp and returned home with a boyfriend and a much-reduced sore. "It was the last time she looked okay." Finally, at the National Institutes of Health, a doctor confirmed the condition as vasculitis. "He said the flesh would continue to disintegrate and that nothing could arrest it. He was telling me the disease was terminal, and, for the first time, I took in that they would die."

For five years, Dana's nose eroded. "I would be lying in bed, watching TV, and I would see light coming through the membrane dividing her nostrils." The nose grew raw and exposed. It oozed and bled. Dana resorted to a prosthesis. "It looked like a nose you buy in a joke store. The glue irritated Dana's skin, and she had to wear glasses to mask the edges. Her appearance was so drastically changed,

I preferred her without the disguise, but with it she could go out. I took her to a makeup expert in Baltimore, who worked wonders. We experimented with hats, clothes, hair styles. She was brave. She even had a special little box for the nose."

Dana died from a virus that entered the raw, nasal passageway and infected her brain. "At the time she was getting sick, Jill was in California and needed a coat. Dana met me at Bloomingdale's, so we could shop, and that's when I saw that she was dragging her leg. She wrote out Jill's address, and I could see she was having trouble forming the letters. I screamed. She admitted that she had been struggling for a while. Dana had the option of a brain biopsy, to see if she could benefit from treatment. I think the situation was already hopeless, and the biopsy is the one thing I have always regretted. But Dana elected it, and it proved, indeed, that nothing could be done, and, on top of that, she was left with the effects of a stroke. She became aphasic. She would say 'yes' meaning 'no' and realize she was saying the wrong word. I was told she had seven more months, and that is exactly how long she lived. We hired therapists to help her walk and speak. But as she grew weaker, I wanted her to die. In the hospital, during the last few days, she was in terrible pain, screaming, and no one could figure out why."

While Dana was dying in one hospital, Jill was in another, gravely ill with a lung infection. "They had to let Jill out so she could say goodbye to Dana. I can't imagine how she must have felt—watching her sister die and knowing she was next. At the gathering after Dana's funeral, Jill refused to appear."

Next Jill grew progressively weaker. "She developed disfiguring warts all over her body and face—a bad sign, since it showed that her immune system couldn't even fend off warts. She had to walk with a cane, and one day, from coughing so hard, she punctured a lung. She was home alone. She could hardly breathe, so she called the police. But the lung never really healed. At the end, she was in intensive care, and a nurse asked if she wanted to be resuscitated. I suppose nothing is worse than having to ask your child if she prefers to be on life support or to die. I felt guilty for wanting to see my children die. Did I think I would have to take care of them when they were seventy? Jill said, 'Don't worry, Mommy, it's no fun anymore without Dana.' This was just before Mark and Wendy were going to be married. Jill called them into her room and told them to have a good life. Then a doctor gave her morphine."

What mesmerized me most was that no affliction disgusted this mother. The girls remained beautiful in her eyes. Natalie's husband, Marty, knew how to pound his daughters' chests, but it was Natalie I saw doing it. In her recollections, there were always three females braided together: enduring ordeals in the hospital, claiming rewards for their trials with shopping trips and fancy meals. I imagined them on a bed, their heads touching, their voices conspiratorial. The girls had graduated from high school with their class, had gone to college and graduate school, had had boyfriends and sex—entrusting their mother with the details. Dana's boyfriend had stuck by her when her nose rotted. "I asked if she wore the prosthesis during sex, and she said she did but that it had once fallen off." Natalie and Dana had laughed at the time, and Natalie and I laughed when she told the story to me.

Natalie could not remember ever being angry with her daughters. I asked if they had ever been angry at her, and she said she could not recall a time. I thought that, perhaps, Natalie had loved her daughters so much—and evenly, not betraying a preference—because they hadn't been emotionally needy; as twins, they'd been able to curl up in each other. Natalie had been the odd one out, never being completely privy to the understanding of twins, and perhaps this unrequitable longing had stoked her affection. Now, in its place was grief.

Many times when Natalie was in the city, she would cut short a meeting, feeling an urge to return home, a reflex she associated with the girls. "When they were alive, I would be driving back from the city, and I would race over the bridge, my heart pounding, my skin hurting. Would there be an ambulance in the driveway? Would I hear coughing or see a red eye?" She feared for the safety of her sons too, wanting to count heads as often as possible. She saw that, after the girls died, she became hooked on crises—manufacturing them, if need be—because they recaptured her daughters. During the period when she was their mother, she'd been at her best: in charge and able to succeed in superhuman ways. She'd been able to avoid ordinary life, and she still hunted for that turn-on. Now, re-assured there were no present dangers and tucked safely in her house, peace was still not assured. She would be thrown back on anguishing thoughts, and the house was mined with pain. When she entered the girls' bathroom, she saw Jill in the tub, so wasted she had to be lifted in and out. In the hallway, she remembered Dana staggering with her cane. From time to time, Natalie talked about selling the house—"To prove I can live *somewhere* else." But mostly she dreaded not being haunted.

At God's Love, after we stood for a while, Natalie would lean on the counter, shifting her weight from foot to foot, her leg and back hurting—a legacy of the famous accident, when Natalie and Marty had been run down by a car on Madison Avenue and cata-pulted through a plate-glass window. Marty had lost some depth perception but had otherwise recovered quickly. Natalie's injuries had been more severe. Her left thigh was severed to the bone, and it had taken months of hospitalization and a year of physical therapy before she could normally resume her life. The accident had oc-curred before the diagnosis of the girls, so, at the time, Natalie had thought that this was the great peril that looms over every family. She thought they had survived. Later, in light of her daughters' suffering, the accident had come to look like a minor twist of fate.

Of course the damage had been inflicted on *Natalie's* body, which made it easier to bear in one sense but also served as an un-welcome reminder that her own flesh was vulnerable. She could not tolerate imperfection. She rose each morning at five-thirty, ran long distances, then cooked for the day, accomplishing a round of du-ties by the time most people awoke. She had always been arresting-looking, and though now, at fifty-eight, little wrinkles surrounded her eyes, she was still striking: her skin taut and her jawline even. The bones of her strong face promised coherence, but she avoided mirrors, disliking what she saw.

She could be harsh about women in general. Threading her devotion to her daughters and her ease with women was an impulse to sacrifice their interests. Her daughter-in-law, Wendy, a professional dancer, was due to give birth, and Natalie objected to Wendy's plan to return to work after the delivery. I wondered how, if her daughters had lived, she would have tolerated their deviations from her life. Would they have ventured far? When Natalie had learned that Wendy was pregnant, she'd confided to me, "I love Wendy and Mark, but it's not the same as if a daughter were having a baby. You know the special bond between mothers and daughters."

"I do?"

"Come on. A mother's love for her girls is *different* from her feelings about her sons . . . or anyone else."

Natalie didn't mean to be declaring that males were less real to her, but in a way she took it for granted that men were an alien species—taking care to place her sons in a roped-off category. She hadn't shortchanged them, she maintained, but sometimes she admitted that Marty had felt shut out. "It was as if no one could penetrate the magic circle I had with the girls." Natalie had not wanted her husband involved in domestic life. She'd positioned him over there, on Planet Money.

Natalie had, more or less, duplicated her own mother's life. Few days had ever passed without intimate contact with her mother, Lillian, who, at ninety-four, lived nearby in a luxurious retirement community. Natalie was on the phone with her mother every day and visited nearly as often, ferrying her to doctors, dropping off clean laundry, replenishing her household supplies. Lillian was blind but otherwise healthy and mentally sharp. Natalie would gaze wistfully at her mother's body, grown frail and bent, and she would remember the dynamo Lillian had been even far into old age. Natalie evoked the weekly parties her mother had orchestrated for scores of friends, who would play cards and eat meals in the family's Brooklyn brownstone—a social hub for the community and the site of the medical practice of Natalie's father, Hugo.

One night at a party, I sat beside Lillian, and then the two of us slipped off to the living room and ensconced ourselves near the fire. Lillian had been a beauty as well, and now, even at her advanced age, a pentimento of loveliness showed beneath layers of time. She too had lost a child: Natalie's older brother, Kenneth, had died of liver cancer at forty-one. Hugo had died when Lillian was eighty, and, until a few years ago, she had lived by herself.

When Lillian recalled her domestic rounds, she did not sound divided. Before marrying, she had devoted herself to her widowed father and raising her two younger brothers. Next she'd raised Kenneth and Natalie, while assisting in her husband's practice and opening her home and heart to Hugo's three bachelor brothers, who lived together in a house near hers. When one of Hugo's brothers was hospitalized, she visited so dutifully and catered to him so solicitously the nurses mistook her for his wife—an assumption she didn't correct. I once asked if she had burned to do something just for herself, and she had looked at me and said, "I never gave it a thought."

She took pains to downplay her trials, and in her militant gallantry allowed a stoic vanity to show. She wanted to appear satisfied, beyond need—and to believe this herself—but renegade desires would flash. She would declare the unimportance of wealth, then drool over the stock portfolios of the German ladies with whom she dined. She presented herself as tolerant: never a harsh word, everyone of her acquaintance "lovely." But in her code, fleshly gratification and the pursuit of personal glory received smart raps on the wrist.

Lillian beguiled with generosity, extending what appeared to be limitless largess. Lillian made herself a model and, by leaking no ambivalence, seemed pure. It would have been difficult to rebel against such an authority, and Natalie learned to mask the parts of herself that didn't match up. Natalie didn't want to wound her mother with dissent or to step outside Lillian's embrace. But sometimes at her dinners—after the elaborate preparations were done—Natalie would look like she had fallen down a rabbit hole. She wasn't made as purely as Lillian to play the martyr. Something else had crept in, something she did not give reign to except in rationed amounts, something connected to dressing with dash and with painting, something her daughters had unleashed, a zone where pleasure could be indulged—although, with her daughters, the pleasure came paid for with pain.

I took Lillian's hand and leaned into her ear. "You look wonderful."

"Thank you, dear," she said, with her crisp enunciation. "Frankly, I don't know why I'm alive."

I smiled at her mordant honesty. She could not adjust to being blind, hated the betrayals of her body. Last year she'd broken a hip and now used a walker. The hip was healing, and, aside from her eyesight, she was physically sound. But everything she deemed substantial was in the past and a function of running a family. Natalie encouraged Lillian to hang on to life with the carrots of her grandchildren's passages: Will's wedding last year and the pending arrival of her first great grandchild. Natalie echoed Lillian's credo: *Live for the family.* But now that Lillian wasn't running the show, family life no longer compelled, and she had not prepared for anything to take its place.

I floated upstairs to the hallway where Jill and Dana had hobbled during their last days. The space was plastered with photographs, arranged as densely as stamps in an album. Papa Hugo's eyes stared pensively out of his Buddha face. There was Mark at seven, perched impishly over a birthday cake. In another shot, the family stood in front of the pool, arms entwined, the boys with long hair and scruffy beards, Natalie and Marty sleek in cut-offs. And everywhere were the girls before their physical decline, two nymphs, resembling Marty, with long, delicate faces and saddles of freckles across their cheeks and noses. They were slender but not frail or forlorn. In the central photograph, they posed on adjacent seesaws, Jill stretched out on one, Dana on another, so that their bodies formed an X, with their eyes meeting the camera. They were sixteen, "their best year." They looked defiant and mischievous, as if they shared a secret that lent them power.

When Natalie evoked her daughters, they didn't seemed real to me because they were unblemished and undifferentiated. Natalie needed daughters perfectly embracing of her. But looking at the twins now, separate from the family and exulting in a loveliness they knew would shortly be destroyed, I imagined the anger they must have felt at such a rotten throw of the dice. Though still included in the chain extending from Lillian and Natalie, they would not themselves become mothers, would not duplicate any woman's life but each other's. The immensity of their loss was equal to the space carved out of Natalie's heart, or maybe she just needed to be chained to the grief. Natalie knew she was obsessed but thought that seeing a shrink would depress her further. Therapy felt like capitulation: proof of her imperfection and another sacrifice for the family. She didn't want to fly right. She didn't want to be cured.

Sometimes, when I miss my mother, I feel the loss of her viscerally, and it is shocking, for such a long time ago—maybe when I was two or three—I came to depend on men to take her place.

My sister, Ellen, has three grown children, earns her living selling real estate, and has had a long marriage. Ellen understands my mother as well as I do, but the shape of her life resembles Toby's, and they do not wrestle about the choices they've made.

When Toby seeks credit for my mind, I yield it to her in a way that shows I am lying. But sometimes, without prompting, I am struck by her humor or touched by her beauty, or I respect the way she tolerates aloneness. I compliment her, and she says, "You don't really mean that," or, "I don't see how you can say that." Or she throws the praise in my face: "Suddenly I'm funny to you. Everyone else thinks I'm funny *all* the time."

My mother met a journalist on a bus and told the woman I was her daughter. "*You're* Laurie Stone's mother?" the woman shot back.

Toby: "I thought she was saying I wasn't smart enough to be your mother."

Me: "She was probably surprised by your age. People often assume I'm younger than I am."

"She *did* ask how old you were."

"What did you say?"

"Thirty. What's it her business? With me you're safe, you're safe with me."

* * *

My mother grew up the child of poor immigrants, living without privacy in cramped quarters. She was bullied by her three older brothers, felt intimidated by authority figures and all non-Jews.

I recently saw a film by Anna Campion, the sister of Jane Campion, who directed *The Piano*. The film, *The Audition*, is a faux documentary about Jane Campion and the sisters' mother, all played by actresses. The mother had once aspired to act, so Jane offers her a role in a film she is making. The mother is nervous in front of the camera and flubs her lines, but when she relaxes she's brilliant. She cannot accept her daughter's praise, however, nor can she tolerate encouragement from others, insisting that she is awful and is being coerced to perform. She recalls a weekend retreat during which mother and daughter practiced "embracing their power." The mother says mockingly: "I never wanted to own my own life."

Early one morning she awakens Jane and asks whether she, too, feels anxious and despairing. Jane says she practices calming techniques and describes them, but her mother cuts her off. She searches the room, her eyes fretful. She gazes at her handsome offspring, and all she can think to say, pointing to her daughter's neck, is, "We should have had that mole removed long ago."

When Jane is typing in front of a window, her mother sets up a lawn sprinkler so that the water beats distractingly against the glass. When Jane readies herself for a bike ride, her mother harps on the dangers of the route but fails to pick up her fatigued child when, later, she sees her standing at the side of the road.

The mother complains about the arrival of guests: "I'm tired of shopping and cooking."

"Don't be a food martyr, Mom," Jane counsels, suggesting that visitors eat simply and be asked to bring provisions.

"You don't care about other people," her mother shoots back.

We see the mother projecting her self-doubt onto the landscape. We see the daughter shaping herself as not-mother, at the same time wanting to give her mother wings and jam her negative scan. Jane wants to compensate her mother for serving as a cautionary tale, but in the daughter's concern, the mother sees only condescension. She doesn't want to think her life needs fixing.

In childhood, I would push the idea of motherhood as far into the future as possible. I would pick a year, say 1984, and figure that by then, in my thirty-seventh year, I would have produced a child, maybe two. I wouldn't want to imagine this time, however, because I would think my life would be over.

My sister says that being a mother was the only thing she ever really wanted, and she had a child within her first year of marriage. My sister thinks that Toby was more destructive to her than to me: "You fought her and got your independence. I was treated like a doormat and I acted like one. Mom said she was protecting me, but she was controlling what I thought and did."

I remember my mother and sister fighting and Ellen sneaking out of the house. I worshipped her daring. My sister was inscrutable, furtive, and to me glamorous in her impenetrability. My mother said that Ellen needed her and that I did not need anyone. My mother said I could be trusted. She did not mean with secrets. She didn't mean that at all. She meant that I could look out for myself, that I was selfish.

My mother was a screamer. She didn't cry, though, while my emotions were written all over me, like a dog's. Toby would say something mean, then tell me not to be sensitive, not to be a baby. I didn't want to do what she said, but I didn't want to be a weakling either.

When Ellen and I were growing up, our father was peripheral, in that way of fathers in the fifties, coming home from work after we'd eaten. When we were small, he washed us in the tub. He woke us for school with back rubs and put us to bed with stories and lullabies, singing in a voice that went sweetly flat. He greeted family members and strangers, alike, with kisses, and he kissed people goodbye. He was smooth-shaven, always a fresh shirt and a cologne-scented hankie. Driving, he draped his arm over whomever was riding shotgun. He manufactured coats for girls—Ellen and I were his models—and several times a year he and the other manufacturers traded items in their lines. Boxes of dresses, sweaters, skirts, and pants were carried home triumphantly. He took my mother to department stores and bought her expensive clothes. It was hard for her to spend money, hard for him not to, even though, as a kid, he had been just as poor.

I was born by cesarean section, an operation for which my mother was not prepared and that left her belly scarred and slightly distended. I would look at the jagged mark on her stomach, thinking she minded it, but she would deny that she cared about her body. She said the pot belly was her fault. "The doctor told me to exercise, and I didn't. I was lazy." I didn't believe she didn't care about her body.

When I conjure myself at fifteen, a brackish taste fills my mouth and a musty torpor blankets the air. In a profile I read of Roman Polanski, he described his experiences during World War II. A Jew in Poland, he was separated from his parents between the ages of eleven and thirteen and had to fend for himself. When he was reunited with his father, the two could not get along, so his father installed him in his own apartment, a measure that scandalized the family but which Polanski claims to have appreciated: "It was a relief. After you're twelve, thirteen, it's too late to have parents. You don't need them anymore." I was seldom coerced to do anything. It would have been hard to coerce me, if anyone had tried. The problem was not being hostage to a crazy person but loving a crazy person.

My father used to say that Toby and I fought because we were similar. I didn't think so then, but he had a point. Neither of us wanted to be mothers.

I was toilet trained by two and a half but wasn't precocious in that endeavor, as I was, reportedly, with walking and talking. My shitting remained a bone of contention. Seldom does a conversation unfold in which it's not raised. My mother will reminisce: "You knew not to crap in your pants, but you did it anyway, stinking to high heaven. I would see this look come over your face. You did it for spite."

* * *

When I was losing my hair, I could not escape the specter of bald-ness. Out of my Walkman would cascade commercials for hair bond-ing. I would turn on the *Today* show, and there would be a panel of balding women. I would take my dog Sasha for a walk, and there, on Broadway, would be a hair ball the size of a fist. I expected it to talk.

On a late spring day, ensnared in hair-panic, I am walking down Broadway when I pass Toby, whom I have not seen in a year. She doesn't notice me, but I call out to her. Still she doesn't regis-ter my presence. I call again, and she turns, hesitates, then smiles. We embrace and go to a café, where my tears spill. "Don't do that," she says, the corners of her mouth curling into a smile.

A few weeks later I pick up the phone and hear a voice so wretched I'm reminded of soldiers in the Crimea with their guts spilling out. Toby has become dizzy and fallen. She says she is dying, but she declares it with the brio of a field marshal leading an at-tack. She demands I come at once, so I get on my bike and ride to her apartment, wondering if she will expire before I get there and whether taking a cab would have been a more charitable act. When I let myself in, I find her on her back in bed. She bellows, "Why won't you believe I'm dying?"

"Wouldn't you rather I *didn't* believe you?"

"You wait for any chance to destroy me. You want me dead."

I don't argue. I wouldn't be convincing. "Lovely to see you," I say, then repair to the kitchen to contend with the mound of vomit she has deposited in the sink. It's chunky, and, as luck would have it, her drain is clogged. She screams that no one has ever suffered such torment, as I slowly ease her puke down the drain, feeling this as retribution against the demon shitter. It takes an amazing amount of time to complete the task, but it is preferable to being with her in her room.

I had experienced my own version of motherhood two nights earlier, when, at three in the morning, Sasha had fallen off my bed and left a puddle of piss on the floor. As I was cleaning it, he scuttled into the living room and took a dump. He whined and fretted. I took him out, where he crapped again. Back inside and up on my bed, he peed. As I changed the linens, it was all I could do not to smack him. I feared he was slipping toward death, and at the same time wished for an end to his messes. Back in bed, he shivered. I covered him. He shook off the blanket and began panting. I made a bed for him in the living room, but he skittered around the floor noisily, while I tried to escape by thinking about sex. At seven he began licking his penis and excreting a bloody discharge. I got him to the vet, who diagnosed a bladder infection and treated him with antibiotics. The rest of the day was consumed with chores and his care. I cleaned the apartment and gathered laundry. Downstairs, the machines were filled. When I was able to secure one, it failed to spin-dry the towels, leaving them soggy, and I discovered that my new lavender sweatshirt was spattered with bleach. It was only one day.

I sit near Toby's bed, reading a newspaper and watching TV, as she drifts in and out of noisy sleep. Several times I go into the kitchen, and her voice rockets out, "What is she *doing* in there?" In Long Beach, we lived in a pressure-cooker house, where she did blow-by-blow commentary on my movements. If I took a shower, she would station herself at the bathroom and ask the door, "Why does she wash so much? She must think she's *dirty*." When my parents went out, I would hunt down the chocolates my mother kept hidden in the bookcase and the cookies she crammed into the back of cabinets. My mother was slender and beautiful. I was a mess.

When Audrey Hepburn died, Toby called. "I'm dying of colon cancer."

"How come?"

"There was a red blob in my stool."

I'm struck by the word *stool*, a term I have never heard her utter, even referring to furniture. She has become clinical, as if prepping for forthcoming medical discussions. I ask, "What did you eat yesterday?"

"Red pepper."

"That was the blob."

"How do you know?"

"The skins of pepper aren't digestible."

"How do you know? I eat red peppers all the time and never see blobs."

"Do you look at your stool, as you put it, every day?"

"No." Momentary relief. "I think it's blood. I'm calling Postley."

"Call God's Love."

"Why should I do volunteer work? I've sacrificed my whole life. Enough is enough."

"I'm not thinking of what you can do for them but what they can do for you. You need diversion."

"How do you know?"

"You're concocting illnesses."

Long inhale. "Don't think I don't appreciate you."

Toby doesn't look at people when she speaks to them but gazes into the middle distance. We are having coffee, when she says, in a faraway voice, "I was a little girl, and a woman came up to my mother and pointed to me, 'She's so beautiful.' My mother shot back, 'She took *my* beauty away.' I felt so guilty. Do you believe a mother would say such a thing?"

"Are you seriously asking me that question?" I try to meet her eyes. "Do you think I stole your beauty?"

"Get out. Of course not. Anyway, you didn't." She sips her coffee and returns to the past. "My sister was the rebellious one. I wanted to make things easier for my mother. She worked hard, under such difficult conditions. I had a job in a department store. I would get paid and run home with the money. I would scrub the kitchen floor because I couldn't stand the filth. She wanted me to spend my wedding night with her, but I said, 'Murray is taking me to a hotel. That's what married people do.'"

Toby says that her father worked long hours in a factory and would come home exhausted. "He would pat my head, to show he loved me, but he had no gumption. He couldn't say 'boo,' much less ask for a raise. He had brains, though, could read and write English very well. His family was much better than my mother's. He was headed for a decent life, but my mother snagged him. That's the story my sister tells. My mother had a lot of men, got herself pregnant, and figured she could hook this schnook."

"Do you believe it?"

Toby shrugs. "My sister hated my mother. She'd make up anything to get back at her. She'd say, 'Toby, don't you know what a witch she is?' I'd say, 'Etta, don't talk that way.'"

I have no memories of my mother and grandmother fighting. I remember them crooning in rapid-fire Yiddish, then laughing and embracing. My grandmother, who would cook for days before our visits, would load my mother down with shopping bags of food. But Toby did not have contact with her mother for the last ten years of my grandmother's life—did not know when or how she had died. Whenever I would ask about the rift, Toby would snap, "Don't dig. You're only interested in pain."

One morning when I was twenty-six, my grandmother called me, pleading for my mother's phone number. I gave it to her, and then my mother called me and screamed, "Traitor." She changed her number. The next time my grandmother called me, she asked where my mother was *buried*, saying she'd read in a newspaper that Toby had died. I assured her my mother was fine and said I would tell her about this call but couldn't give her the new number. My grandmother did not call again. I had seldom seen her since childhood, and she spooked me now.

I knew she had come from Poland, near the Russian border, but not why she'd emigrated. Now Toby says wistfully, "She was sent away from home by her mother, who kept her older daughter with her. They were killed during the war. My mother had all those kids, plus abortions and two babies who died before I was born. I wasn't supposed to live, either, but she willed me to survive. That's how she talked. She saved Ellen too."

"What do you mean?"

"When Ellen was born, she wouldn't eat, or she'd eat a little and throw up. The doctor said it was from my fear. I was anxious that I couldn't do anything right, and Ellen could feel the tension in my body. She was skinny, like a frog, and Daddy was traveling, so I went to stay with my mother. When she held Ellen, the baby ate."

"Why did you stop speaking to her?"

This time Toby doesn't cloud over. "She called saying she wanted to see me, that she was afraid she was going to die. I thought she wanted me, and I was happy, but it was a trick. She was looking out for her sons, always the sons. Saul's daughter was getting married, and she wanted to make sure I'd come to the wedding, give them money. As a kid, I couldn't bring a friend into the house because my brothers would threaten us and throw things. My mother turned them into bullies, let them do whatever they wanted. They were her men, substitutes for my father. I didn't go to the wedding, and I never let my mother bamboozle me again."

Listening, I note a pattern in the three sets of sisters in my family: my grandmother and her older sister; my mother and her sister Etta; Ellen and me. The mothers had clutched their first-born daughters with special ferocity, and at least two of them, Toby and Ellen, had started off sickly. The three older sisters—Toby, Ellen, and my grandmother's sister—became their mother's twin and felt suffocated. The three younger sisters—my grandmother, my aunt Etta, and me—were given freer rein but felt cast away.

I say, "Grandma couldn't treat you better than she treated herself. You were everything to her, but the world said that women were nothing, so you were both nothing. Sometimes your mother was hateful. Sometimes she was lovable."

Toby nods, then her face goes black.

My mother and I are on Broadway. She is seventy-eight but looks ten years younger, with her bleached blond hair, smooth skin, and youthful skirts. She is recalling a trip she and my father took to Pakistan. "He couldn't get over a haircut he got for twenty-five cents. Where were we? You see, I can't remember anything. I have that disease. What the hell is it called?"

"Alzheimer's."

"That's what I have."

"Not yet."

"How do you know?"

"You're not stupid enough."

"By then I'll be too dumb to understand what I have."

We duck into Shakespeare & Company and find an atlas. Toby looks up Pakistan and cries out, "Karachi. That's where it was." Back on Broadway, she takes my arm. "I'm walking toward Ninetieth Street, and it's very windy. Suddenly something is wedged between my legs. I look down and there's a head. It fits perfectly. I look again and see, no, it's a wig. Then this woman comes flying toward me, thanking me profusely." Toby's face fills with horror. "She had only a few, scraggly pieces of hair and a sort of tape down her scalp. I guess that's where the wig got glued."

She looks at me hopefully, wanting to charm me with her urban bumpkin routine, though she knows I am losing my hair.

"You could be talking about me that way in a little while."

"*That* won't happen to you." She whispers, "You look good, knock wood. I don't compliment you as often as you would like, because to me that's like asking for trouble."

We walk past Zabar's. "Goddamn that place. I got lured in and bought chocolates yesterday, and now I'm afraid to eat them. Last time my cheek blew up. Remember? I'll give them to you."

"Okay."

"But will you *eat* them?"

"I'll eat a few, and I'll give some to Natalie. She loves chocolate."

"Nuh uh. You can't have them. You give everything away."

"You mean the candy has to go through my body, so you can eat it vicariously?"

"Exactly."

She sashays off, flaring the hem of her stylish coat, with its stand-up collar that frames her face. "What do you think? I just bought it."

"It's beautiful."

She shows off the satin lining. "See, I took it from that old woolen coat Daddy bought me twenty years ago. Look how I sewed it in. The coat was a steal, not that I need to save money, only why should I throw it away?" She slips a pendant out from under her scarf, a chunk of turquoise, encased in filigreed silver. "Do you like it?"

"It looks like a mezuzah."

"You have a point. I can always put it over the door."

She wants to go to Burger King, where the coffee is watery and cheap, the way she likes it, but agrees to go to Edgar's when I say the waitresses come from Israel. She hungrily studies the pies and cakes at the front of the shop. When we're seated, she says, "I heard on the radio that people who overeat and gamble and drink too much have compulsions. What are compulsions?"

"God, Mother, why are you playing dumb?"

"I'm *not*."

"Okay, let's look at your compulsions."

She stops, affecting a mask of earnestness. "Oh, you mean when I drift off? And there is something else. Oh yes, when I interrupt people and jump in and talk about myself. That's very bad."

A waitress brings coffee and biscotti. Toby tries them. The waitress asks how everything is, and Toby says, "The coffee is too strong and the cookie is too hard, but food is of no importance to me." I take a cookie, and Toby says, "I see you as a little girl, like it was yesterday. You were wearing this coat that Daddy made. Everyone wanted it, because it looked so good on you. It changed his business. He became very popular after that. You wore the coat to a party and at night I found little frankfurters in the pockets. You said, 'For later.'"

"I still take food from parties. *There's* a compulsion for you."

"Why would you do such a thing? You can afford to buy food."

"It tastes better."

"It makes you look like a beggar."

"I feel like a beggar often." But she isn't looking at me. She's drifted off. I pay the bill, leaving a few dollars as a tip, and her eyes bore into the money.

She shakes her head. "You have to impress strangers. You think they'll love you." As I help her on with her coat, she leans in close. "Why do you hate *me* so much?"

When I picture my mother during my childhood, she is sitting in the den, holding a newspaper, staring into space.

When I picture my father, he is smiling because I've entered the room.

My mother says, "Your father recognized your talents right away. He said, 'Toby, she's a smart kid.' I said, 'Really?'"

I miss Toby even when we are together. There is always something missing.

On the phone she says, "I'm not leaving you any money in my will."

I think: Your dying will be enough of a gift, but it isn't true. She is only reminding me of how much I want her things, want her. The will is her last dangled hot dog.

After I left for college, she would disown me whenever we disagreed. The argument could be about Vietnam or the way to pick a cantaloupe. I would cry, and she would say, "Why do you take me so seriously?" After we'd reunite, she would deny she had ever been angry. She'd say, "All the hatred is in you."

Now she says, "I'm afraid to turn my back on you. You would kill me, like those Menendez brothers, and say I abused you."

"Why would I kill you if I'm not in your will?"

"For spite."

When Gardner was alive, I would call him in the morning to announce my existence. Now, sometimes, I think of calling Toby, although she becomes irritable at hearing my voice. The reliability

of her aversion and of my disappointment doesn't drain my desire.
I imagine (nothing else accounts for the repetition) that I can make
her love me. On the rare occasion that she isn't the first to reject,
I come face-to-face with my distaste for her. When the end of apart-
heid was announced, she thought it an atrocity for black people to
have their rights. I feel defeated by wanting to be loved by such a
person, and I cannot remember the way she makes me laugh. I have
not been loved enough, and I am insufficiently loving.

I had a lover who for years staged sadistic scenarios with me.
His name was Benno. He excited me, even just thinking about him.
He still does, although there have been other tops. The first time
we were alone I was on a couch in his apartment. He knelt beside
me on the floor. Then he parted my lips with two fingers and slid
them into my mouth. My chin went up, and something leapt in my
stomach, a snake out of a basket. He rubbed my gums and ran his
fingers along the edges of my teeth, pushing my jaw open. His fingers tasted salty, from pretzels, but I'd heard him wash his hands in
the kitchen before coming in, as if he were planning the move ahead
of time. I was wet without knowing why. What he was doing was
vaguely unpleasant, but I could feel my moorings coming loose, and
I liked that, the surprise, being caught off guard, being proved wrong,
being taken by the hand.

My lips went tight in resistance, as if I had to show that, or
maybe I wanted to resist, to see how he would surprise me again.
He pushed my teeth farther apart, inserting a third finger into my
mouth. It sent a charge through me, although I felt more uncomfortable and more directed by his hand, but the feeling of being
forced wasn't repellent, the opposite, pleasurable. It made me cocky.
I would have laughed if I could have. I felt that what was happening was my doing, mine, something about me that was having my
way with him, my way.

In and out his fingers slid across my tongue. I closed my eyes
and sucked. It was hard to enclose the objects in my mouth, which
now weren't fingers but instruments of control, whether his or mine
it didn't matter, or maybe it did, but it was okay because I was giddy.
I closed my teeth, feeling like a horse with a bit in its mouth. I
clamped harder, in order to hurt him, but I was afraid to exert too

much pressure, not because of what he might do in retaliation but because of what I might be capable of. He pushed my teeth open again. His hands were strong. He was a swimmer, lanky and dirty blond, his body almost hairless except for a fine downy goldness. Gardner's body was the opposite: brawny, big shoulders and chest, arms and back. Benno was closer to me, thin with muscle underneath, nerve endings close to the surface, hip bones jutting. When he kissed me, he kept his fingers in my mouth.

He played with my face, as if smudging the features. He put his mouth over mine, not a kiss, more like a patient breathing ether. He plunged his tongue into my mouth, and I swallowed. He kissed me until my lips felt sore, and I imagined my face becoming puffy and open. I held his face, licking his mouth. He took my hands, kissed them, and pinned them over my head, then he opened my sweater, button by button, thrusting his mouth onto fresh skin.

During sex he was focused on my arousal, wanting to discover my corridors of sensation, to establish new ones, probing me with fingers and tongue. He sucked my nipples, tugging at my pubic hair. He licked my eyelids while arousing my vagina with his fingers. I got lost in his hands. He slipped his cock inside me, straddling my hips, and stayed like that, not moving, not letting me move, making me feel that he knew me, parts I could only discover through him. The knowledge was in his flesh. This is where he lives, I thought, in sex.

He was less welcoming of my avidity, unlike Gardner, who could relax in my hands, allow me to tease out his pleasure. Benno's armpits had a clean, clay smell like earth after a rain. I licked the silky hair there. I devoured his cock with my mouth and hands, licking salty droplets from the tip. You could in those days. His cock was big, long and thick. Too long for a comfortable fit when he thrust into me. I maneuvered so I was over him, moving up and down, controlling the depth, but he couldn't stay hard. I wondered if, literally, this man had to be on top. He pinned my hands as he reversed our positions. He took lubricant from the drawer of his night stand and anointed my ass, then slid a finger up inside me, as he had thrust fingers into my mouth. He said, "Open for me, open for me everywhere."

I wanted to stay on his bed, although days earlier I'd had the same feeling with Gardner. It was the first time two intensely erotic relationships had arisen simultaneously. In the morning Benno said, "I knew you had a taste for submission, the way your head shot back when I put my fingers in your mouth." I submitted to that, but I didn't say so out loud.

Benno, alone, determined when we would see each other and what we would do. This made me angry, but once he agreed to sex the anger would seem to melt. I didn't know where it went. I was driving toward his capitulation, for it seemed, almost from the beginning, that he was resisting me. It didn't occur to me that he might have different feelings about our sex, might not like what we did or his role in the doing. I knew the sex excited him, and it confounded me that someone would squirm away from that. It surprised me, too, that though at first Benno had taken pains to seduce me, once he'd accomplished it his goal became to toy with me, hoping perhaps that I would resist him again and he could repeat the original scenario. He was an architect, interested in literature and art, and he liked to spin theories about culture. He said that when he met me he'd found me haughty, a little dismissive. It had made him angry, but he'd also liked it.

The first few times we had sex, his dominance was restricted to foreplay. He talked about things he wanted to do to me in a matter-of-fact way, as if suggesting he'd like to tie my hands and command me to kneel before him naked contained no kinky edge. He had no interest in exploring the meaning of our excitement, what it said about our pasts and characters. He dismissed psychoanalysis, maybe because he thought it would shame him, the things he might discover, and he thought that shame would make him too self-conscious to go on. If I introduced these subjects, even out of bed, he bristled scornfully. It was as if I were laughing at him, and in a way I was, because he was too smart to be this blunt. The dumbness was willful, like so much about him I recognized in myself.

The first time he drew me across his lap, I felt exposed. It was daytime, and light streamed over us. I said, "I have fat on my ass." He said, "I like the fat on your ass." He was looking at the part of my body that had most reviled my mother, the part where the shit came out. I was grateful he wanted to explore and lick me. I liked doing the same to him. Gardner was free there, Benno not. Benno didn't permit me the same reign of his body he wanted over mine. It was okay. I was with him now.

He ran his hands gently over my buttocks and thighs, so that the hairs feathered up and it seemed there was a force field around my hind quarters, as if a breeze were blowing, though the air was still and warm. He pressed down on the small of my back with his left hand. My body tensed. I liked not knowing what would happen because I did know. His right hand drew back and slapped me sharply, making a satisfying sound, like a tennis ball hitting the sweet spot on a racquet. The sting was pleasing. I took it for caring, a response that was automatic, something as natural to me as checking a mirror before entering a room. He paused between the slaps, circling my flesh with his palm before again coming down hard. He didn't hit me more than I could stand. I didn't know what that was.

When he tied my wrists or told me to kneel and lean over an arm chair, I sometimes felt embarrassed, as if we were staging a charade. But after a while I would lose my self-consciousness. I liked the thought of his leaving marks on me, even though I told him not to. During sex, I did not feel in his control, rather that I was casting a spell with my compliance, my appetite, goading him to betray his girlfriend with these infidelities.

Once, he sat on a chair in front of a mirror. He told me to bend over his lap. I didn't. He drew me into the desired position, sliding his hand between my legs, up into my vagina, and with his other hand gripped my neck. Open your eyes, he said. I saw us in the mirror. I was already wet. He had two fingers up me, and I thought my wetness would engulf us. Look, he said. He jerked back my head. Two tears escaped my eyes, from the pleasure and from the sight of my face screwed up and open. A finger slid into my ass. It felt like silk.

He would make me come, and then he would come, remaining inside me and draping his limbs around mine. We would breath together, a warm, fleshly mass. Semen would drip from my crevices, and it would feel gooily comforting. I would slide my hand along his backbone, counting the ridges. When he withdrew from me, I would slip his penis between my fingers, first one, then the next, then the next. Stretched out, with his eyes shut and his chin curling to one side, he would doze. A path of blond fur traveled from his pubis across his belly, up his sternum, and fanned out between his breasts. His skin was firm and clear, except for a series of scars on his hands.

"Where do they come from?"

"I smashed my hands through a pane of glass to stop my mother from crying once. I used to scrape my hands with a compass point in school."

He propped himself on an elbow and slapped me across the face. The sting felt familiar, although no one had ever done that before. "I like hurting you," he said.

I thought he was saying he loved me.

During our scenes, if I teased him or laughed, the mood would be broken and the session would end. I would be dismissed. If at some point I cried, he was charmed. From time to time he did say, "I love you," and I would feel relief, as if I could get him to care for me apart from what I was willing to do. He was close to his girlfriend and I was with Gardner. There was no chance of a relationship apart from clandestine sex, but it rankled me that he didn't want one, in fact protected himself from the possibility. That, more than anything, made him powerful. His advantage had been established almost immediately, and as soon as he claimed it we played the same scenario outside bed as on it, but while, in sex, I felt excited and victorious—even when I was being bossed and controlled—outside sex I was enraged.

Occasionally I would call him, and he would tell me to come up, or he would call me, and I would go to him. Most of the time he preferred to have sex after a chance meeting. Our spheres were close enough for this to happen periodically. He wanted to feel that the meeting gave him no choice. He toyed with me so that my desire was the first to spill over and all he would have to do was direct me. I would feel myself getting wet almost as soon as I laid eyes on him. I would wait for him to speak, and when he did I would wait for him to suggest a rendezvous. If he didn't, I would feel humiliated, assaulted, and I'd vow not to put myself in that position again. But weeks later we would meet, and the machinery would switch on. If he felt me slipping, he would behave seductively, and if he felt his advantage, he would up the ante.

We had known each other three years and were on a park bench on a freezing day. We were necking furiously when he said, "The next time we have sex, I will beat you." If I had not been sitting down, I would have swooned, so intense was the pleasure that radiated to my extremities.

"With what?"

"A belt, a riding crop."

"How can I agree?"

"It's up to you."

He wanted me to go home with him then, but I declined. I was late to meet Gardner. I thought that Benno had put an end to our scenes, that he had given me a condition I could not meet.

I don't remember the exact circumstances that prompted my next visit, but I can taste the need that would well from some shakiness in another part of my life, becoming an urge to grasp for love or conquest and at the same time be denied. I didn't think about the emptiness in advance. I didn't really want Benno as a mate. The thought of being his girlfriend held no charm. Though intelligent, he wanted an audience more than a conversation. He could become long-winded and grandiose. And since I didn't conceal my impatience and since my approval mattered to him, I could be as deflating to him as he was to me. It was nice being mean, though I could see how one would tire of it.

Once I was in a trance state, the thought of being beaten was as exciting as any other kind of sex. In a trance, my desires didn't feel crazy, didn't smack of damage, though they did feel perverse in a way that, in a reckless mood, I would have wanted to brag about to a girlfriend—lord over her my adventurousness—and with men use as a piece of seduction. I felt shame, too, although that went in and out like a shaky radio signal. I wondered about Benno entrusting me with his nature, for he was doing that, even though he acted like our activities were a standard feature of how men and women really were if they could be honest. I scoffed at this posture and at his unwillingness to gauge how his competitiveness and aggression shaped his other relationships.

Before going to Benno's apartment, I worked out at the gym, then took a sauna, imagining what he would do to me and realizing that probably, afterward, I wouldn't be able to show my naked ass in the locker room for a while. I breathed in the image, as if I were contemplating gifts, for that is what the marks seemed to me: a love letter. I perfumed myself, then constructed an outfit as close as I could manage to fetish gear: garter belt and hose, silk teddy, slinky black minidress, heels. When I presented myself, Benno said he was touched.

We went to a restaurant, where I moved food around a plate and discussed a play, but my thoughts were on the discomfort of the garter belt and on the pleasure to come, which by now was mixed with apprehension, not that Benno would hurt me but that I might not like being hurt enough to excite him or me. It was there, in that dilemma, that I could feel my surrender, for it didn't matter what I wanted. I wanted to give myself to his plan, and it struck me how conciliatory I was in these moments, how generous, the same way I was in sex, in a space free of judgment. In sex I wasn't weighing what I was getting against what I was giving, wasn't worrying that I would be cheated. I extended whatever the lover desired. Gardner treated people that way outside bed, not looking with scalpel eyes. Benno was like me: trained on power.

Once, on a walk, he spoke about his mother. Her name was Tally, and she had strawberry blond hair, blue eyes, and a slim, strong body. She'd been a competitive swimmer in her youth and throughout Benno's childhood had spent an hour each day in the pool. He said that when he closed his eyes he saw her in a tank suit, absentmindedly stroking her flat stomach. She had bragged about going back in the pool three weeks after his birth. Benno thought she had married in defeat, some time after she'd begun losing races.

I imagined his mother drawn to underwater sounds, musical and mysterious. To her the air was heavy and land a place where she felt sluggish and ungainly. I thought of her as unquestioning, not knowing why she'd stopped winning races—whether she'd lacked the talent or the drive. But while swimming her laps, questions had slid from her mind.

There was a thin scar across Benno's right cheekbone. You had to look closely to see it. When he was twelve, he'd sauntered home one night past midnight, refusing to say where he'd been, and his mother had slapped him, cutting him with her diamond. When she saw blood bead to the surface, her face had filled with horror, and Benno said he was glad because in that moment she'd become vivid instead of distracted. He said he had wanted to move toward her then but had stood his ground. A scene flashed through his mind, one he'd replayed often. He would see his mother walk into the ocean and submerge herself. He would watch, scared she might do something terrible. Waiting, he'd want her to sink, and he'd imagine her hair floating like seaweed and her face becoming soft and malleable. Then he'd think that she truly wanted to die, and he'd rush into the water and drag her out.

Benno opened a bottle of wine. We sat on the couch, face to face. He filled a glass and took a drink, placing his lips against mine, releasing the liquid into my mouth. He did it again. I kept swallowing. We were in a zone stripped of language, certainly of conversation. When he spoke it was to direct me. He said, "Take off your dress but leave on the teddy and stockings." He said, "Stand in the middle of the room and face the wall." I did as he ordered, glancing at him over my shoulder, and he told me again to face the wall. I felt ridiculous, me who loved to be looked at but didn't like following commands, even this one, and yet I complied, because it was what I had come to do. I was squeezing my body together, for fear it would spill over. But the effort was useless. All I could do was wait.

After a while he approached me and said I looked beautiful. I became wet in the breeze of his movement. I wasn't drunk. I wanted to take in what we were doing. What we were doing was so outlined for me it was a memory before it was a memory. He traced my collar bone with his tongue, tilting back my head so my neck was exposed. He circled it with his fingers. I said, "Don't," and he stopped. He said, "I want to fuck you in the ass." I liked hearing the words. I said, "It will never happen."

"Why?" he coaxed.

"You're too big."

"I can open you, so it won't hurt. I can do it gradually."

"It will never happen."

He let me kiss him, lick his face, though he had other plans before we went to bed. With a scarf he tied my hands behind my back, so tight I could not wriggle free. He led me to the couch and took me across his lap, positioning his erection so it jutted into my crotch, and I felt as if it were my erection, mine. I would have liked to freeze the moment: me stretched out in silk, his body warm against my skin, me not needing more range of movement, completely aroused. He spanked me hard, as if he were out of control, and I liked the intensity and my inability to move. He acted for us both, his fury expressing mine. The hurting felt so good I had no awareness of any other feeling.

Then he reached under a couch cushion and withdrew a belt, a hammer, and a nail. My first instinct was to laugh out of appreciation for his planning. That he had hidden something for me felt tender. He stood me up and carefully removed my remaining clothes. The hammer and nail confused me, though I wasn't afraid. I was never afraid. I trusted Benno, who had never lied, never gone back on his word.

We walked to the bedroom, then he took the ends of the scarf and nailed them to the top of the door frame. I felt ridiculous again, and I wished I didn't. It seemed churlish, like turning up my nose at a meal he'd prepared or a gift he'd gone out of his way to find. But there it was, the place he wanted me to go, to go willingly, a place I didn't want to go and that he knew I would find unpalatable, for he knew when he was bending to my will and when he was thwarting it. He wanted me not only to endure his test but to enjoy it, to come around, shed my skin, become a creature he'd transformed. He wanted me to be what I was not, in the same way I wanted it from him, from Toby, from everyone else on the planet, probably, but myself.

He said, "I will beat you ten times." I said, "Okay," or I said nothing. I didn't see the point in bargaining, and part of me was curious to discover what would happen. The other part resented being trussed in this position—standing on tippy toes with my arms stretched above my head and my ass in the air with no other body bracing it—and resentment began eroding my arousal. The feeling was closer to melancholy that I would never get mine from Benno. I would keep forgetting that, but now that the shabby reality was weighing in on me, I felt sad about being who I was.

My flesh already tingled from the spanking, so when Benno said, "One," and snapped the belt across my ass, I let out a disgruntled "ouch" that I think he liked. Before each whack he called out the number, and by four I was into it again, the weirdness more than the pain. I looked at Benno over my shoulder. He encouraged me to hold on, sweetly, the way you would a child you were encouraging to take her first leap off a pier. He paused between the blows, giving me time to recover but also drawing out the ordeal. By seven I had no problem with my position, the embarrassment fading as the welts on my ass rose in relief. It took so little time for almost anything to seem normal.

At the eighth whack, I cried out loudly because he was going over sore flesh. He smiled with a kind of crazy glee that I was letting him do this and he talked soothingly, as if we had to see the project through together and beating me was as hard for him as for me, and maybe in a way it was because, really, he was more out there than me, owning how much he wanted to beat the crap out of people, which I did, too, but he was showing it, raw and naked. Together, too, we were stepping off the cliff of ordinary life and finding ourselves intact. If I was in a trance, it was one of clarity. I could have held my own in a philosophical debate—hands tied and ass stinging—between the whacks.

The ninth and tenth lashes were amazingly painful, and all I could think about when he released me was the damage he'd done. But I had no chance to look in the mirror, for Benno ripped off his clothes, pulled me onto the bed, and made love savagely, as never before. The act wasn't merely devoid of finesse, it seemed impersonal, and maybe that's what the beating had been intended to accomplish: turn me into something generic, not me with my opinions and separateness.

I behaved well. It was still sex, after all, and I would not have dreamed of hurting his feelings by conveying my disappointment.

Not only that, it would have been bad sportsmanship; there weren't supposed to be guarantees. It was sex after all, where, good or bad, I would rather be than anywhere else, where I liked myself the most, feeling an ease and confidence I felt nowhere else. Benno got me going, and I came, but right after I started thinking about my ass and how I would need to cool it for a while with Gardner, who was conveniently out of town that week. After Benno and I were done, he guiltily appraised the marks he'd left, saying they didn't look that bad and massaging me with lotion that was somewhat soothing. Actually, the soreness was the best part, the part that still charged me and that I knew would continue when I left, when I was home, when I would watch the marks fade and feel a disconnected sense of connection.

Benno was tender as I rinsed off in the tub and while I got dressed, telling me how touched he was by my surrender, although I don't know if he used that exact word, by my what, willingness to give to him, to give, for that is what he felt I'd done, and I could see from his perspective it looked that way, and I felt a little false in remaining in my role the whole time, but I really didn't know what else to do and I was sad again, sad the way I always was when I hung up the phone with my mother.

My friend Helen is trying to get pregnant and at forty-five isn't having luck. Earlier in her life, she quit an unhappy marriage, learned to manage on her own, and fell in love with a man with whom she lives. She was a successful dancer and became a massage therapist. About her childless state, she says, "I was too fucked up to entertain motherhood earlier." I feel the same about myself but take a different tack with her. "We were the first generation of women who didn't *have* to embrace motherhood. We demanded all the choices we won. Even though maybe you and I won't get to live out everything, lots of women do." I tell her about Ariella, a beautiful nineteen-year-old who has taken care of twin boys for the past year. Ariella is learning to sing and has been told she can act, but she is painfully lacking in confidence. Ariella confided, "I know I have to make a life for myself before marrying and having kids, but I could so easily immerse myself in the care of children. With the twins, there are no strains on my abilities. Nothing makes me feel insecure. It's a drug."

At the gym, I tread the StairMaster beside a writer named Dean, a man my age with a twelve-year-old son and a wife named Danny. Danny, a biologist, earns more money than Dean, who makes his living as a teacher, and yet Danny assumes the bulk of the child care. I ask Dean if he considers this fair, and he says, well, if he thinks about it, it isn't, but he has little enough time for writing and Danny, who isn't driven creatively, has no need to work beyond her job. She would like more space for herself, but Dean won't cede it to her, since it means sacrificing his writing.

On other days, I lift weights with a cardiologist named Jim DeWitt. In addition to seeing patients, Jim teaches two classes each semester, supervises students, and writes short stories, two collections of which have been published. He says, "I have been married to two different women," meaning that his wife was one kind of person before becoming pregnant and another after. He says they began their relationship as social mavericks and now conform to conventional sex roles: He goes to work, while Lannie stays home and takes care of nine-year-old Molly. Lannie had been a professional caterer and now paints. Jim says he is surprised by his wife's desire to devote herself to their child. He would prefer that Lannie had a full-time job and shared the financial burden, but in another breath he admits being pleased: "I'm glad Molly is being raised by a devoted mother."

In another conversation he goes further, deriding the mothers of Molly's classmates, all of whom work. They strike him as harried and inadequate. "Feminism," he declares, "has failed them."

I feel he has attacked me personally, which, in a way, he has, but more to the point, as if his attitude has prevented me from becoming a parent, which is not the case, since none of the men with whom I considered having a child expected me to sacrifice myself. Fighting with Jim, I don't have to think about my envy of women who can just take the plunge. But it's less the women I envy—at least consciously—than men like Jim, and the envy is malevolent. I don't want to be in Jim's place, with a wife and child, but I hate him for his entitlement.

"Feminism hasn't failed them," I flare. "Feminism has given them room to change the family. If these women have been let down, it has been by husbands who shun parenting. The difference between those men and you is that they chose women with ambitions in the world comparable to their own, and although they may not be up to the challenge, at least they have engaged it."

I married Nathan at nineteen. Nathan—who wanted to be an architect or a photographer but instead went to law school—had a vision of our marriage. I was to attend graduate school, earn a Ph.D., and become a college professor with flexible hours: "So you'll have time for the kids. You can write on your days off and on vacations." I wanted to be Jack Kerouac and sleep on the Spanish Steps. I kept a diary and wrote poems and stories whose brittle tone did not mask their sentimentality. I was good at analyzing and arguing. I went to graduate school because I was afraid of doing anything else.

In 1968, Nathan was eligible for the draft, though he could get a deferment if he had a child, a decision about which he wasn't apprehensive. Far from it. He had been adopted and longed for a blood tie. He was tuned in to children: petting their cheeks and pitching his voice just right. He introduced the idea of my getting pregnant while I was taking a shower, and as the water streamed down, it seemed like ribs on a cage. I countered with the suggestion we join the Peace Corps or defect to Canada. I was willing to live in a remote village in a country I'd never heard of rather than get pregnant. I was willing to forfeit my citizenship, but to have a child, well, why didn't I just stretch out on a slab like Tess of the d'Urbervilles and die.

Nathan and I were accepted into VISTA, but we didn't go. There was a shakeup in the school system, and he landed a job (and a deferment) in the Oceanhill/Brownsville section of Brooklyn, teaching second grade. He taught a gaggle of kids to read; he calmed their fears, made them laugh.

After we split, he married a woman who did not work and who raised their two kids pretty much full-time. I went to London and met Graham, who sold drugs and his body. He lived in a ground-floor flat in Chelsea, with a toilet in the yard. After we'd been to-gether a few weeks, I hitchhiked around Ireland and came back to an empty flat. A note said he was at a rock concert in Somerset, so I snoozed on the bed, only to be awakened, Goldilocks-fashion, by three cops. Didn't I know there were drugs here? Where was my passport? I pulled my trench coat around me, but they didn't need that flourish to see what I was. "You don't want to be messing around with the likes of this," they counseled over tea in a sandwich shop. I said, "I'll never see him again." The next morning I found Gra-ham waiting for me in bed.

As a four-year-old in home movies, I am naked above the waist, throwing pebbles into a stream, staring into the camera my father holds as if I've never known innocence. "You're a hot kid," Toby used to say. "It's written all over you." She sees something true and disturbing. Ellen won't eat as a baby and is therefore like her, a creature whose appetites are masked. I came out hungry.

My father kept his condoms in the top drawer of his bureau, behind his cuff links and hankies. They were in a big box, because he always bought in bulk. I was maybe seven when I discovered them, lined up in neat rows, their scrolled shapes mysterious and alluring. I didn't know what they were, but I knew they were sex— the way secrets are sex.

My friend Deborah says, "You look at men so uncritically, you forgive them everything." My mother did not hit me, while my fa-ther spanked me. He pressured me to be magnanimous toward my mother, no matter what she did. When I objected, he would get all Lear-like and red-faced, calling me ungrateful and listing all the wonderful things he'd done. The night I got married, we were walk-ing to the rabbi's office, which was around the corner from my parents' apartment, when my mother launched an attack on Nathan's parents. Their crime: asking if two of their friends could attend the ceremony. Toby had said no. I wasn't given a say. It was Toby's wedding, though she wasn't really into it, the way she'd been into Ellen's, and I couldn't blame her, because I wasn't into it either. I was afraid of marriage the way I was of becoming pregnant, but at least with marriage you could get out.

Toby fumed at "the audacity" of Nathan's parents. I defended them, though I didn't like them, myself. I was stunned that she couldn't be nice to me. It hurt so much it lent the wedding a symbolic power it might otherwise have lacked. As we rode the elevator to the rabbi's office, Toby screamed at me, "Traitor," and after the ceremony my father blamed me for the blaze and said he never wanted to see me again. The scene was so Oedipal it was comical— my dad dismissing me as I was leaving him—but I didn't know it was Oedipal, so I didn't laugh. I never told him how I felt, for what would have been the point? This man did not apologize. While I could despise my mother with unstinting freedom, it felt unsafe to hate my father, even for a short time.

I was thirty-two when I hooked up with Gardner, forty-four when he died. He was twenty-six years older than me, with three grown children and a couple of grandchildren. He was graceful, funny, inexhaustible. He did not always keep his word. He did not stand up to bullies, and he squandered his talent on doomed projects. I tried to leave him several times, thinking I should be with another man, have a child with someone else. But I could not stop curling into his side.

Sometime in my thirties, I began sitting near kids on buses and staring at the down on their cheeks. I would lean in to smell them, amazed at their ability to walk and talk. I would picture myself arriving home to a little girl, the kid jumping up at the sound of my voice, her face radiant. Or the two of us would be walking the streets hand in hand. I was seeing myself with Toby, when being with my mother was a delight beyond words. Ellen would leave for school and my father for work, and I would loll on my parents' bedspread, as Toby slipped her breasts into a brassiere and slid nylons over her legs. Outside we would squeeze hands in little pulse beats, meaning, "I love you." She was the prettiest mother in the chicest clothes. We shopped, had lunch at the Automat, trooped to the park with shovel and pail. Then every afternoon, after Ellen came home, my lover dumped me.

In Wellfleet one summer I went to a dinner with Natalie and Marty at the home of a couple with two small kids. Four-year-old Trish claimed me for her own, and I was charmed by her as well. She thrust herself onto my lap, then herded me to her play room in a loft above the dining room.

"Which one do you want to be," she asked, presenting her doll house family, "the mother, the father, the sister, or the brother?"

"The friend."

"Okay, you're John. I'll be Nancy. Let's vacuum."

"Let's play with the dog."

"His name is Ruffie."

"Let's go to his house."

"We can't."

"Watch." I put John inside the dog house, and after a moment Trish sent her figure there, too. John slithered out the window and climbed to the roof. Nancy did the same, then she suddenly leapt off the building and soared through the air.

Trish's brother, Nick, clambered up the stairs. He was six: bright and mischievous. He sent the figures hurtling into car crashes and boating disasters, an ironic glint in his eyes, as if he were intentionally playing the boy. I spent an hour with the children, who were imaginative and uncomplaining, yet my attention drifted long before I left. From the loft, I could see the dinner guests below, hear bits of their conversation, and I felt as I had in childhood, when I'd been sent to bed but was still within earshot of the family. I would sneak out and position myself in the hall, where I could see a sliver of TV—until I was caught.

* * *

One day my friend Nora asked me to watch her kids while she
visited her mother. She parked her van and placed one-year-old
Sarah and three-and-a-half-year-old Zack in a double stroller, and
I wheeled them to Madison Avenue. The morning was mild and
clear, the kids entranced by the panorama. I thought: I can do this.
I'm on the streets, thinking my own thoughts, the kids are happy.
I sipped cappuccino outside a café while Zack petted a Scottish
terrier and Sarah wiggled her feet until her booties flew off. I wheeled
the kids to Betsey Johnson, and they were peaceful while I priced a
cat suit. But outside the store I saw a hunk chaining his bike to a
meter. It was all I could do not to go up and say: "This is not who I
am. I'm playing a part."

Toby is on the phone, regaling me with the eating habits, bus routes,
and medical histories of strangers, when I blurt, "Cut to the chase."
    "You're so impatient. You sound like an old maid."
    She doesn't mean that I've never married or that I've been
deprived of sex but that I haven't reproduced. When I was a kid,
she would describe childless women as "trees that haven't borne
fruit," saying they were "dried up and shriveled." Their bodies had
failed them, and they had failed their bodies.
    Whenever I'd confide to Toby that I was thinking of having
a baby, she would say, "I feel sorry for any child you would have.
You lack the patience. A child would interfere with your work.
You're an artist." She did not call me an artist at any other time.
At these moments, it was difficult to know if I wanted a child or
only to prove her wrong. I wanted to beat her at everything.
    On Saturdays and Sundays, the Metro Diner is bustling with
families. They crowd the booths beside the windows, and as Sasha
ambles along, I watch them. The tables are spread with newspapers, French toast, waffles, eggs, and sausages. Everyone looks
comfortable, casual, swathed in sweat suits and turtlenecks. No
one is rushing to be someplace else, and I feel cut off from the
human chain.

If I'd had a child with Gardner, the financial responsibility would have fallen to me, for Gardner barely scraped by. I feared that my dreaming time would disappear. But the last few years of Gardner's life, we played Russian roulette with birth control. I thought I would have the baby if I got pregnant, but in my fantasies the child was mostly with him. The baby would be sleeping or playing peacefully while he painted. I would be home, fourteen blocks away.

I liked the idea of being a parent. What I couldn't bear was being the mommy, the humiliation of that, the nauseating identification that was so basic I felt it in my gut before there was time to be dismayed.

When I was a teenager, my mother redecorated my bedroom with furniture and paintings I loathed. I protested, and she said I would be leaving for college soon; I should consider myself a boarder. In truth, though, often our parts were reversed, with me the one not jettisoned but in flight. In third grade, I attached myself to Linda, to whose rambling house I was magnetically drawn and whose playful, patient mother, Ellie, I adored. I didn't want to hear Toby's tires crunching on the driveway. One spring my parents went on vacation and left me with Linda's family for three weeks. It was bliss.

I tried to make Linda as jealous of me as I was of her. I would tantalize her with stories of summer camp, until the year we were eleven and she was allowed to go. I was a camp veteran, Linda a newcomer though a crack athlete. She needed my allegiance, and I abandoned her. It seemed crazy, but I couldn't resist it, swanning in the attentions of my summer pals. Numbed by my desertion, she sank, and by the time I sobered up, it was too late. She hated camp and would not forgive me, although it took two years for her to pull away completely.

Well into my twenties, I dreamed of the two of us on the beach, holding each other, grown up, though I saw her only once after childhood, an awkward reunion with a tense, young woman who had become a gym teacher besotted by bonsai plants. I remember the ride I took to her house when I was thirteen, a last-ditch effort to win her back. I went to the utility room for my bike, wheeled it along the narrow passageway, held the door open with my hip, sticking my right foot out to brace myself, and drew the bike over the threshold, which sometimes caught the back wheel. The bike was black with pink iridescent streamers at the handle bars. I remember the peculiar noise the gears made as I wheeled it, not the usual whirring sound but a sharp click, which I could not fix. I wheeled the bike across the flagstone patio, the nicest part of our claustrophobic back yard, on which sat a great octagonal slate table, topped with a ruffled Plexiglas awning. The hedges were twenty feet high, obscuring the house behind and creating an illusion of privacy that was broken whenever our neighbors, out in their backyard, spoke above a whisper.

Linda and I hardly ever played in my neighborhood, except to explore the canals and pester the horseshoe crabs that gathered by the shore. Some were dead but you could never be sure. We would study one, thinking it a goner—a big muddy blackish monster with a six-inch, serrated tail we called a stinger. Then the crab would start to move, slowly but determinedly, twitching its tail, not liking to be inspected by two little girls with a stick. Sometimes the boys who shot BBs would terrorize us, lifting the crabs by their tails, twirling them around their heads, and pitching them at us while we screamed.

We lived at Linda's house and at the ocean down her block. We played on a log embedded in the sand that became our boat, for we could perch on it, staying dry while waves surrounded us. Being islanded made us shriek with joy. Linda's cheeks were pink and downy, with a deep dimple in each. Her hair was crisp and brownish—wild. Her mother said she could never do anything with it.

I rode to her house and waited for her on the lawn. She looked more surprised than pleased to see me, but we walked to the beach, and in the dunes I cried telling her how sad I was that we were no longer close. I knew it was hopeless. I knew that she was lost the day, a few months earlier, I discovered my first period in the upstairs bathroom of her house and she told me that she'd had hers for a year. When I asked why she hadn't told me, she mumbled something about not wanting me to think she was "different," but I knew she'd kicked the habit of confiding. When we were little, I'd said we would marry when we grew up, not being able to imagine anyone else. Later, during sleepovers, we'd discovered our bodies with each other, staging naked shows under her desk lamp. I was captain of one of the kick-ball teams that played after lunch, and my first choice was always Linda, the strongest kicker, the fastest runner. She sat across from me dry-eyed and embarrassed, trying to comfort me by saying we *were* still friends. I would not give her up without a fight, though I could see in her puzzled eyes that the mission was futile.

In bed with men like Benno, I can be with my mother as I know how to be with her: alternating hope and despair. Outside bed, I relive the scenario with women, with four friends in particular: Alana, Mira, Ruth, and Joy. All are writers: brilliant, ambitious, and successful. Three are straight, one a lesbian. Two are stylish, two anxious about their looks. None has had a satisfying history with men. I hooked up with them in my early thirties, during the initial stages of my relationship with Gardner. I don't see any of them now, but the breaks are recent. These relationships sizzled, sputtered, and dragged on for more than fifteen years.

The friendships are romances gone bad. At first I'm treated like a puzzle piece the woman has been missing. I'm invited to dinners and parties, made privy to her deepest secrets. It's like being seduced by a man, except that when things go wrong—and even when they go right—my anger takes a different form with women than with men. My aggression toward men is open, with a seductive edge. Its rawest forms are pursuing married men and my own infidelity to a partner. In enticing a married man, there is nothing so thrilling as his first surrender, where I get to cut a woman too. If, out of bed, a man is ambivalent toward me, I leave.

The ambivalence of women, on the other hand, ensnares me. I think I deserve it. My anger is so devious that even the target doesn't always know what has hit her, only that a dart is impaling her forehead. Sometimes I "help"—present a slap in the form of a caress: sorting out the woman's problems, offering advice about how to fix her life. I parade my sexual conquests. When I seduced the husband of one of Joy's closest friends (though we didn't actually fuck), I was disappointed that she didn't cheer my accomplishment. What was her problem? Nobody was putting a gun to the guy's head.

When my troubling quartet of friends complained, I listened, feeling doomed by my nature and vowing to reform. It was hard for them to say what irked them, other than my self-absorption. Their tendency was to withdraw, and they weren't curious about their power.

Alana, more than the others, made me feel small. She was older than me, more achieved, a woman who strode through the fields of Manhattan chopping down dumb people with her machete. My eyes told her: "You are big." Hers said: "Yeah, that's right, I have a big mind and you have a little mind, and that's the way it's gonna be no matter what. You will never gain admittance to the table of worthies." What she could openly admire—in a way that made her feel squirmy in her overweight flesh—was my figure, clothes, and confident way in the kitchen. She liked making me the girl.

I knew things had soured by the fourth year of our friendship, though I hung in for thirteen more. (Think of every bad marriage you've known.) Alana had a cottage on the north shore of Long Island. Gardner and I drove out a few weeks after my father's death and spent a weekend. Gardner needed to return to the city. Alana asked if I would stay and asked if I could keep Gardner's car—if he'd be willing to go back by train. He said sure, and I told Alana, whose car was in the shop, that I'd spend a few more days with her.

I thought she wanted me, while in truth it was the car. Gardner went home and the next day Alana unveiled her plan. In a voice raised an octave and lurching along like she, herself, were jammed in first gear, she told me that Holly Trask was visiting a friend in the area, not close, about thirty minutes away. Alana was invited to the gathering but not me because Alana had met Holly's friend only once and didn't feel comfortable asking if she could bring a guest. Holly was Alana's latest conquest, although she was diffident, so Alana was wooing her with special intensity. Alana wanted to know if I would mind—and she hoped I wouldn't, hoped I would understand this had nothing to do with her feelings for me—but as a friend could she borrow Gardner's car and leave me alone for the day, relaxing or working on that article I'd said I had to write anyway?

Let's freeze the moment. Alana is pulling her hands through her blond bangs. She's reaching into her shirt pocket for a cigarette, tilting her head to the side and smiling out of the corner of her mouth as she asks for this favor, lying exactly the way I would to a lover I was about to cheat on and was offering the excuse for why I couldn't meet him at the museum as we'd planned but needed to check out a book from the library and would hook up with him at the movie. The analogy isn't exact because while I can't be with two men at the same time, Alana, who isn't fucking me or Holly, *could* bring us together if she wanted. That's where I get stuck, that she doesn't.

I don't act on the impulse to say no, I'm going back to the city, screw you. I don't want Alana being this cheap to me, so I pretend—I must pretend—that she's asked something reasonable and I am being petty to mind. I say sure, take the car, and she drives off, and I think she'll be gone a few hours but she stays away the whole day, until dinner time. I am alone for eight hours. I work and tell myself I'm getting something out of it, but as the hours creep by I seethe, not knowing whether I'm angrier at Alana or myself. When she returns, I don't tell her how I feel, for fear of losing her completely. I never tell her how this day works on me, that it's the beginning of my hating her in a personal rather than general way, as I sit on the lawn, reading stories by Ruth Prawer Jhabvala, writing on a legal pad, listening for the tires that don't sound until it's too late. It is too late when I give her the car.

A year ago at a theater festival in Montreal, I met Rick. He spoke first, outside our hotel, a wedding ring glinting on his finger, and I told myself *don't*. The next afternoon we sat together during a play. *Don't*, I said. We worked out in the gym and then had coffee. He directed regional theater in the Southeast and Midwest. A solo piece he'd worked on was being presented. We showered, and he came to my room before the next show. We sat on chairs. He had been married for twelve years. He had a stepchild, his wife's daughter, but she was grown and at college. He moved to the floor near me and took my foot in his hands.

He had never been unfaithful, but he did not seem anguished. We would be in Montreal for ten days. I said: "We get to say whatever we want, whenever we want, and the other one has to listen."

"Agreed," he said, and we went to buy condoms.

We talked about theater and our lives. He was a middle child, the peacemaker and anchor in a family with alcoholic parents. Until he left home, there had been no space for his imagination. When he was evasive with me, I tugged at him, and he did not pull away. After a rehearsal, I met him on the street, and he pushed down my sunglasses, wanting to see me looking at him. We bathed together. He said we were dogs. When it was time to part, I told myself to let go. When I entered my apartment, it had never felt emptier.

I drove to East Hampton to pick up Sasha, who was staying with a friend. I made my way to New England, to see other friends and more plays. Upon my return, two weeks later, there was a letter from Rick—chatty and amiable. Not romantic. I thought fine. He sent tapes of his work. I sent my novel.

He wrote cards and letters regularly. He called. I liked thinking I was on his mind. If weeks passed without contact, I told myself it was hopeless and felt the old sadness. At Christmas he sent a present. A few weeks later he called. He would be directing a play in Atlanta. The theater would put me up for three nights if I'd see rehearsals and offer feedback. He would be busy, but we would have time. I said it was crazy. He said he could handle it, could I? I said it was a mistake and booked a flight.

I told myself the trip was a lark, a bit of travel, a new scene, but all I could think about was Rick. At the gym, I inhaled men. I read gay porn, mesmerized by the inventory of body parts. In Montreal, Rick's hotel room had been on the third floor. I imagined myself leaping up the wall and smashing through his window. I wrote with energy. I was wanted by a man.

Before leaving for Atlanta, I learned that my friend Ned was dying of AIDS. He wrote for the *Voice*, mostly about theater and the epidemic. I had known he was HIV positive from the time, in the mid-eighties, he was diagnosed. But I believed he'd live. He was only thirty-six. I believed everyone I knew who was sick would live. For a long time Ned had evaded symptoms, but in one of his last pieces, he wrote about a virus that was now destroying his cerebellum—the part of the brain that controls motor responses, like breathing and swallowing. I left messages on his machine, sent notes. He didn't respond.

My time in Atlanta was as charged as it had been in Montreal, only now I was more besotted. The play Rick was directing was by Anna Lively, a memory piece with Southern Gothic strains. Rick lent it tension where it might have been sentimental. He pumped confidence into the actors and had the same effect on me. I forgot what was wrong with what we were doing, my life. I said, "I love you." He said, "You hardly know me." He said, "I will be in New York in March, with Jennifer. Will you see me for one afternoon?"

At home my mailbox became hot. I told myself to let go, spending more and more time at the gym. When I rode the subway, I didn't bring a book, knowing I would only stare into space. A box arrived from Charleston. I dragged it out of the elevator and tore it open in the hall, finding a basket of cakes, cookies, chocolates, and cheeses. I felt embraced, though the card wasn't a love letter. Rick sent a Valentine in the form of a jigsaw puzzle, which I had to assemble in order to read. He said I was entering his dream life. In another letter, he said I was consuming his waking thoughts. I wanted him to move to New York. I thought about the ways I could help him get work, not knowing if I really could. I wanted him in a way that did not admit doubts, though they flickered at the margins: worry I'd be sorry if he said yes, sorry I'd been a party to busting up his marriage, sorry I'd chosen a man I loved fucking but otherwise hardly knew. Could he hold his own against my will?

Ned grew too ill to be alone, so his lover Cary organized a schedule of visitors. Cary said that, eventually, Ned would suffocate: "I wake up every hour to see if he's breathing." When I arrived at Ned's apartment, the front door was unlocked, and he was sleeping on the couch. I called his name and touched his shoulder.

He opened his eyes with effort and shot me a lopsided smile. I hadn't seen him in several months, so his condition was shocking: his body frail, his face scaly, his left arm and leg limp, as if he'd suffered a stroke. He could not hear out of his left ear, and he had double vision, unless he shut one eye. His speech was difficult to decipher, but he kept repeating himself until he was understood.

I thought of Natalie's daughter Dana, with her brain infection and strokelike symptoms. I cried, saying I was remembering Gardner, and I recalled a trip that Gardner and I had taken with Ned. Ned had asked me to review a play in the Berkshires and had come along on the trip. On the drive, Gardner had regaled us with stories of his exploits as a naval aviator and his days in the New York art scene during the fifties. The three of us ate dinner in a funky fish place and after the show sneaked Sasha into the Williams College dorms. Ned had been single then. He was dark-haired, compact, and slender, favoring jeans and white shirts rolled up above the elbows. He had a slinky, catlike way and a readiness to be silly, but he was shy and he stammered at times. He let people know, through a sly merriment, that he was glad they existed. Every Christmas he presented ingenious presents to his friends and decked his apartment with a Milky Way of candles.

I filled him in about Rick, and he was all there: his sense of humor and intelligence intact. The illness would not touch these parts. I told Ned he could be grateful for that, flashing to the dementia that had seized Gardner when his calcium levels had spiked. At those times, Gardner had seemed swallowed in the terror and rage that otherwise did not surface. Ned had trouble swallowing, and he drooled. I feared contact with his saliva and felt ashamed of my anxiety, but every so often I slipped into the kitchen to wash my hands.

Rick rang my buzzer at one-thirty, and I was waiting in the hall when the elevator door opened. We embraced and did not let go. I said I wanted him to take us seriously and that I was willing to spend part of the year in Virginia. He did not flinch but said he would have to think. I said to take as long as he needed. This was the time for us to consider, but I could not continue as before. He said he thought about us all the time. He brought me yellow roses and a silk shirt. I cried when he got ready to leave, and he wiped away the tears, running his hands through my hair and saying it was hard for him, too. When he left, I plunged.

He called on Monday, admitting he was scared. I said, "Of course." He sent me a note saying he was haunted by demons. I knew the next time he called would be the end, and it was. I said I wasn't angry but I couldn't bear contact. I felt relieved to have things settled, until the next day, when I woke up looking forward to nothing, fearing nothing. It was late March, and the days were mild. I had thought spring would be unbearable if Rick and I ended, but the weather was soothing.

The next time I saw Ned, he had more difficulty speaking, but he was alert. First thing, he wanted to know about Rick, and when I told him it was over, he coughed up, "Better sooner than later, if it had to end." I relayed *Voice* gossip, and we talked about friends of his whose absences were perplexing. I told him I suspected that they were afraid of their helplessness, the knowledge that they couldn't do anything to change his fate. I had seen it with Gardner's sister, who had not visited him in the hospital. Perhaps such people did not believe they were going to die and didn't think they needed to rehearse it. Ned's face was hollowed, but there was a beatific quality to his eyes, an expression terminally ill people often assume of horror and empathy—as if they are registering sensation at a speeded rate. I felt Ned could see through me, which made it easier to express my predicament to him: the way understanding kept bouncing off, rather than penetrating, my psyche's oldest commands. He choked out a sentence saying he liked hearing about my life. He said that connection was all a dying person really wanted because that was all that could really be given. Not hope, not remedies. So there I was, suffering because I was being myself, and there was Ned, unable to walk, barely able to speak or swallow, gagging when he sipped liquids, but momentarily attached to life by my hump. I felt light, for it seemed that contact was all we had and all that mattered and that the rest that I did not have, well, it wasn't painful for the moment.

Recently my shrink asked—in a way not meant to be accusing but that had felt like an indictment—when I thought I was ever parental, able to mentor people, or maybe she meant just able to be there dependably. Maybe she meant being selfless, the way Natalie had been with her daughters, wanting to be a fountain. I had been able to care for my dog and for Gardner when he was sick, but I couldn't say that being needed was an unalloyed joy. With Ned, though, I didn't need to feel needed. I just didn't want to turn away.

The next time I visited, he was sleeping in the living room, with a hospice attendant present. I sat by his bedside and spoke into his good ear. He was attentive, seeming little worse than the week before. His speech was more slurred, but he kept diving for air and huffing out words. I drew an alphabet board, so he could point to letters and spell out words. I asked what was on his mind, and he spelled, "I don't feel cheated." Then he spelled, "I wish I'd written more," as if to say he *had* been cheated. I said that was what all writers thought. I said he'd inspired love in his odd, distant way, and asked how he explained that? He smiled and spelled out, "I'm not demanding."

The next time I saw him, he was weaker and could barely communicate. A tank of oxygen was beside his bed. He looked wasted and haunted, his body shriveled to fetal defenselessness. He could barely grasp a pen to point to letters. I took his hand, but he could not squeeze mine back. Trying to speak, he became frustrated, but finally I understood that he wanted ice cream. I fetched a pop from the freezer, and he ate it, slurping and licking with determination, his sense of taste remaining keen—even exaggerated—in the dwindling of his other powers. I helped him hold the pop, and cream dripped down his chin and over my hand. I cleaned him. I asked if he wanted his back rubbed, and he nodded, turning onto his stomach with his arms over his head, a position I found erotic, which made his proximity to death all the more visceral and the tissue dividing being and not-being all the more fragile. I worked on him for a long time, and he purred as I traced his body with my hands. It was open to me now, though in the past we'd seldom touched.

He died three days later, a Saturday, at 9 A.M., with Cary by his side and his best friend Eleanor there, too. He had been admitted to the hospital the previous day, wanting any shred of life still available, not foreseeing the anguish that awaited. He had been denied food for the previous two days and was ravenous and enraged, believing that he could swallow, though in fact he was inhaling food into his lungs. A feeding tube had been inserted into his abdomen, but it had been hooked up incorrectly, so his stomach continued to gnaw. Although the problem was corrected, Ned did not wait for its benefits. He spent his last hours in a morphine euphoria, then he stopped breathing.

The funeral was on Monday, a brilliant, cloudless day. A caravan of cars made its way to a mausoleum in Queens, where Cary's father was interred. Ned had loved Cary's parents, who were accepting of their son's gayness. Ned had not come out to his own parents, who were devout Catholics, and they had resolutely kept at bay not only their son's gayness but also his AIDS. They had blinded themselves, even though they'd visited Ned and Cary many times and knew that their son was terminally ill. Ned had spared them the disclosures, sparing himself too, but the silence had been depressing. When his parents had visited, he'd felt run through the wringer, especially by his mother, who refused to acknowledge his condition and instead chitchatted about neighbors and her pet canary.

Ned's siblings, to whom he'd been out, were at the ceremony, amid a crowd of Ned's friends. We placed purple tulips on the coffin and spoke of him, evoking his AIDS activism and his love of Cary, and the words sailed like arrows into Ned's parents. They stood near a marble wall and, small as they were, seemed to shrink further and recede into it. It was hard to feel sympathy for them and difficult not to. They seemed only now to be registering the extent of their son's journey from them, searching in this man they did not know for the baby who had once been as recognizable as their own flesh.

* * *

It is June. I remind myself that I want someone with whom to share my life, but the thought becomes feathery. I dream that Rick has a male lover in addition to his wife. The male lover is possessive, and Rick has difficulty fitting me in. My shrink offers: "You think you're not man enough for him, that you don't measure up. The reason you couldn't have him isn't because he has a wife but because you are too puny."

Natalie and I are on Broadway when we run into my mother, the first time the two have met. Toby is outside the Burger King, smoking and staring into space. I call out, "Mom," twice, loud. She is orbiting in a different warp, her lipstick half chewed off. When she registers my presence, I introduce her to Natalie. She doesn't say "Hello" or "I've heard so much about you." She dives into a monologue, pointing to me and saying to Natalie, "You have no idea how gorgeous she was as a baby. I was afraid to go out with her because someone might steal her." She glances at me. "Remember that boy in the A & P? You were five. He said, 'She's ruined me. How can I marry anyone who doesn't look like her?'"

When Toby leaves, Natalie says, "She does seem crazy. She doesn't look you in the eye, and the drifting off. I can see she was pretty, though, the dimples."

That night Toby calls: "I liked your friend. She's genuine. She won't stab you in the back."

Toby calls a week later: "Postley is concerned about the congestion in my lungs."

"Does he know you smoke?"

"Are you crazy? Do you think I would tell him a thing like that?"

"How many cigarettes a day?"

"Seven."

"If you quit, your lungs would clear."

"The last time I did, my body blew up."

"You can control what you eat."

"It's not the eating. It's the metabolism. At my age, you blow up if you stop smoking. It's a fact."

"So you'll blow up. At least you won't die."

"You wish for my death every day, but it won't do you any good. You're still out of the will. I wrote a new one. I swear."

She says that Ellen's daughter, Stephanie, who is going to be married in the summer, is planning to start a family right away. "Ellen is going to quit her job and move to Boston. She doesn't want to miss a minute with her grandchildren. She said, 'Ma, you're coming with me, even if I have to drug you. I'm not leaving you alone.'"

"What would you do in Boston? You know how you love New York."

"Of course, but you don't understand what it is to be alone. At least the other one cares if I live or die. If I get sick, I have no one to make me a cup of tea. You don't speak to me for months. I'm going to depend on you?"

Another day Toby calls: "I'm on the phone with Ellen, and I feel my teeth getting loose. I eat a sweet potato, and I get scared, so I call the dentist. It's Saturday, but he says he'll come from Jersey. Imagine that. I go up in the elevator, and I see him in his coat, opening the door to his office. I go running over, and as I thank him, my teeth fall straight out of my mouth onto the carpet. I pick them up. I'm embarrassed, but I'm more relieved I haven't schlepped him there for nothing. I hand over the teeth. 'See?'"

I laugh out loud, and she laughs, too, and we will not stop. "I wanted to be a WAC," she says, "because I loved the uniforms. I would have looked good. You would have seen pictures and been proud."

* * *

I am perched in the window of Starbucks on a Saturday night, gazing at the Broadway parade, which is Noah's ark, everyone strolling in couples: arms entwined, faces expectant, children in snugglies. I have five male friends who are married to women twenty years younger than they are, men who were wild and are now having babies.

I am watching a dog tied to a parking meter, its head jerking this way and that, its tongue peeking out, its ears cocked and nose aloft. When another dog is scented, its tail wags furiously and its paws pounce.

Kids are sitting on the sidewalk in a circle: two girls and three boys, early twenties, with backpacks—classic vagabonds, with long hair escaping rubber bands, and wrists and ankles encircled with macramé bands. They are smoking cigarettes, thinking they own the world, which they do, and I slip back to the cannibal me, sleeping on the Spanish Steps. It is so alluring to be unformed, to curl up, to be stopped. After Benno tied my hands, he cradled me sweetly.

According to Santayana: To be happy you must have taken the measure of your powers, tasted the fruits of your passion, and learned your place in the world.

Sitting in the window of Starbucks, I have a clue.

Pipe to the Head

JERRY STAHL

SOMETIMES THE SMELL OF FLESH COMES BACK TO ME. BURNING FLESH. The way the glass pipe singed my lips when I couldn't let go, when I could not get enough smoke in my lungs, could not suck hard enough to obliterate the awareness of where I was, what I'd become, what the rest of the world was shrieking, whimpering, and hissing at me through the walls or out of the blinding sky while I was scorching my own mouth to keep from screaming back.

This is true. I have whole months I can't recall. I've managed to retain squibs, details here and there, but mostly, it's not unlike a fainting man's memory of the swirls in the ceiling: the last thing he sees on the way out, the first thing staring down at him when he comes to again.

When, in the midst of a ten-year smack run, I had the bright idea of countering my heroin addiction with rock cocaine, I lost whatever tenuous shred of control I'd managed to maintain up until then. It made sense, at the time. I had no veins that hadn't caved: I'd burned out my neck, my legs, my feet, my arms, and the backs of my hands. There was a good vein in my dick, but the one time I tried it, my fingers shook so much, in the grips of some junked-out stop-and-go palsy, I missed by a mile and my balls swelled up like distended apricots. They stayed that way for a day and a half. I wasted three good bags of dope.

The thing is, I hated crack, so of course I couldn't stop. After the first high—those two or three blissful, arrhythmic minutes—you spend the rest of your time trying to get it back, chasing that neuro-orgasm, until you end up some quivering, tweaked-out heap, hearing voices and trying to pluck leering pygmies out of your eye-balls. Years go by.

Oddly, there's one memory of the period—more like a vivid, staccato movie trapped in my brainpan than an actual memory—of a week or so spent mired in the narcotic Amazon of downtown LA. I can't tell you exact dates. I only know it was around the time I started shitting blue. I'd come to around ten or eleven in the morning having chugged tureens of Robitussin DM to counter the effects of the crack I'd smoked the night before. I'd guzzle two or three bottles if there were no downers around—this was, you'll re-call, my stay-away-from-the-needle regimen—and end up spray painting the toilet an electric cobalt every three and a half min-utes before hobbling back to my mattress and sinking to a twitchy sleep again.

But where was I? I start remembering this stuff and it's like I start reliving it, and when I start reliving it it's as if the same mind-set, the same muddled, toxic-smog-in-the-skull that sent me career-ing through days so racked with confusion and disgrace it was all I could do to drive in a straight line, without swerving to avoid vi-sions of my father's corpse or crawling babies in the street, returns full-blown to my psyche.

But I was telling you how I got lost. How I hooked up with a recent LA County jail graduate named Sammy and ended up los-ing a week or so in the wilds of MacArthur Park, the Cecil Hotel, a Travelodge on Olympic Boulevard and other Stations of the Narco-Cross on the downtown drug circuit.

What happened—and my windshield, I have to repeat, is still a bit filmy—what happened is, I was stumbling around in my usual fashion, trying to cop on Sixth and Alvarado around noon, when this snaky black dude showed up and insisted he knew where to get the good shit. The real down, bonaroo brain-fuck stuff.

Which I guess he did. Because the next thing I remember, it wasn't morning anymore. It was ten o'clock at night. The same day or a day later. And it was me, Sammy, and a strawberry named some-thing like "Rulette," who could not have been more than fifteen, sacked out on the toast-colored, cigarette-burned bedspread of some no-doubt five-star motel. (A strawberry, for those of you who've led less festive lives, is a young lady who will do anything for crack. This usually means giving head, but it can also mean, you know, *any-thing*. . . . That's her job.)

After copping a couple handfuls of rocks that morning, I agreed, under some kind of weird duress, to stop in at said motel with Rulette and Sammy. Thinking, no doubt, to complement my otherwise ho-hum semi-existence with a taste of *that* reality—and get some better drugs.

Sammy, see, was a funny guy. Animated to begin with, he shifted to hyperspeed at the prospect of a pipe in his mouth. I mean, I'd seen him around. He was a guy who hooked—that is, hooked up a buyer with a seller, for which socially redeeming pursuit he'd receive a hit, a piece, three or four rocks, maybe half of everything, depending on how intimidated whatever sorry basehead he was playing turned out to be.

Anyway, here we are in this roach parlor: Whiteboy Me, Small-Time Sammy, and this sloe-eyed junior high dropout whose vocabulary seemed to have shrunken to only the necessary. In this case, three words: *Gimme pipe . . . C'mon, gimme some pipe.* Or maybe that's six. But never mind. Trap La Toya Jackson in a sewer for three weeks, withdraw food and shower privileges, and you have a handle on Rulette. She wore a sleeveless Lakers T that came to her knees, and when she reached a hand out for a rock I saw her arms were full of red blotches. Sammy saw me looking and slapped her arms away.

"Ain't that ugly?" he barked, shaking his wafer-thin head and spitting on the carpet. He was always spitting, like he had some-thing in his mouth he just couldn't get out, but not for lack of try-ing. "Thass what happens you suck too much rock. S'all that fucking salt in the baking soda, that shit they use to cook it up. Hound them hotcakes long enough, you get all that Arm and Hammer shit runnin' roun' inside. You get the sodium poisoning."

He took the docile crack ecstatic's arm, barely wider around than a tube of toothpaste, and raised it proudly.

"Gotta smoke a whole hell of a lotta yimyom to get them blotches. Ain't that right, baby? Gotta suck that glass dick a beau-coup long time."

He let her arm drop limply to her side, then whipped his head around and cackled. "She ain't that old, neither." We both looked back at the skinny, sullen girl slumped on the ratty bed. Everything in the room shone a weird shade of yellow. Bright yellow gone to grime. It smelled like whoever'd been there before us had died and stayed a while, without benefit of embalming fluid. Sammy baited the child some more. "Straight up, girl, your mama must have given you a pipe to suck on in your crib 'stead of a damn bottle."

That's how it was. I remember this day, with weirdness on all kinds of levels. Not the least for how I tried to tell Sammy that the credit card paying for the room was stolen. The name on the card was GERALD STAHL. While mine, I told him, was Hank Snow or Buddy Blitz, I forget. The thing is, I felt like an impostor. As ever. (It didn't matter what world I was in: Yuppies or Writers, Husbands, Daddies, or Dope Fiends, I didn't belong. I was the Universal Faux-Boy.) I wanted to be a down gangster like him. To live, or so it seemed from the outside, a life devoid of ambiguity, driven by rawer discomforts than alienation and self-loathing.

In short, I wanted to be a *bad* guy, instead of a *fucked-up* one. On the Great Chain of Cool, evil—or at least *criminality*—seemed infinitely sexier than angst. And passing my own American Express card as fruit of a successful mugging marked my way of fitting in. You didn't want to look lame, you know, in front of a guy like Sammy. Enhanced by chemical stimulant, I outdid myself describing the surly customer I had to hit upside the head with a tire-iron. Oh sure, he put up a fight. He grabbed me by the Adam's apple, see, tried to bite my nose off. I believe I may have even dragged my victim out of a car, a chocolate brown Beamer, and stomped him for holding out. His wife, who happened to be a beautiful redhead, with a throat wrapped in diamonds, actually wanted to come with me. That's how damn macho I was.

I don't think Sammy bought my little saga. Gaunt as a med school skeleton and puke green, I doubt I could have mugged a coma victim. I might, at most, have scared someone into giving me their wallet—*"Hand it over or I'll bite you, motherfucker! You don't want to catch what I have!"*—but the likelihood of overpowering anybody larger than the late little suicide, Herve Villechese, was far from likely. On the other hand, he didn't press me. Out on the street, lying is just another form of breathing. Everybody does it. Nobody takes it personally. . . .

So there we were: just a couple of OGs and their moll, fresh into our first rest stop, when Sammy tells me, "Listen up, homes, we gots to do the *farm thang.*"

"Farm thang?" I heard my voice come out weirdly high, like some wannabe homeboy trapped in a helium vault. "We ain't smoked more than a couple rocks, and you're going Greenjeans on me." I don't know who I thought I sounded like, but it didn't impress my partner.

"Fuck that, man. Talk normal. We pick this strawberry fresh, you know what I'm sayin'?"

"Well, kinda . . ."

"C'mon man, you brain-fucked or what? *Shee-it!*"

"You don't mean . . ." I believe I actually gulped. "You don't mean with *her*, do you?"

"Whassa mater with Rulette? She got teef, don't she? Most of the ho's down here don't even have no teef."

"Yeah, but Sammy . . ."

"Shee-it," he said again, shooting me the look that only a streetwise African-American can give a Caucasian like myself. "Guess I gotta show you everything, huh?"

He sneered just long enough to let me know the immense respect and esteem in which he held me. Then he began speaking in distinct, insulting monosyllables.

"First, you stick this glass dick in yo' mouth. S'called a pipe, see?"

As he talked, he swiped at my pocket and grabbed the thing, a standard-issue, straight-from-the-street, three-inch stem of charred brown glass, a tattered chunk of Chore Boy copper—the bit through which the actual cocaine is sucked—burned gray-black and still jammed in the tip. He waved it for a second, then shoved it in my mouth, nearly chipping my front tooth.

"Okay. You got the pipe, now you get the bitch."

He grabbed the girl, who'd been slumping dully against the wall, staring off. She seemed flimsy as a rag doll. But less enthusiastic. I watched in a kind of horrified stupor.

"Don't worry, this is what she do. Suck the cock, get the rock. Straight bidness. Yo, Ru . . . party-time!"

The girl gave an unsmiling shrug as Sammy took hold of her shoulders. He pushed her down till she kneeled on her bony knees, then pulled my thighs apart and shoved her between them. He reached for my zipper and yanked it down before I had a thought to resist.

"Okay, whiteboy. Now you put your joint in Rulette's mouf. . . . You can do that by yourself, right? Shee-it, now I'm gonna slam you a big motherfuckin' rock. A *big* motherfucker! Yeah, baby. I fire that up, you start suckin' while she suckin' on you."

To this day, I don't know what accounts for my strange passivity. Or worse, maybe I do. . . . It wasn't like I was actually intimidated. More like I'd become too apathetic to care at all about my own behavior. Let him shove me around a little. Let him insult me. Get me to do something I had absolutely no interest in doing. I couldn't have cared less about sex, let alone my once-vaunted liberal views about the exploitation of women. The fact was, I didn't care a whole lot about anything, as long I could get high enough not to have to. The fatigue engendered from hauling around all that desperation made questions of dignity or appearance as irrelevant as fashion. Any behavior was fine as long as there were drugs at the other end. There was such infinite relief in just *not having to think*, it was a kind of drug in itself.

"All right," he hollered, breaking into a one-toothed smile. "All right, now we all set up. You go 'haid, homeboy. *Go 'haid!*"

He hit the lighter, watched while I inhaled and Rulette began her listless oral assault.

"Thass right. Thass right," he repeated, going over the instructions like a father coaxing his child on his first bike ride. "Keep that damn pipe up! Keep your join in Rulette's mouf here . . . Uh huh! Uh huh! Let my girl do that skanky dick. You jus' take a huge motherfuckin' hit while she chomp your johnson. All right," he sang, watching while it all unfurled as planned, dancing a peculiar little jig on the motel carpet. "All right, you farmin' now, pardner! You shoot your thang while you brain be blowin' sideways, you farmin' *bigtime*!"

And so I was, in a way, alternately pounded by a pleasure that made me choke back vomit and launched into some sideways world where green-eyed insects peered at me from nests inside the walls, their writhing pupae spilling from the plaster while I sucked and gasped, blinking from the acrid smoke pasting my eyeballs and the twin dead voids in the eyes of the child in front of me. I touched her cheek—it felt like gum on a sidewalk—until that hot sad swamp of a mouth seemed to swallow me whole and the world went black and I twitched into a falling dream and back awake to klieg lights and cackling laughter and the television blaring in the next room, or maybe the next city: "Oprah, I knew mother had a problem, I just never knew what it was . . ."

There were a couple more motels after that. Somewhere I lost my wallet, then we lost Rulette. I saw her step into an El Camino with a couple of Mexican guys, then saw her Lakers T-shirt fly out the window as they tore around the corner of Sixth and Union. Then we ran out of options altogether. That's when we hooked up with another local, a brother named Delmore we picked up in front of the Cecil Hotel, and things got weird.

Sammy and I were waiting on San Pedro, I don't know for what, and Delmore came running out of the hotel holding a telephone—a whole telephone, ripped right out of the wall—followed by a screaming Armenian in a wifebeater wielding what looked like a hacksaw in one hand and a garden trowel in the other. I never figured out about the trowel. But Sammy said he knew D. from way back, so we followed him around the corner to the alley where he ducked beside a pair of burned-out car seats waiting for the Armenian to chill. I remember a rat nosed out of the stuffing, glared at me, then skittered over my curling toes and through the broken glass and piss-stink into the alley's shadows. I remember how much I wanted to follow it.

"Get me nine bucks for this phone," Delmore told me, by way of introduction, "there's a lot of dudes won't mess with a phone. Me, I always grab that motherfucker. That motherfucker always be good for half a rock. Get Big D. 'least a taste of that hamburger helper, you know what I'm sayin'?"

"Delmore always be thinkin'," Sammy said. "I be knowin' his ass since forever. We used to get high with Rick James."

"*Way* high," Delmore snickered, and then they both fell out laughing.

"Yeah, oh shit, *yeah* . . ." Sammy slipped into a coughing fit and kind of choked his words out. "Don't be giving *that* nigger any matches to play wif. That motherfucker get lit up, he like to start burnin' on some bitch's titties. I seen 'im waste half a pack of Kools just firin' 'em up and puttin' 'em out on some poor ho's nips." His voice went husky, he was doing his homeboy Rick: 'Gonna light me some cherry-bombs, fellas. Gonna light me some pretty-titty cherry-bombs . . . !' Shee-it, thass why they locked his black ass up."

"Spooky dude," Delmore agreed, nodding with either disgust or appreciation, I couldn't tell.

They shot the shit in the alley a few more minutes, then Delmore and Sammy came up with an idea: We'd rip off a crack crew he knew five blocks away. We'd take my car. I'd drive and do the talking. They'd hide in the back. A swell idea all the way around.

At the time I still had my Cadillac. One of those ugly mid-eighties models with the boxy rear, painted a heinous goldfish-yellow the human pompadour at the used car lot called "Champagne." This was the squarest ride in the world. The perfect retired accountant vehicle. Ideal for the Young Dope Fiend on the Go.

Every time I started to say, "I don't think this is a good idea" or "maybe we should wait," Sammy'd lurch west and smack me across the back of my head. I don't know why I let him hit me. He did it in front of Delmore. In front of people in the street. "Where's the motherfuckin' lighter?" *Bam!* "Yo, gimme a motherfuckin' dollar" *Bam!*

It would have been humiliating if I were capable of humiliation. But I wasn't. The emotional sensors were burned out. I couldn't feel, period. Even self-loathing was a flight up; it would have required awareness. And by now whatever anger, whatever trauma or disappointment or dread had driven me to drugs in the first place had been obliterated, along with any shred of ego, by the drugs themselves. I just stumbled along. Like some cracked-addled cousin of Lenny in *Of Mice and Men.*

Until finally, idling at a red light on the way to our first stab at taking off a street dealer, he whanged me on the back of the head, and, without thinking, I whanged him back. Caught him with a backhand across his mouth. This time Sammy broke into a smile. "My boy! My boy's learnin'. My boy do fine in the joint. Ain't no motherfucker gonna take his white ass for prime steak pussy . . ."

"Yeah," said Delmore, with a strange little chuckle, "but I bet he look real fine in a slip."

They cracked up again and I just kept driving.

I realize, now, how all this sounds. How insane. But when you're out there, in that psycho-toxic whirl, when all the lights are blurry and all the sounds are far away and one foot just marches unsteadily along behind the other, normal standards don't apply.

The truth is, maybe I wanted the shame. Maybe I needed to break through the barrier of my own self-loathing, sink into some whole other region where I was not just shit in my own mind, *I was shit in front of the world,* beyond even trying to put up a front—like some ash-dappled Saddhu stumbling through the streets of Calcutta. Slap me. Berate me. Pluck the fucking dollar bills out of my pockets and spit in my face. Just as long as you give me drugs. I was, at this point, one of *those people* you see in the street, not quite scabbed and drooling but not, you know, "normal" either. The kind you look at, as you edge to the other side of the pavement, and wonder: *How did he get that way? What the fuck happened to him?*

* * *

Don't ask on what block our mini-criminal venture actually took place. It was dark. I was loaded. And, by then, more than a little distressed by the burning that accompanied my piss since Rulette's loving ministrations. At every chance, I dug my penis out of my pants to check it out, wholly convinced I'd be sprouting a lesion the size of a dung beetle any second. I don't know what the deal was with the strawberry's strawberry mouth. Like Grandma Essie used to say, *"You don't know where it's been."* (Except, in Rulette's case, I had a pretty fair idea. Which is what scared me . . .)

It hit me, in some random flash of clarity, that I was about to commit a dangerous act, a stupid, violent, potentially fatal act. I've never been scared of death—that is, of *being dead.* What scares me is the *process* of dying; or worse, living on with my lips eaten away, my intestines in a plastic bag, or my ass running with bed-sores, a hyperaware flesh cabbage. (In my hairiest scenario, I'm lay-ing there, looking comatose, while all these people—people I used to think were, you know, *friends*—mill around talking about me. They don't know I can hear. And what they're saying: "I never really liked him." "Did you ever notice he had this *smell?*" "He was a bigger asshole *without* the drugs." confirms some bone-deep sense of myself as a total loser, a deluded skeek who believed, despite a monstro streak of self-consciousness and doubt, that there were at least a few people he could trust. Only to find out, when they stand there chatting over my veg-tone flesh, that this was just another delusion. Something I'll have forty more years, as the nurses change my bag and mock my penis, to contemplate thor-oughly.) In other words, I didn't want to do it. But I didn't want to do anything I was doing. This didn't stop me from doing it, though. I could not go on and I could not stop; I'd hit the Sam Beckett phase of addiction.

But *that's how it happens.* One minute you're fine—fucked up but *okay* with it—the next you're neck-deep in a world you don't want to have anything to do with. *And don't want to leave.* Because that's where the drugs are. And that's how I ended up at the corner of Crack and Eightball, at two in the morning. Me and this car full of paraphernalia, crack crumbs, empty balloons, and my two new, friendly African-American perps, Sammy and Delmore.

The first time we tried the Drive and Jive, my already crack-ravaged heart nearly slammed out of my chest. The young homeboy who leaned in my window, handing over the rocks, looked like the coverboy for *San Quentin* magazine, Mexican mafia issue. He had a head shaped like a small cannonball, shaved to the scalp, with a single tuft up front so soaked in *Tres Flores,* fave pomade of the Eighteenth Street set, that the sharp, sweet stink of it burned my nostrils. Three tattooed teardrops showed below his right eye. But I could never remember if those meant "I dusted three people" or "I did three years in the joint." Either way, the thought of reaching in my pocket, pretending to pull out a wad of cash, then snatching the product and stunt driving off into the night packed about as much appeal as gargling lightbulbs. Of course, I thought about suicide all the time. But that was on *my* terms; I didn't feature some adolescent Vato doing the job for me.

In my haste, and idiocy, once I'd made the grab I jammed the car into reverse and slammed into the crate behind me, an idling fruit truck, before peeling out and barely missing another cluster of entrepreneurs halfway up the block. There was yelling. Frantic Spanish. I saw a doll fly by the window. Then somebody fired something—Sammy said "sawed-off" in a voice so casual he might have been reading from *Newsweek*—but whatever it was did nothing more than scare the shit out of me. Which is just as well. I had Triple A (I was prepared), but I didn't know their policy on bullet holes.

Flushed with success—we'd fishtailed around the block, where it was suddenly, eerily quiet—I wanted to shoot back to the motel and hose off. I'd never felt a rush like that. Never. Just pulling it off without dying—hearing that *boo-yah* rattle the windshield and blast a trash can—got me high as a weather balloon. I was dying to get fucked up again. All the more so as the thought that the *cholos* we'd borrowed drugs from might have a few amigos in La Eme began to worm into what passed for my consciousness.

By the time we got three blocks away I felt like I had a face full of piranhas. Paranoia gnawed my spine. I imagined gang signs flashing corner-to-corner from here to Tijuana, somehow spelling out WHITE GUY WITH MOLES . . . UGLY CADILLAC . . . SHOOT TO MAIM.

In no time I imagined entire posses just dropping what they were doing, abandoning their lookouts to track down the *blanco* in the piss-colored Coupe de Ville. But my crime partners—whose job, I now realized, consisted of baiting me into doing this shit, then laughing about it and taking half the drugs—were of a different opinion. Entirely sanguine.

"I gots ta see Scotty," Delmore kept grunting. "I want that mofo to beam me up! I *gots* ta see Mister Scott . . ."

He'd been babbling that, almost nonstop, since we got in the car. But I'd paid it no mind. Crackheads say all kinds of shit. I've sucked the glass dick in rooms where guys dug their heads under pillows, where they locked themselves in closets with .38s, where they talked to their dead mothers for three hours after two puffs. And all of it, of course, between the endless minutes spent plucking the carpet for crumbs, looking for white flecks of anything— plaster, dandruff, calcified mouse-droppings—to put in the pipe and smoke. Delmore's deal was standard *Star Trek*. Which was fine. Until it meant I had to take a bullet in my ear for getting his ass up to the fucking *Enterprise*.

Now, though, I was ready to prevail. I was the one driving, after all. However newly spineless and devoid of will I might now find myself. Except that, on the way back to our rent-a-dump, half-way down some unlikely sidestreet, there they were. The perfect marks. Two skinny hombres who could not have been more than fourteen. Waving us down like a couple of long-lost friends. I pulled over and they rushed the car.

"*Cuánto? Cuánto?*"

The skinnier kid wore his flannel shirt down to his knees, over pressed khakis so wide he could have housed a family of six. He had the rock out of his boxers and in my face before I'd even hit Park.

"Um . . ."

"All of it!" Sammy chimed up from the back.

"Thass right," Delmore seconded, "we want all that mother-fuckin' kibble. Jus' lay it all out. My man here got the cake for all this shit."

Both passengers leaned forward. Sammy loomed so close I had to inhale the jail-stench still on him, a fetid cocktail of cigarettes, BO and stale drawers.

Skinny handed the stuff over, and this time I hit the gas without ever pocketing the rocks. He was still doling the shit out when I floored it and the stuff spilled into my lap. The kid's wrist smacked into the window frame. His homeboy expected the move. He must have. We hadn't made three feet when the crash caught me cold. The rear windshield shattered in a spray of diamonds. A brick clunked into the front seat, but I was still thinking *shotgun*, like before, and tore forward blind, my head down, my only thought that now I had a Caddy full of loose crack and a dead black dude in the backseat.

"Fuck," I heard myself screaming. *"Fuck!"*

"Yo! We done *game* their tortilla ass . . ."

"Adios, burritos!"

It was Sammy and D., not dead after all. The two brothers thought the whole thing was funny. Delmore laughed so hard it sounded like screaming. Sammy's came out as a kind of groan, and his eyes kept meeting mine in the rearview. At some point daylight had rolled in. I had this sudden image of the three of us: a tweaked-out candyass whiteboy driving a pair of homeless black—one still sporting his county jail wristband, one schlepping a stolen telephone—in a bigass Cadillac with the rear windshield caved in by a brick. Why not, I thought, just make a giant sign for the cops and tape it to the trunk: DRUG ADDICTS—PLEASE ARREST!

We rolled around for what seemed like hours, smoking and driving. We didn't go right back to the motel because of the feds. Or the CIA. Or maybe the Mexican mafia, La Eme, again. I forget. Whatever, Sammy was sure they were after us and Delmore swore he could hear them on his phone, despite the wires dangling off it connected to nothing. Whenever I saw a helicopter I got sparks down my spine. On some level, I knew this was rank insanity; on another, my nerve ends were so scraped raw, so many faces danced in my peripheral vision, that every tree trunk might have been a man in black. Every car that whooshed by seemed charged with menace, packed with handguns and cell phones, steered by sneer-

ing gangsteristas or law enforcement professionals who smirked
when they sailed past.

Finally, we pulled into a deserted parking lot, under the
Hollywood Freeway, and took turns firing up our ill-gotten booty. I
wanted to fix, too. I had the rig in my boot and a chunk of tar I'd
been carrying around. I could never bring myself to leave shit in a
motel. I wanted it *on* me, and the idiocy of sliming around festooned
with bloody paraphernalia rarely crossed my radar.

Somehow, after we finished our narcotic repast, I found
myself back in traffic, and it was rush hour. That happens on crack:
You go in, you go out, you come to, and all the entire time you may
have been parked on a couch—or aiming your car down Wilshire
Boulevard at five in the afternoon. Which is where my own frayed
little magic carpet dropped me off. My eyes just seemed to fly open,
at which point the pipe popped onto my lap and the sizzling rock
fell onto my crotch, instantly burning through my foul pants and
down to the skin of my dick. I scooped up the white boulder, screaming, then jammed it in the pipe, rammed it in my mouth, and
slammed into the back of the RTD bus in front of us at the same
time.

"*Shit!*"

My head hit the wheel. Hard. I banged a gash in my forehead and had to check the rearview to wipe the blood out of my
eyes. But I could not stop long. While my passengers hooted—this
was high comedy to them—I swung through the lane to my left,
cut down the nearest sidestreet, nearly smashing a grape-colored
Mazda, and got away without slowing to look back.

How could I? It was five-something in the afternoon. I had a
pipe in my mouth. A syringe in my shirt. Crack chips and dope
crumbs stuffed in my pockets, lumping my socks, and no doubt all
over the floor of the car. It was beyond hopeless. The problem was,
in the accident, my front end had been fully accordioned, and my
car could barely stagger forward. Black smoke poured out from
under the hood. It was Bhopal on wheels, and I was steering.

Sammy howled directions back to Travelodge. And the three
of us ducked inside after stashing the car around back behind a
mysteriously abandoned semi. I don't think I killed anybody, but

for all I know some triple amputee tipped out of his handicap seat and flopped like a hooked trout until he died—all because yours truly fucked up and hit the gas and bailed.

Things were careening out of control. I was doing shit I never dreamed I'd be doing. And it was only a matter of time before I'd start paying the consequences. Paying more, at any rate, than I had already paid. Like every other erstwhile middle-class fuckwad, I'd always wanted to be black, always wanted to give some physical form to the cartilage-deep alienation I'd felt since I was seven and found out first grade was pathetic and my parents geeks. (They didn't *make* me feel worthless, it just seemed sort of a given, like gravity or having two elbows.)

That's the thing. I loved the adrenal weirdness of being *Out There*, in the Street, doing my narco-business. But what I really dug was the idea of justifiable rage. (If you were black, you *had* to be mad, but what was a well-fed whiteboy's beef?) I envied the inherent and imagined grace and cool and built-in badass status. I wanted to be intimidating, and all I could manage was disturbed. But still . . .

Now that it was *on*, unfortunately, now that I was running with a couple of genuine ghetto-bred jailhouse nightmares, it wasn't like I was any cooler at all. In fact, I was lame beyond all concept of lameness. Why? Because, for one, I imagined this up-close-and-personal proximity to my African-American pals would render me a sort of honorary brother. Or, more mortifying, I thought at the very least it entitled me to some sort of lowgrade Mac Daddy status. In fact—there's no way around it—these motherfuckers were as tore-up and out of it as I was. The only difference being, my brothers-in-basedom enjoyed less padding between their asses and the concrete. And they'd taken a lot more falls.

But so what? My needs were simple: I needed to be fucked up, and I needed to be out of it—in every sense of the term. If there was a world I belonged to, by virtue of race, birth, class, or education, there was no surer way to blow a hole through the other side of it and tumble down than sucking in a brainful of cocaine smoke and letting it douse everything in my skull before blowing it out again.

This wasn't about "getting down with the brothers," this wasn't about turning my bourgeois back in a bourgeois gesture before scuttling back to my bourgeois life. Not even close. This was, for better or worse, about obliterating all the options. Climbing up to the top of the high-dive and draining the pool before diving off. (Does this make sense? *It doesn't matter*.) I just wanted off the map, out of the game. Call it transcendence through jeopardy. Bad as things got, I never found anywhere I belonged more than among those who belonged nowhere.

And that's it. There is no more outside status, or at least, in my case, no more outside-*feeling* one, than that of stumbling sleepless and incoherent around a neighborhood of souls for whom you are, at best, invisible, and at worst, one of a countless legion of skeeks stomping the concrete looking for one more hit, one more fix, one more momentary chemical nullification of their own existence. It's not merely, as Dr. Johnson would have it, that "he who makes a beast of himself gets rid of the pain of being a man." It's that he who gets so high for so long doesn't give a fuck *what* he is. At the other end of all that pain is a certain freedom—you're never coming back, because, if you're doing it right, you can't even remember where you left. And I was doing it right. At least for a while.

It was just after this, against all odds, that I caught a break. After three days and nights holed up in the motel, I decided I had had it. I'd been up seventy-two hours. It was time to go. So I snuck out of the room. The Korean manager, I'm sure, was less than thrilled to accept a check from some pie-eyed bobo bleeding from the eyebrows. But I slipped him a twenty along with the bad paper and he chilled out. He was, he confided with a five-tooth smile, just filling in.

Here's when I got lucky. What happened, see, is that the Caddy wouldn't start. I turned the key, jimmied the ignition, opened the hood, waved my palm over the engine and spun around three times. Nothing. And so, as if I were still civilized, I pulled out my Triple A card, summoned a tow truck, rode bitch with the driver back to Hollywood and dumped the car in a boarded-up Exxon station before proceeding on foot to the apartment I'd sort of forgotten I had. . . .

The next morning, when I straggled back to Chez Exxon, the land yacht was gone. There was another gas station across the street, and thinking I'd got turned around—my senses were so dulled, after years of dope and coke, I just assumed I was wrong about everything—I checked that one too and came up with nothing more than strange looks from the Egyptian owners. Imagine! Some poor fuck had actually *stolen* the damn thing.

In a sudden fit of legitimacy, I reported the theft to both the LAPD and my insurance company. And, to my infinite delight, LA's finest called back before the day was out to say they'd found the car. But—and here the lady dispatcher's voice lowered with real grief, heartfelt empathetic regret at what our society had come to—but whoever'd made off with my pride and joy had banged it up pretty bad. (I had not, needless to say, reported my earlier tête-à-tête with the back of a bus.) What's worse, she continued darkly, dope and paraphernalia were found all over the car. The thieves must have been *drug addicts*!

"It looked like a bad dream in there," the policewoman sighed sympathetically. All I could do was click my tongue and sigh right back. Just a couple of decent people trying to make sense of an indecent world. "It's a shame what's happening to this city," she offered. "They said it must have been a pretty car, too."

I said it was and thanked her. Then, heart pounding in a frisson of guilt and glee, I called back Allstate and asked them to put a rush on the check. They'd seen the police photos and declared the Cadillac a total loss. The blue book for my make and year came to fifty-two hundred dollars.

The whole episode had left me pretty shaky. But I learned my lesson: no more crack. That shit was just too self-destructive. Enough was enough.

I'd spend the five grand on heroin.

My Father's Picture

CATHERINE TEXIER

I WAS ABOUT FIVE YEARS OLD WHEN I SAW MY FATHER'S PICTURE FOR the first time.

My mother put the picture in front of me on a table and said: This is your father. I remember how her voice sounded forced, dramatic, angry. The accent falling on the last word, *père*, in French, the *p* exploding out of her mouth like spit. In the background my grandmother sat in her big, tapestry armchair, knitting one of her lavender sweaters, humming her disapproval with guttural sounds.

I remember how the words, *ton père*, sounded like an insult. How they suddenly emerged from the murky waters of a secret, never to be pushed back into hiding. How they would haunt me. How I wished I'd never heard them in the first place, how I never wanted to hear them again.

I remember not wanting to look at the picture and, when I did, my cheeks and chest burning with shame.

My father's picture was a small black-and-white snapshot with dented edges, two and a half inches by three and a half. It was slightly overexposed, washed out. A young man was standing in the sunlight, slender, his eyes pale, squinting, his hair swept back in a careful wave, wearing an argyle sweater and a pair of flannel pants. He looked like a complete stranger, someone who didn't look at all like me.

I am describing that picture from memory. The last time I saw it was after my grandmother's funeral in Paris. I was looking at the family photo albums and filling a shoe box with odd snapshots and other mementos that I wanted to take back to New York. That photo, of course, was not in any photo album. It was lying at the bottom of a drawer with a loose bunch of other forgotten snapshots. I could swear I took it and sneaked it to the bottom of the shoe box. But maybe I didn't, because I can't find it anymore. It seems to have vanished. And my memory of it seems to be receding, too, my father's features whitening, fading into the background until all that remains is the outline of the argyle sweater and a pair of clear eyes floating up from the past.

Ton père. So I had a father. The secret of my birth was finally revealed. My birth wasn't something that had been concocted between my mother and her parents. There was a stranger involved, too. And he was mine. My father. Out of the blue I had made him exist. It was all my fault. As if father and daughter formed a disgusting, shameful bond.

My mother said his name was Michel Seulliet. That he was a doctor. At the time that you were conceived, she said, he was a medical student. *Conçue* is the word she used. *Conceived* is a word she would often use in connection with my father. And of course it was exactly the right term. His contribution to my existence was just that: the conception. He is from Auvergne, my mother went on, the center of France. You are from there, too, half *auvergnate*.

And I felt the chill of that unknown heredity thrown upon me like a mantle of ice.

My school was a few blocks down the street from my grandparents' house where we lived. It stood in the middle of a shady garden on a curved corner lot surrounded by a wrought-iron fence. Ecole des Lacs, it was called. Run by nuns. My grandfather would walk me or drop me off with his car. Sometimes my uncle, who also lived with us—he was twenty-five years old and just out of business school—picked me up on his Vespa after Saturday morning class. In the morning, when we arrived at school, we had to take off our shoes, put them in our cubbies, and put on a pinafore and a pair of slippers for the day. In the afternoon, when school was over, we had to do the whole thing in reverse: take off the pinafores, remove the slippers, put the shoes back on. There was always some pushing and shoving and giggling. One day a kid from my class asked me out of the blue: *Il fait quoi, ton père?* What does your father do? I had been dreading that question. Kids were always asking about everybody's dad. It was important, a way to define each other socially. Moms were assumed to be housewives. My father? I have no father. But I didn't say that. I didn't miss a beat. I said: He is a doctor. And the kid was satisfied, went on putting on his coat and shoes.

But I was caught. It was a lie. There was no doctor in my house, nobody who could qualify as my father. I had given that kid a completely wrong idea of what my family was, and who I was. Next time the kid would probe further: Is this old man who drives you to school your father? Is this man with the Vespa your father? And I would have to lie some more.

After that I asked my grandfather to drop me off a block away from school, or if my uncle wanted to pick me up, he had to wait for me down the street, a little way off, so that nobody would see him. I determined that no kid would come to my house to find out the truth.

There was no father.

No one ever asked me again about my father. I thought some-times some of the parents looked at me funny, but then I thought *everyone* looked at me funny. I just assumed everyone knew, even though no one said anything. Especially since no one said anything.

Years and years later, when I first thought about looking for him, meeting him, it was this absence, this invisibility that held me back. How does one bring to life a ghost?

It is not even that this man had left no trace. He had never been there in the first place. Nobody in that house, nobody that I knew had any connection with him. He was nobody's husband, nobody's son-in-law, had been nobody's friend. I, who had never even seen him, had somehow caused him to be. Had caused all the trouble. Without me, nobody would ever think about him, would even remember him.

My mother didn't say anything else about my father that day. She didn't say whether she had ever been married to my father or not, she didn't say if she had ever lived with him, she didn't say if she had loved him, or if he had loved her, she didn't say what had happened to this man. Maybe she assumed that I knew. And in a way I did. I didn't bear my father's name, but her name, and all the administrative letters she got were addressed to Mademoiselle Paule Texier. I was just learning how to read, and I knew Mademoiselle meant that she was not married. Later she bought a gold ring that she put on the ring finger of her left hand so that people would think she had a husband. I am sure she did that for me because, as far as she was concerned, she didn't give a hoot.

We were in the dining room of my grandparents' house. My mother had put the picture on a side table under the bay window overlooking the front garden. To the left of that window was a veranda draped with wisteria, and under the window two red bushes of rhododendrons in full bloom, and beyond the bushes was a large round lawn, and beyond the lawn, two massive chestnut trees flanking the front gate. We had just moved to that house from an apartment near Paris. It was a white, turn-of-the-century villa, in a plush and leafy suburb, typical of Paris western *banlieue*: two- or three-story houses with slate roofs and deep, secret gardens enclosed by stone walls.

The day we moved into that house, I climbed up to the first floor but the steps were so steep and narrow that I was scared to come down, and I had to sit on the little triangular landing and wait for someone to rescue me. That landing had a perfect view of the front door and hallway. Later, when my mother would come back late at night and my grandparents were waiting to ambush her in the dining room, I used to tiptoe to that landing and stand in the dark and listen to their screaming insults and fights.

It was already the fifties, but it's as if we were caught in a time-warp. My grandfather was born in 1885 and my grandmother in 1893. And there was no question that this was not a modern household: There was no TV, a record-player was not introduced till much later, when I was a teenager, and a strict routine ruled every moment of the day, not only the alternation of meals and work and rest, but also the days of the week: laundry on Monday boiled and stirred by hand in a tin washtub heated by coal, ironing on Wednesday, fish on Friday, there was a day for polishing the silver and the copper and another day to do the windows, a day to make jam from the garden plums and quinces in the big copper cauldron, and so on.

My grandparents were from Vendée, an Atlantic province just south of Brittany, perhaps one of the most fiercely Catholic regions of France. Vendée is known for the rebellion of the Chouans against the French Revolution, its reactionary attachment to the old values of Church and royalty, its suspect embroilment in super-stition and magic. Actually, our family had been pro-revolutionary in 1789, but a thick cloud of dark beliefs hung over the house, most of them emanating from my grandmother, who professed an inti-mate acquaintance with the devil.

Sex, in particular, was the evil weed that had to be uprooted. Both my grandparents were obsessed by my mother's sexual life. My grandfather's mother had left her husband and small children to run away with a lover in Indochina, only to return seven years later to have another child with her husband, and both my grandmother and grandfather, who were first cousins, had been traumatized by the scandal. The memory of that adventure hung silently over our household. My grandparents spied on my mother, listened to her phone calls, clocked her comings and goings. In their psychodrama she was the fallen woman, the whore, the bad mother, and I was the innocent victim. But I didn't feel like a victim, I felt like the dirty product of my mother's freedom. I was—literally—sex incarnate.

My mother played her part to perfection. She bleached her hair platinum or dyed it red, wore pink lipstick and glittery nail polish and wore tarty clothes à la Marilyn Monroe: waist cinched so tight she had to loosen up her wide belt a couple of holes after eating, spike heels, breasts pushed up into a deep cleavage, and mascara out to there. She drank too much and smoked cigarettes and danced and went out at night and had affairs and generally outraged bourgeois propriety. She probably didn't have the wild sexual life she was given credit for: She told me that often she didn't come back home because she had had dinner at a friend's house, and if she missed the last train back to the house, she would stay over for the night. According to my grandmother, demure wives trembled for their marriage when my mother sailed through a party, her breasts balanced on the cups of her push-up bra, followed by an entourage of men. Whore! Husband stealer! my grandmother hissed behind her back.

By the time I was born, my mother was thirty-two, so she had had plenty of time to hone her part, including the time to have outgrown it. She had another life—she worked full-time as a secretary for various American firms, as she spoke fluent English—but at home, she was locked into an unchanging role, that of a provocative teenager, driving her parents crazy.

I hear the key in the front door. My mother's coming back late, well after dinner's over, after I have already gone to bed. I imagine her tiptoeing across the hall in her stockings, her shoes dangling by thin straps from her fingers. My grandmother steps out of the kitchen, her hands screwed on her hips, lips pinched to a thin line. Where have you been, tramp, she spits. Who do you think is taking care of your daughter when you're out slutting?

At this point, I have stolen out of bed and have perched on the triangular landing. I stand in my flannel nightgown, watching. My grandfather emerges from the dining room, shuffling in his slippers. He hollers: What do you think this is, a hotel? My mother tosses her coat in the general direction of a chair, misses, doesn't bother to pick it up and swears right back at them. *Vieux con. Vieille salope.* Asshole. Old bitch.

And they say: *Tu n'es qu'une putain.* Whore. Look what you're doing to that poor child. *La pauvre enfant.*

I wish I had her guts. Look at her. Her body erect, chest pushed forward, head proud. Not scared. She's not scared of them. She doesn't give a damn. She defies them. I'm jealous of her nerve, of her sexiness. When I will finally claim that sexuality for myself, with a vengeance, it will be with strangers at first, or far away. To her and to them I will stay the good girl, chest caved in, shoulders a little stooped, a disguise. For a long time, I will not attempt to dethrone her to her face, terrified to confront her on her turf, and that, when I do, she would never forgive me.

In French the word for rage is the same as for rabies. To be rabid is to have *la rage.* My mother's got the rage. She's got foam on her lips like a rabid dog. It comes out in spittles of saliva rushing after her words. *Vieux con,* she says again. Asshole. I go back into my bedroom before anybody catches me. She furiously runs up the stairs and stomps into my room. I am already back in bed, hiding under the blankets. Are you awake? I know you're awake. She whispers, but there's a threatening edge to her voice. I pretend I am asleep. She hesitates for a moment, then walks out. I can hear her swear all the way to the third floor, where her bedroom is set up under the eaves. I hear her door slam. Then it's my grandparents' turn to come up the stairs and close their door. Their bedroom is right next to mine. I have the largest bedroom in the house, one window at each end, overlooking the front and back garden. They treat me like a princess, like I am the second coming of Christ. They love you more than me, she says. I don't want them to love me more than her. I know I am a fake. I don't deserve their love. I am all twisted inside, and I suck up to them so that they won't reject me. They're all hypocrites, she says. You're the only one who loves me, the only one I love. But I am a hypocrite, too. I fake it so that they love me. So that she loves me. *Je t'aime, toi,* she says fiercely. And what I hear is: You are my love, you are mine, all mine. And I can feel her breath all over me, her lips on my cheek, her hand on my head feels like a lover's touch, and I shrink inside, petrified, afraid to be sucked in, swallowed whole into that monstrous love.

When she's safely back into her own room, the silence falls and expands. It spreads in thick layers like the suffocating smoke of a fire. You think the flames will singe you, but it's the smoke that ends up smothering you.

I have no idea why the subject of my father was brought up that day. Years later, when I was a teenager, my mother told me there had been a correspondence—an exchange of letters and mailings of pictures—going on between her and my father since the time I was born, but not directly. Apparently a priest by the name of Père Donjon, a friend of my father's family, had agreed to play the part of go-between and serve as a mail-drop in utmost secrecy. I don't know why the correspondence couldn't have taken place openly, unless the two families were opposed to it. Unless, once again, the circumstances of my birth had to be kept secret, something that could be mentioned only backstage.

Anyway, it seems that at a certain point, my father—perhaps pressed by the priest, or by my mother—had wanted to see me. So I can only assume that my mother consented to "prepare" me. I cannot understand the sudden appearance of his picture, otherwise. She must have been setting about "breaking the news."

But then, nothing happened. The picture was only a peek into another reality, the fact that, like every child, I had a father.

He was never mentioned again. Except on the occasion of a particularly vicious fight between my mother and my grandmother. Only then would the dreaded name be uttered, followed by: *le salaud!* the bastard.

I didn't ask about him after that day. *Mon père*. Even now, forty years later, they feel like forbidden words. No, I couldn't have said those words then. I would never, even to myself, have said: my father. Naming him would have meant appropriating him, while the silence surrounding him was meant to erase, to nullify him, as if, by some bizarre sleight of hand, my mother had been both mother and father, or had conceived me with her own father, or perhaps, after all, I was an immaculate conception. For a long period, long past the usual time to be confused about the "facts of life," I thought babies came out of their mothers' belly buttons.

I remember when I first applied for my passport, on my birth certificate, in the space for the father's name, someone had written by hand: *inconnu*. Unknown.

I could never remember my father's name, nor quite forget it, either. It was hovering somewhere at the edge of my memory, carved in a slightly bastardized form until one day—long after I had left France, after I had lived in New York for more than fifteen years— I asked my mother if she knew how I could get in touch with him and she whipped out his address from an old book and wrote it down for me. After another full year had elapsed, I thought I might want to write to him, but I couldn't remember his name properly. For some reason, I always remembered it as something different. Seuillet or Seulier instead of Seulliet. *Souillé* is what I heard in my mind, a French word that means soiled, dirty, fouled, sullied, and Seuillet, a near-homonym to *souillé*, is the name I gave to the operator when I called information in the French town where he was supposed to live, in spite of the fact that his name was correctly spelled right in front of my eyes, written on a torn piece of paper in my mother's handwriting. The operator told me no one with the name Seuillet lived in that town, and until I finally realized my mistake and got the proper listing, I was seized by two conflicting feelings: relief for not having to confront him, and deep sadness and regret that we might never have a chance to meet.

My mother's breasts. They're always in my face. Maybe it's my height. I am seven or eight. I see them in the opening of her robe. Moving, free under the fabric. Alive. Always at eye level. I see them in the bathtub, when we take baths together. Her body, so much bigger than mine, her breasts, two buoys at the edge of the water. I stare at them. The round nipples, the big round globes, swollen. The granulous bumps around the nipples. In fashion magazines editors love to classify women's bodies with little drawings of breasts, buttocks, face, hands, fitting into squares and circles and triangles. As if it is reassuring for a woman to know she belongs in a certain category. As if it justifies everything. I am a pear-shaped woman, and what are you? Me? Oh, I am a triangle. It gives you an identity. Breasts can be apple-shaped or pear-shaped. My mother's breasts are definitely apple-shaped, but larger, the size of grapefruits: huge, they seem to me, and perfectly round, aloft in defiance of all gravity. They float on the surface of the bath water. With a spray of freckles in the cleavage. The granulous bumps are turning into goosebumps. The nipples stand erect, a few inches from my own flat chest. I pull away from her. It's cold in the bathroom. It's winter. The windows are all steamed up. My shoulders are shivering. I lower myself into the water until it reaches my chin.

When she gets up to soap herself, water drips from her in big gushes, drips from her curly, black bush, cascades from her hips, way above me. When I look up, I see droplets balanced at the tip of her nipples. Again I want to turn away, but I can't help staring at her. She lifts a leg and balances her foot on the edge of the bathtub. She runs the soap between her legs. I see far under her thigh, too far.

Her hand goes in and out, swallowed up to the wrist. When it comes out, her pubic hair explodes into white bubbles, then, weighted by water and soap, it hangs like a goatee. In between the strands of beard I see the lips of her sex, red. They make me think of a rooster's comb.

Her sex in close-up, oversized, imperious. And me receding, small, shrinking chin-deep into the bathtub.

I look away from her. Then back. Then away again. Then back to her hand.

She's done. Stands up. Turns the shower full blast on cold. She loves cold showers after a hot bath, says it "reinvigorates." Tightens the skin. She teases me with the shower head. Frigid drops reach my face. I cower at the end of the tub. She splashes cold water all over herself. Steps out of the tub, grabs a towel and rubs herself raw, with great, big huffs. Her breasts shake, her thighs quiver. Her whole body, powerful, seems animated from within, as if the breasts were going to take off and squash against the wall. She laughs at me staring at her, still immersed in the tepid water.

She doesn't know what she stirs up in me, the rage for feeling so small next to her, so transparent, so nothing, the rage that later will make me throw my hands around her neck and squeeze, squeeze hard, meaning it, trying to choke the life force that once again threatens to submerge me, my fingers a bracelet of flesh encircling her flesh that is finally yielding to me; the longing to be a sex queen, to thrust my tits out and my ass out and my cunt out and feel the force grow from inside of me, too, furiously, delectably.

Allez, viens, viens, sors, she says, oblivious, as always. Dipping her hand in the water and splashing my face, like we're both having a great time.

I cover my face with my folded arms, refuse to move. I'm not playing her games.

Finally there's a rapping at the door.

Vous avez bientôt fini?

It's my grandmother. She bangs and rattles the handle, finds out the door's not locked and marches in, carrying my panties and

undershirt on her arm. She eyes my mother from the back, her freckled shoulders, apple-shaped behind, my mother's drying her hair,
not a stitch on.

Contempt and repulsion drip from my grandmother's lips.

Aren't you ashamed to parade around naked in front of your
daughter?

My mother turns around. Her breasts jiggle for a second, then
stay still, pointed in the direction of my grandmother, like two
torpedoes.

Mind your own business, she says. I'll take a bath with my
own daughter if I want.

My grandmother looks back daggers from her steel-gray eyes.

Come, *ma cocotte*. Her hands drape a towel around my back,
clutch at my shoulder. She steers me away. Away from Evil's ways.
Come and get dressed. You are going to catch a cold. Come, I prepared your clothes in your room.

Sometimes it feels as if we are two prisoners in that house,
but I get better treatment than her because I suck up to the jailers
instead of rebelling like she does. She's the noble heroine who stands
up for her rights, while I am the opportunist. I'd do anything for
survival, and it fills me with shame.

I hang my head down and follow my grandmother, me the
favorite, me the innocent, me the traitor.

Old monkey, my mother shouts after her.

Years later, when I was pregnant with my second daughter and
my mother was already in her late seventies, I saw those breasts dangling in my face again, although this time I was taller than her, but
the effect was just as powerful. My grandmother had died, the old
house was being sold, and my mother was packing and sorting things
out. I was visiting from New York, on my way to the South of France,
and she had thrown a dinner party, inviting one of my cousins and
his family. The table was set in the garden behind the house, and
she was trying to turn an old abandoned bathtub into a barbecue
pit, to cook the steaks. It was July, it was hot, she wasn't ready.

I see her rushing out into the garden, wearing only an apron tied behind her back and nothing else, swearing at herself, at time running out, swearing, like she always has, when things don't go her way. *Putain de merde! Saloperie! Salope! Ah, la vache!* Her voice growling like that of a drunk sailor after many cigarettes and whiskeys.

And here come the breasts, again, hanging now, not defying the laws of gravity anymore, but still formidable-looking, still packing a punch, barely hidden behind the bib of the apron, dangling, jiggling, as she leans over the bathtub and tries to get the fire going with a pair of bellows, her white, naked behind not so apple-shaped anymore, turning into a pear now, but very much *there*, perfectly framed by the dainty knot of the apron strings and the two flaps covering the thighs.

And I feel the same rage, to see her body take center-stage again, and the same jealousy that she's got the guts to defy convention and I'm not sure I would, not like that. My mother the lone ranger, my mother the diva, my mother the nutcase. My mother larger than life and fighting impossible, quixotic battles.

While we linger around the tub, sipping on our chilled white wine, among the fading roses and the garden going to seed, the sun sinking low over the stone wall at the back, she keeps insulting the pile of wood that refuses to catch fire, as if only to spite her, cursing at it: Fuck! Fuck! Fuck!

Finally my cousin inquires if she needs help. And she furiously drops the bellows and wipes her forehead with the corner of the apron. Defeated.

After the bath I watch her descend the staircase, sensually wrapped in a silky robe in shades of peach or apricot, loosely tied at the waist, a pack of Craven A in her hand. She is my role-model, unattainable, glamorous. She holds the stage and I watch. Sometimes I put her high-heeled shoes on, of course, and her dresses, and I parade down the stairs like a princess, but in the mirror I look gauche, small, hopeless. Everything hangs like on a deflated balloon. My grandmother, who has spent her morning cooking jam, peeling vegetables for lunch, making the beds, catches another patch of naked skin between the lapels of her robe.

Cover your chest, she says. You should be ashamed to show yourself to your daughter like that. That poor child!

I doubt my mother feels any shame. A rush of pleasure, rather, to get my grandmother going so easily, but I don't think the word shame belongs to my mother's vocabulary. I, on the other hand, feel the shame as if I were the one parading around showing too much flesh, in a house obsessed with sex.

My mother shrugs and walks on. I follow her like a trained poodle, adoring and slavish. I have a poodle, a brown Royal called Xerès, that wags its tail and follows me around, so I know. She sits at the dining-room table and pours herself a cup of café au lait. She spreads fashion magazines all around her, takes her time with breakfast, slowly savors it to the last drop and crumb, then lights a cigarette and gets a bottle of nail polish from the bathroom while I watch her.

My grandmother follows the smoke to the dining-room. She appears at the door, her teeth clenched.

Smoking already! Tart! Look at you. What an example for this child. Shame on you!

My mother doesn't bat an eyelash. She's busy painting her nails an iridescent shade of mandarin. Coils of blue smoke curl from the cigarette balanced at the edge of the ashtray. Her nail polish, her red hair, and her flesh-colored peignoir make her white skin glow in the same peachy-gold light.

Your father was a wimp. *Un faible*. No balls.

To have or not to have balls is the ultimate measuring stick for my mother. Everybody who talks about her says she's got balls. One of the guys. *Un mec*. But my father, no. *Pas de couilles*. No cojones. Or, anyway, just enough to conceive me. I am older now, old enough to know about men and to be instructed about their shortcomings. Old enough to hear the details.

The details come piecemeal. They are still coming. Back then I never asked. Talking about my father would have been like stirring up the dirt, admitting that I came out of illegitimate, dirty sex, not dutiful conjugality. I wouldn't be the innocent anymore, but the child of lust. Later, when I was in my twenties, I started asking my mother questions, wearily, but irresistibly, like one approaches a still-active volcano.

I am trying to remember the words she used in French. *Lavette. Dominé par sa mère.* Henpecked. Mama's boy. *Réservé. Déprimé.* Withdrawn. Depressed.

They met at somebody's wedding. Mutual friends. I tried to imagine a May wedding, June wedding. 1946. The war just ended. Celebrations still in the air. The women wearing wedged shoes, printed dresses cut at the knee, little short sleeves gathered at the shoulder seams. My mother had her hair twisted in two big rolls over her forehead, the rest hanging to her shoulders. The men's suits had wide shoulders, wide lapels. Wide trouser legs. I imagine a garden party in the afternoon, the sun slanting over the gaily printed dresses, the red fingernails around the champagne glasses, the red, red lips, the expensive smells of Madame Rochas and Joy, the tiny pillbox hats teetering at the edge of the tall hair. And the dance, after sundown, on the lawn, the band playing blues standards, bastardized. And then a waltz, and the two of them getting up, swaying into the balmy air, him following her, following her laugh, dazzled by her smile.

The two of them, a little tipsy, walking down the alley to his car.

But maybe it was a summer wedding, late August, or early September, after everyone is back from vacation, from their country houses or the seashore.

In the first case, it was a six-month affair. In the second, it lasted three months.

Because I was conceived in early December, and when she found out . . . well, when she found out . . .

I want you to know I never had any intention of committing suicide when I found out I was pregnant, my mother tells me, inexplicably.

What she did do is consult a woman who dealt in herbs. The herbalist prepared a concoction, told her to take it, wait a few days. It didn't work. I hung in there, not to be dislodged.

Then, she had an epiphany. She'd never had an accident, never been pregnant before. She actually thought she might never be able to have a baby. And now the miracle had happened. She was delirious with joy. Telling me the story, she hands me this detail victoriously, as proof of her great love for me.

They talked about getting married. A hasty marriage. Do the honorable thing.

Here's how it went, according to my mother:

The two families met to discuss the possibility of an alliance. His mother, an overpowering, iron-fisted lady of small nobility and big arrogance, wanted to keep him for a better prospect with a proper virgin, not some older tart who slept around, and she slammed her foot down.

Pas de mariage!

He hid behind his mother's skirts.

An older woman, pregnant, a tart!

Oui, maman.

I forbid you! You'll ruin your life!

Oui, maman.

My grandfather took one look at the lot of them, upended his pipe over an ashtray, leaving a little mound of ashes at the bottom, and turned on his heels.

You don't belong with these people, he told my mother on the way back to his car—an almond-green Panhard with chrome fins. I don't see you making a life with this loser. We'll raise the child. Don't you worry about it.

In this version, my mother is not an abandoned *fille-mère*, as goes the old French expression, daughter-mother, eerily appropriate in her case, but she's the superior one who rejects a lesser suitor. The family's face is saved, at my expense. I end up being the daughter of a less-than-nothing.

The other version is the seduced-and-abandoned maiden, and although my mother alludes to it at times, her teeth clenched in fury, that one was quickly discarded.

You couldn't tell, from my father's photograph, whether he had balls or not. You couldn't tell if he was a wimp, if it was true that he was a mama's boy.

You could tell only that he had clear eyes and that he was dressed in the fashion of the time with a certain flair, and that he wasn't bad-looking, maybe even good-looking.

Whenever I came across that picture I saw the wavy hair, the crease of the pants, the diamond patterns on the sweater. I had to force my eyes to travel to the face, the mouth, to focus on the eyes. Creep. Creepy guy. Wimp. *Veule.* Weak. Pushover. No balls.

I felt my cheeks turn bright red, felt the hot flush, and quickly put it back with the other pictures, shuffling them all together so that I wouldn't remember where it was, so that it would get lost.

At night, before going to sleep, I make up a substitute family: a mother wearing a navy-blue suit and a blond chignon coming to tuck me into bed—she looks like one of the models in the magazine my grandmother subscribes to, *Modes & Travaux*, a French *Ladies' Home Journal*, poised and sweet and calm and the epitome of the *bourgeoise*—but I can never put a face on the father.

There is a man in our house, but it's my grandfather. He's got a strong chest and skinny legs and a steel-gray crewcut and a pair of round, tortoiseshell glasses. In earlier photos of him, the ones from before the war, a stiff bristle of a mustache sprouts between his lip and the base of his nose, like Charlie Chaplin in *The Great Dictator*. There are two self-portraits of him, hanging in my bedroom, painted just a few years apart: one with the mustache, one without, both with a shock of jet-black hair, both looking stern and manly.

From him I learned the meaning of these words:

Freethinker, pantheist. An atheist, he explained to me, is someone who believes in nothing. He was a pantheist. Although he never went to church, he believed that spirits lived in nature, hidden in the trees and the clouds.

Bakelite: he was the CEO of the French subsidiary of the American plastic manufacturing company, and there were Bakelite boxes and ashtrays in veined or freckled greens and browns scattered all over the house.

Poetry: he knew whole poems of Baudelaire and Apollinaire and Verlaine by heart and recited them at the dinner table. Ditto with Victor Hugo's epic poems, his favorite, the one entitled *Hernani*. He liked to fill his chest and his mouth with its martial rhythms.

Painting: he called himself a Sunday artist and spent all his weekends painting in the studio he had installed in the attic, or, in nice weather, he took his easel with him to Paris or the countryside.

There is no doubt about who my grandfather is. A man in the classic tradition. A patriarch. Presumably, he's got balls, *lui*. And a broken nose courtesy of an amateur boxing championship, which makes him look like Jean Gabin. He belongs to another time. The nineteenth century, my mother says disparagingly, but it's more like the first half of the twentieth. And his belongings are artifacts of that time: a Remington typewriter, c. 1930, its black keys set in small steel circles; an ivory-handled compass nesting in a case lined with purple velvet and inscribed: BARBOTHEU, 17, rue Béranger, Paris; a small round box in green Bakelite; a Persian lamb hat like those Khrushchev used to wear; three or four pairs of hand-stitched suede gloves, small for a man's hand; several notebooks from his days at engineering school, with handwritten notes in sepia ink, now fading to a pale ochre; his boxing pictures from around 1910, in which he and his opponents are wearing soft leather, lace-up shoes, and leather helmets; the pictures of his Duesenberg, of his Citroen 15; his long gentleman's umbrella, with a curved wooden handle, and a fabric elegantly printed in a small green and brown pattern; his leather-bound volumes of Baudelaire and Victor Hugo; his art books of Impressionist paintings; his collection of Mickey Spillane and Chester Himes in Gallimard's Black Mask imprint.

I have brought some of these objects here with me, to New York. His self-portrait—the one without the mustache—in oil on a piece of canvas board is hanging in my study.

* * *

Which one is my father, the young man with the pale eyes and no balls or the amateur boxer?

Whenever someone asked me about my family, I wouldn't say: I don't know my father, or, I have never met my father, but: I don't have a father.

The storm broke a few minutes after I came back from meeting my father. It was a devilish storm. A summertime storm, a Mediterranean downpour. Brutal. Rain crashing down, thunder rumbling, lightning striking the electric lines, popping the fuses. Torrents of water gushing down the narrow streets like mountain rapids. The sky purple, dark, pouring itself out.

I listened to the storm beating down from my bed in my mother's house in Provence, dozing from the wine, from exhaustion.

There was wine, at lunch with my father, white wine, and sultry heat.

Driving back on the winding road cutting through the Esterel from Grasse, all the windows rolled down, MC Solar turned way up, blasting his witty rap rhythms on the stereo. The dark sky bearing down on the mountains. Hypnotic ribbon of road, curving and winding its way through the hills. Shifting gear. Brake/clutch/gas and back. Back and forth at each curve like a dance. Feeling no pain. Not feeling a damn thing.

Once in a while there was a flash of my father's piercing blue eyes, forget-me-not blue, fresh and clear, his only distinctive feature—why didn't I get the blue eyes? Céline, my older daughter, complained when I told her—and a surprising smile that clicked on and off at odd moments. The eyes and the smile: some remnants of forgotten charm, floating away from his beaten face like a stray raft.

It must have been him that I saw, the *monsieur* with the white hair sitting in his car, door open on the passenger side, right across from where I first parked, along the *pétanque* court, at the foot of the village. But I turned away. I wasn't ready yet. I crossed the lawn toward a little café and went to the bathroom, and when I came out I asked the *cafétier* where the castle was because our rendezvous was at the Restaurant du Vieux Château.

The name of the village is Cabris. It means young goat, or kid, in French. It's a small perched village in the Esterel Mountains, a few minutes away from Grasse, the perfume capital of Provence, about a couple of hours from where my mother has moved, twenty years ago, in a similar perched village, overlooking a similar scenery of pine forest, vineyards, and olive groves.

A year and a half after my mother had given me his address, I sent a letter to my father. It was January 11, 1995. I don't know why that day, but it had to be the result of some subterranean process that had been going on for years and burst forth after the new year. The letter was word-processed, impeccably printed on my printer, and it read like a piece I might have composed for posterity. In it I wrote that I felt like the narrator of a romance novel or a potboiler. I didn't know how to address this man directly, I had to use literary language. It took him three weeks to answer me, and during this time I checked the mailbox every day as if waiting to hear from a lover, and when his letter came I locked myself in the car and wept.

He had an old-fashioned, slanted handwriting that reminded me of my grandmother's, and he called me Madame, which offended me. Madame is what people called my grandmother. My mother was always a Mademoiselle. The letter was short, one and a half pages on airmail paper. He said that I had awakened an old wound and told me about his losses—his first wife, his younger daughter who had recently died in a car accident. It was all very factual, sober, a little thin, the pain held back, a life summed up in a handful of dry lines.

It wasn't what he wrote that made me cry, but that he had answered me at all, and that by doing so had finally acknowledged my existence, recognized me.

After that letter he sent several cards, one for Christmas, one to thank me for sending him pictures of my family. The covers of the cards were all identical, featuring a bouquet of flowers painted by a Dutch master.

In Cabris, I ended up parking farther up the road, right below the restaurant, not because I didn't want to walk but—I only realized it later, when it was time to leave—because I wanted a quick escape when it would be over, hop into the peppy little blue Renault, pump up the gas, and hightail it down the street, leaving him in the dust.

It was still early. In his letter he had suggested 12:30, I had written back 1 P.M., to give myself a little more time because of the jet lag. It was now a quarter to one. I gave my name to the waitress and told her a *monsieur* was expecting me. She said the *monsieur* had been around already and had left. He had said he would come back in a little while. In the meantime she seated me at a table.

Like in most restaurants in Southern France in summer, the tables were set outside, on a large terrace, each one shaded by a big parasol. The parasols were blue, the tablecloths white, everything still in the hot midday air. I couldn't see the castle from where I was, only the bluish green of the pine trees, the grayish green of the stiff bushes covering the rugged hills, the rows of vineyards undulating down the valley.

Some of the tables were occupied by families of tourists. At one sat a man in his sixties with a strong face and wild salt-and-pepper hair and tan hands and forearms and a quick, easy smile, and I thought why can't this be my father. And then I looked at all the men in the restaurant and nobody else qualified age-wise and I felt sad and fuck you and never mind. There were manicured bushes on three sides of the terrace and I started craning my neck around them to see if I could spot him coming from the road.

Then I saw him.

* * *

I see this guy, the right age, seventyish, a little bent around the shoulders, like his head is too heavy for his back and neck and life has beat him down, pearl white hair combed back, white slacks, white loafers, checked red and white short-sleeved shirt, a navy blue jacket thrown over his arm, a little black bag in his hands— the kind that some French men carry around, but that American men would find too effeminate, too European. I take it all in, in a flash, because he is walking back and forth behind the bushes and I catch a glimpse of him and then he's gone, and again another glimpse and he's gone again. The white slacks, the white loafers: that spells Florida to me, but we're in the South of France, and men in hot countries go for the white and the French Riviera has its own little Miami style.

I watch him, so hesitant. I can see him clearly every time he paces out from behind the bushes. He sits on a bench, he stands up. I'm not sure if it's the same man who was sitting in the car earlier, but I have a feeling he might be. My heart sinks. He is painful to look at, lost in his thoughts, head forward, nose down. It has to be him.

Yet I don't want it to be him.

After still more of this back-and-forthing I can't stand it any longer. I can tell he is suffering, and I want to give him a break, so I ask the waitress if he's the *monsieur* who's come earlier, and she looks up in his direction and she says, yes. So I ask her to tell him I am here.

He comes around following the waitress and I stand up and hold out my hand and say his name, forcing myself to say it clearly: Michel Seulliet? and this time I say it right. His eyes open wide like he can't believe it's me. And he looks okay from up close, I mean the smile is kind of nice. But he looks nothing like that old snapshot.

He kept staring at me with a disbelieving look and finally he said: I thought you were blond, from the pictures.

I touched my red hair and said: It's henna.

And then I said, what pictures?

We moved to sit at another table because there was a patch of sun coming down on the first one, and he wanted to be in the shade and it was fine with me.

What pictures? I said again when we had sat down, wondering wildly if my mother was still in touch with him and had sent him recent pictures of me. But he just said: The picture you sent me. And now of course I remembered it. It was a Polaroid taken when I was pregnant. I wasn't a blonde in it. I had long dark hair and I was wearing my glasses, and a crimson red top, and my arms were folded behind my head. And he said, You look better than in the photo, and I took it as a compliment although I kind of liked that picture, and I said I had cut my hair since then and it was curlier now. And then we didn't know what to say.

We were staring at the impossibly long menu and I just couldn't decide, it had like fifteen entrées, so I went for something simple, melon and *loup*, which I think is called bass in English, and right away he ordered the same, as if he was relieved I had made the decision for him. I think he didn't want to embark on anything too fancy, either. Then he ordered white wine and I ordered a bottle of Badoit. Badoit is what everybody drinks at meals in France, it's like San Pellegrino water, light and fizzy. And the waitress came and poured the wine and the water and we busied ourselves with our glasses. And then again we didn't know what to say.

I picked at the bread and drank little sips of wine and kept throwing these sidelong glances at him, trying to make him out, hoping to glean signs that he was okay. Like when we had sat down he had said: Call me Michel, everybody calls me Michel, or maybe he said that later, when we said goodbye, just before I took off, pumping the gas and slamming the gear shift into first, second, third in ten seconds, while he waved at me.

So we talked about my trip, the jet lag—I had flown in the day before—my life in New York, a trip he had taken with his wife to New Orleans, organized for retired physicians from the Nice area. We tiptoed around each other, holding our breath. I wondered if it was harder for him than for me. For me it seemed easy, as if I was standing at the edge of myself, to be looked at and admired, but untouchable.

Without the blue eyes he would have looked defeated. Not physically defeated. He looked fine: healthy, tan, trim, rosy cheeked, alert, youngish, actually. No, it was the attitude. Or maybe it was all in comparison with my uncle who, at seventy, is a tough guy, still on top of his game—or at least, would like you to believe so—or compared to my grandfather, the undefeated welterweight in amateur championship. Or maybe I wanted to separate myself from the weak, the wimp, the pussy-whipped. Watch him from the vantage point of the strong.

Certainly he had no macho swagger. Modest, almost. Shy, yes, shy. He didn't try to impress me. Maybe I would have liked him to turn on the charm or something. I certainly did. I had finally claimed it for myself: sex as seduction, sex as armor. There was no way I was going in there with this guy, my father, and not turn it on.

And that way I wouldn't allow him to hurt me.

The first thing he told me was that his younger daughter had died in a car accident five years earlier. She was thirty-five and a Jehovah's Witness in Toronto. That sounded like bad news to me. I don't mean the death—although he certainly looked like he hadn't recovered from it—but the Jehovah's Witness part. Creepy. He thought it was creepy, too. And I could feel myself becoming sarcastic and judgmental. What kind of family produces a Jehovah's Witness? What kind of freaks were these people? I remember now the line my grandfather had supposedly used about my father's family: You don't belong with these people. Maybe this was the way I looked at him too: with arrogance and contempt.

From that point on, it was a deluge of dramas: His first wife had died giving birth to that same daughter, his sister had died in another car accident the year before, and you could see that it had all gotten to him, all these tragedies. And I didn't know what to say about all that; I think I didn't want it to touch me.

He was a total stranger after all, an elderly *monsieur* with white hair combed straight back and a pinkie ring, whom I had just met a few minutes ago. And in a way I wanted him to remain that way, not too close. A stranger.

So I drank a little more wine and ate a little more bread and listened to him some more.

I am good at that, listening. It's easy. You don't have to reveal yourself, and you can bide your time. People feel they can trust you, they open up and pour out their hearts. But sometimes it's too much, you don't want to take in all that.

He told me he had been a pediatrician, that he was retired, and that through the church he visited old people's homes as a doctor. But even that failed to bring any kind of enthusiasm. It's as if his life had been on tracks from the get-go. He'd moved to the South of France because his parents had started building a house there, and then he'd found a practice to buy. He kept putting himself down. I did quite modestly, he said. For a moment I thought he wanted to diminish his accomplishments so that I wouldn't think there was any money to inherit. I didn't like having that thought. It was too cynical. He was probably only disillusioned. I wonder now if he meant that he had nothing of himself to give me. Maybe he thought he had wasted his life. That would make two of them. My mother also thinks her life is failed.

Then I told him my life was great and everything was going super-duper and couldn't be better, and I was drooling with enthusiasm and joie de vivre. I was determined to be cheerful and sexy to the finish. Let him not see the cracks, see how scarred— and scared—I really was. How humiliating, how weak. I wasn't going to join him in his misery. I wasn't going to be a wimp, too. But maybe I couldn't open up to him because I didn't know what he would do with that. I didn't trust him. I didn't see any reason for trust.

We went on eating and drinking and I thought: This thing is not taking off. This is not going anywhere.

So to cut to the chase, I asked him about the circumstances of my birth. That was a sore spot. You could see he had gone over it again and again. And that the version he had decided to tell was the one that was the least painful for him.

I was twenty-five years old, he said. I didn't know what I was doing. I was in medical school. I met your mother and we were maybe a month together. I barely remember her. (For anyone who has met my mother, if only for two minutes, that is hard to believe.) I barely remember that time.

He sounded pained to have these buried memories jolted by my presence.

I listened to his story, and inside of me was this hysterical laugh. A giddy, nervous laugh that I had to repress. All this drama I had heard about, the whole business of a botched abortion, talk of marriage, the meeting of the parents, the priest serving as go-between, and my father barely remembers the affair. He barely remembers my mother. And I don't know if I believe him or not. Because it's possible, just possible, that he's sincere, that he's blanked it all out. That he doesn't remember making me.

I had no morality at that time, he says.

Which I take to mean that he was sleeping around in those days and had no sense of responsibility.

At this point we are well into the fish, which is delicious, and I steal a quick look at him, and I see that he is dead serious, no irony at all.

But now I have straightened out and I believe in God, he goes on.

It didn't sound quite as awful as the way I am putting it down. Not like a born-again Christian. More modest. He actually didn't seem as rigid as that. He didn't seem like a hard man. And for a moment I softened, I almost liked him. He didn't seem mean. More like lost and tired, and maybe his belief in God was a core that kept him together, because later he told me that he was depressed, but he was a survivor. A survivor: that's a word I had used about myself, a word that is used for concentration camp victims, cancer victims. It gave me the chills. I wanted to be more than a survivor, someone who hangs on to the edge of life by her fingertips. And it occurred to me that both he and my mother were using the same justification for their lack of responsibility toward me: They had both been victims.

I pulled out pictures of my two daughters, Chloé and Céline, from my backpack, and he showed me pictures of his children and grandchildren. I wondered if he had brought them for me, or if he always carried them with him.

Now we looked like a couple of relatives poring over family snapshots in the middle of the lunch left-overs, and our meeting seemed innocuous, innocent.

I took the pictures of his children and stared at them one by one. There were only three children left, since the younger daughter had died, and there they were with their respective husbands, wives, and kids, and none of them looked like me at all. But you can't always trust pictures, and I asked him if he saw any resemblance. He said no.

I don't know why it mattered to me to look like him or like them, maybe because it was so abstract otherwise, sitting next to this man, how did I know he was my father? What if my mother had slept with a different man around the same time? When I went back to my mother's house, later, I sat in front of the mirror and tilted my head up and at an angle and thought I recognized something in the line of my nose and the space between my nose and my lips that made me think of him. But it was so elusive, a flutter, a mirage, as if for an instant his spirit had entered me, and a moment later my features reassembled themselves and I couldn't capture him anymore. He had vanished.

Are you going to tell your children you've met me? I asked him.

I knew his wife knew and she had encouraged him to meet me. He told me that she had said to him, you cannot reject her. You have to meet her. I didn't like hearing that. Why couldn't he decide to see me by himself? The henpecked husband. Why did he persist in fitting the bill? But suddenly I was imagining meeting his family, my half sisters and brother. It was an idea that flashed through my mind while I looked at their pictures. They looked fine. Not repulsive, like some families can be. Not too stuck-up. I could stand being in the same room as them and finding out who they were, if we had something in common, some quirk of behavior, like twins separated at birth.

I don't know, he said. We don't want to make trouble, do we?

In French, the way he put it was: *On va pas faire de pataquès, hein? Pataquès* meaning trouble in Marseille slang. Trouble, problems, anything that would disturb the smooth texture of life's façade. The good bourgeois axiom that my grandmother was fond of. Although he is from Auvergne, the center of France, my father's lived in the South probably for more than forty years, so it makes sense he would use local words. But still *pataquès* sounded like a cheap word to me.

No *pataquès*.

Right. So it was okay to see me, but I wasn't to make trouble, waves. He would see me on the side, but nothing would change in his life.

I didn't say anything. I had already been a pack of *pataquès* all my life.

I didn't feel the anger. Just a sudden stillness. And then the word rolled around in me like a wave. We were already making waves, and the waves were in me. So I had to shut up, stay quiet once again, erase myself like he had erased me from his memory? Did he fear that I would expose him, shake up his life to its foundations? And of course I could, pop out of the blue like a jack-in-the-box and reveal myself to his children. Like a flasher: See what your god-fearing father's got inside his pants? The moment passed. Was I coming to him out of revenge? Did I want to make *pataquès* for him?

I didn't know what I wanted. Maybe to be acknowledged and embraced.

He, on the other hand, seemed to want to sum up his life for me, look back at it for my benefit from the prospect of his seventy-two years.

So I listened. Over the fish, over the glasses of wine, over dessert, which was fresh raspberries dusted with sugar. Over the tiny cups of expresso.

Life is all about routine, he said.

I disagreed. Life changes all the time, I said. Life is unpredictable.

He shook his head.

Je suis un pauvre type, he said. I am a poor guy, a loser.

I believe he meant: You didn't miss anything. He meant: I couldn't measure up, it was my failure, not yours. He meant: Don't ask me to answer to you.

I didn't know what to say.

Because your father's failure is your own. It's a wound you carry around with you all your life, and you cover it up and make up for it any way you can, but it can never completely heal.

I drank some wine and polished off the raspberries.

He looked at me sideways and flashed one of his quick smiles, as if his lips had been an elastic, pulled, then snapped back.

You must be disappointed in me, he said.

I looked at him. Why do you say that?

But I knew why. And he was right. Of course, I was disappointed. But I couldn't tell him that. Disappointed for what? I didn't even know I had had fantasies, expectations. To acknowledge my disappointment would have been to acknowledge my need of a father. Someone to lean on, to look up to.

I don't know, I told him. I don't know how I feel.

And he said that it was normal, that he didn't know, either, and that he was intimidated by me. I can't let myself go, he said. I am very nervous. And I felt sad for him. He was only a failed human being, after all.

I told him I was nervous, too.

Of course, he said, it's normal.

And we didn't say anything more for a while. But it wasn't the same silence as before. It was a little bit more comfortable. Companionable. As if we were both admitting our shortcomings. Our fragility. And I was grateful that he allowed himself to show his vulnerability. Even if I couldn't show him mine.

Finally it ended. It was around 3 P.M. I went to the bathroom and put on fresh lipstick and checked that I still looked like myself in the floor-length mirror, the black espadrilles, the off-white linen pants, the sleeveless top, all carefully picked to strike the right note, not too overtly sexy but not too understated either, and I was still in one piece, and I hadn't changed, and that surprised me. I was free. I wasn't really his daughter, not in the sense of these complicated entanglements that one calls father/daughter or mother/daughter relationships. I didn't have to see him again if I chose not to.

When I came back to the table he said: We should leave before the storm hits. The restaurant had emptied out. The sky was hanging low, bulging with dark heavy clouds.

He picked up the bill and paid with his credit card and walked me to the blue Renault, which turned out to be parked strategically well.

I opened the car door and we started to say goodbye, and he said, Call me Michel, everybody calls me Michel, even my grandchildren. I thought that maybe we should kiss but I couldn't do it. Maybe I was angry that he had not lived up to my hidden fantasies, that he couldn't change anything in the course of my life. I would have liked to be able to kiss him.

He was standing there, a little bent, slight, clutching his little black bag.

I wanted to get away, leave him behind.

Au revoir, Michel, I said, and we shook hands and it felt as if we would never see each other again.

I sat behind the wheel and pumped up the gas and made a U-turn and waved at him from the open window and went first, second, third in ten seconds flat, and I saw him standing by the sidewalk in the rearview mirror, looking at me, and when I drove down the lower road, I saw him get into his car, right across from where I had parked originally, along the lawn, and I honked my horn and waved my hand at him and he waved back.

My mother was making paper flowers with my four-year-old in the living room when I walked in the house. I didn't tell them where I had been. I went to my bedroom and lay down. The storm broke a little while later, and through the open window rose a smell of honeysuckle and wet soil freshly tilled. When the rug started getting soaked from the rain, I got up to close the window and I watched the sulfurous sky spilling itself out, and then I lay down again and I closed my eyes and I listened to the sound of crashing rain for a long time.

Contributors' Notes

Jane Creighton has published essays in *The American Voice, Gulf Coast, Mother Jones, Ploughshares,* and the anthology *Unwinding the Vietnam War.* Her collection of poems, *Ceres in an Open Field,* was published by Out & Out Books. She is an assistant professor at the University of Houston Downtown. "Brother," an earlier version of which appeared in *Ploughshares,* is from the manuscript *My Home in the Country.*

Lois Gould has written eight novels, two works of nonfiction, two satires posing as children's fables and a collection of personal essays. A frequent contributor of articles and reviews to *The New York Times,* she initiated that newspaper's personal column "Hers" in 1977. In 1996 *The New York Times* published "Mommy Dressing," Gould's memoir about her mother, the fashion designer Jo Copeland. Anchor/Doubleday will publish this in expanded form in 1998. Gould has taught fiction writing and the art of adaptation at New York University, Boston University and University College Dublin, and has lectured and taught all over the world. Her first novel *Such Good Friends,* an international bestseller, was adapted to film by the director Otto Preminger. Gould's most recent work, the novel *No Brakes,* was published in 1997 by Henry Holt & Co.

Phillip Lopate, a native New Yorker, was born in 1943. He is the author of works of fiction, nonfiction and poetry, almost all of which have been autobiographical in subject. He has edited the anthology *The Art of the Personal Essay* and is ongoing editor of *The Anchor Essay Annual.* Lopate is the recipient of a Guggenheim fellowship and two National Endowment for the Arts grants. His memoir *Being with Children* received a Christopher Medal; his collection of personal essays, *Bachelorhood*, was awarded a Texas Institute of Arts and Letters Award for Best Nonfiction Book of the Year; and another collection of personal essays, *Portrait of My Body*, was named a finalist for the PEN Speilvogel-Diamonstein Award for Best Essay Book of the Year. Lopate holds the Adams Chair in Humanities at Hofstra University and lives with his family in Brooklyn.

Jerry Stahl's memoir *Permanent Midnight* was published by Warner Books in 1995. The movie version, starring Ben Stiller, will be released in 1998. Stahl's fiction and nonfiction have appeared in British and American *Esquire*, *Playboy*, *Buzz*, *The Village Voice*, *LA Weekly*, and a variety of other places, and his health column, "A Year to Live," appears in *Bikini* magazine. His short stories have been included in the *Pushcart Prize Anthology* and have received the Transatlantic Review Erotica Award. Stahl's screen credits include the cult films *Café Flesh* and *Dr. Caligari*. He has also written for television.

Laurie Stone is author of the novel *Starting with Serge* and a collection of writings about comic performance, *Laughing in the Dark: A Decade of Subversive Comedy*. She is the theater critic for *The Nation* and has been a regular contributor and columnist for *The Village Voice* since 1975. Her literary memoirs have appeared in *TriQuarterly* and *Ms.* In 1996 she received the Nona Balakian Excellence in Reviewing Award from the National Book Critics Circle, and she is the recipient of a grant in creative nonfiction from the New York Foundation for the Arts.

Terminator began writing stories in his head at seven and started to put them on paper at fourteen, when his therapist, Dr. Terrance Owens, asked him to help him teach a class about drugs, hustling, and life on the streets. For encouraging his work, he thanks his mother, Eric Wolensky, Dennis Cooper, Bruce Benderson, Joel Rose, Catherine Texier, Sharon Olds, Laurie Stone, Mary Gaitskill,

Karen Rinaldi, Henry Dunow, and Tobias Wolff. His first novel is forthcoming from Crown.

Catherine Texier was born and raised in France and now lives in New York City. Her first novel, *Chloe l'Atlantique*, was written in French and published in Paris. She is the author of two novels in English, *Love Me Tender* and *Panic Blood*. Her work has been translated into nine languages. She was co-founder and co-editor, with Joel Rose, of the literary magazine *Between C and D*, and has co-edited, with him, two anthologies of short fiction: *Between C and D* and *Love Is Strange*. She is the recipient of a National Endowment for the Arts Award and a New York Foundation for the Arts Fellowship. She just completed a book-length memoir.

Peter Trachtenberg is the author of the memoir *Seven Tattoos* (Crown, 1997) and *The Casanova Complex*, a book of nonfiction. His essays and stories have appeared in *Chicago, TriQuarterly, Poets & Writers, BENZENE*, and the electronic journal *word.com*, and have been broadcast on National Public Radio's "All Things Considered." He also performs his work at clubs and theaters in New York City. A winner of the Nelson Algren Award for Short Fiction and a fellowship in fiction writing from the New York Foundation for the Arts, Trachtenberg lives in New York City.